# MEMOIRS OF A MILITANT

## Sharply and to the point

**Kevin Halpin**

PRAXIS PRESS 2012

Memoirs
of a militant
Sharply and to the point
Kevin Halpin

Praxis Press
Unity Office
72 Waterloo Street,
Glasgow, G2 7DA
Scotland

T: +44 141 204 1611
www.unitybooks.co.uk

ISBN 978-1-899155-05-7



Pictures: Kevin Halpin and Platform Films/CP

Edited by E Barrett. Design and layout K Coyle and L Lam.

Printed in Great Britain by Russell Press, Nottingham

# Contents

# Acknowledgements

This book came about when I was on a delegation of the Communist Party to China. The three other delegates were general secretary Robert Griffiths; John Haylett, the *Morning Star* editor at the time and Emily Mann, a gifted and talented Communist journalist.

While flying from one end of China to the other I sat with Emily and chatted about the CP and the struggles of working people. She said that listening to me she had found out a lot more than she had back in Britain - and I should write it down. I said I'd think about it, and she offered to type it up for me. A very brave offer, as my handwriting is atrocious, so I forced myself to write in unconnected letters to make it a bit easier.

I needed some pressing by Emily, but I did it, writing a few pages a week just as I remembered workers and the issues. She and her husband Richard kept me going by saying how much they were looking forward to the next 'instalment'.

Later Emily introduced me to her brother James, who continued typing up my stuff and also did the first revision. This was invaluable because, not being in my game, his questions showed me where I had forgotten to explain something which I had rather arrogantly assumed that everyone would know.

Finally it was done. I wasn't convinced that it was worth reading, but a couple of close friends said I should get on with it, so an NUJ comrade of Anita's and friend of ours, Eddie Barrett, subbed and edited it. Shortly after that by chance I bumped into my good comrade Kenny Coyle at the TUC and remembered he had an imprint – Praxis Press, so he's the one you have to thank for being able to read it now.

And I thank him and all those, most recently Andrew Murray, who made it happen.

# Preface

My shopfloor life began at the age of 13 and continued when I was demobbed in 1948. During the second world war, trades union organisation was maintained often by indomitable women brought in for 'war work'.

Remember, after the Second World War when I was demobbed I worked in a virtual jungle. Workers were laid off from their jobs at the whim of their employer; 'better put your hat on, Bill, they're sacking the old uns' was a jokey remark based on fact. Friday, the foreman came round with your pay packets and your employment cards. In woodworking shops you got an hour to grind your personal tools; not out of generosity but to be sure when you next got a job you could have a quick start to benefit the employer.

At that time thousands of manufacturing firms suffered from the fuel crisis and laid off thousands of workers. I say, 'laid off' but in reality they were sacked, finished. Long before the fight for jobs, people expected to be tapped on the shoulder, told to pick up their cards, and they were gone. The fuel crisis was used to bar employment to shop stewards and militants. The job of building trades union organisation started then: the fight for recognition, permanent employment, sackings to be resisted, the shorter working week.

The battle was often derided by the press. If you were amenable you were a good, stocky figure. If not, then you were a burly loudmouth. Many trade union leaders detested the rank and file movement and clashed with its leaders who came to the fore on the basis of improving wages, hours and having a voice in your working days.

However the so-called 'bad days of the 70s' were about bad employers, not bad workers. The TUC went up to 14 million members on that basis of confidence. There's been a great deal of talk about trade union militancy in the 'winter of discontent'. Some members of the media made a profession out of propaganda against working people. I have written as someone on the inside who took part with or supported working people who were raising their heads and demanding to work with dignity in the third of their lives which they spend at work, with a say in hours, how they worked and their pay.

Many fights were to get rid of casualisation. Take the motor industry – after the October Motor show and the buying there was a slack period with massive lay-offs until spring. Shortening the working week without loss of pay was one victory. Cutting hours to keep the factory with a united workforce even though hours paid were cut was an attempt to thwart lay-offs and a return to casualisation. Big advances were made; but today employers and government are trying to turn back the clock.

I have written of my experience in the building up a trade union membership of more than 14 million; now reduced to less than 7 million by closures etc. But one contributory factor in that reduction of membership is the loss of confidence in trade unions, through their being unable to win disputes because of anti-union laws, one of which is banning sympathy strikes, or what we rightly know as solidarity. There are still millions not in unions who need organisation.

I hope this book can help to give back confidence to win. It reflects my life and the thousands of workers who gave me backing. I congratulate them and thank them for their support. This, then, is the personal story of the growing movement. It is written not as a history, but as a narrative of one who was both derided and attacked, and whose members gave him confidence. It is about them that I write.

Often whilst speaking to people about their past experiences they insist that they will write it down; it would make a good and an interesting story. Leaders such as Mick McGahey, Derek Robinson, Bernie Steer and many others all said this at one time or another, but never did it. Well, for what it's worth, I did.

# 1 Early years in Preston

I was born in Preston in January 1927, eight months after the failed general strike. My mother was from Oswaldtwistle, near Accrington in East Lancashire; my father from a poor quarter of Dublin – the Coombe. They were both strong and loyal Catholics, and yet were also both in trade unions.

My father was a goods porter at Preston station. Once a month he put on a collar and tie to attend his union branch meeting, but he forbade any mention of the National Union of Railwaymen (NUR) General Secretary Jimmy Thomas, who sold out the strikers in 1926.

My father's job as a porter meant prosperity or famine. When a box of fish from Fleetwood burst as it was being unloaded the railway claimed for the accident on insurance and the fish was dished out cheaply to the company's workers. It was best when this happened with a crate of strawberries.

My mother was a weaver in one of the town's cotton mills. The weavers' union had been a foundation of Chartism. Many national trade unionists meet in Preston, but I wonder how many go past the Corn Exchange (now a night-club). Outside, erected by a progressive council, is a monumental sculpture of soldiers firing on and killing female cotton mill workers during the general strike of 1842.

I checked it the other night but I couldn't read the inscription in the dark. A knot of youngsters asked what I was looking for and when I told them they recited the words by heart: 'Four weavers in 1842, shot while demonstrating against wage cuts and for the 'Charter' of democratic rights ...' They must teach them well in Preston.

Lancashire was divided between cotton-spinning towns and weaving towns. Preston was a weaving town dominated by Horrockses. All the mills had royal titles – the Queen Victoria, the Alexandra – or were named after some military victory or other.

I had two sisters; Mary was the eldest, then Joan; and a brother, Denis, or Michael as he preferred to be called. They were each four years apart by the 'Grace of God', or good timing. The girls were very bright.

They grew up during mother's time and had been well educated; I believe to university standard. My father hated them because they were always writing: 'Girls educated is a waste of time,' he would say. I used to wonder how Mary and Joan managed it. I once had a conversation with an NUR delegate who had good north-country knowledge. She explained that my mother would have had some clout. Weavers earned much more than railwaymen and Mary Alice Roberts must have had the guts to stand up to John Joseph Halpin and educate her daughters. I would have liked to have known her later, when I was a communist.

Grandma Roberts had also been a weaver in the mill. She spoke Lancashire dialect so sharp I thought she was speaking another language. Very often that was the case: she would use an Anglo-Saxon word when we would a Norman. Grandfather Roberts had died leaving Grandma destitute.

At first she lived with us. It was crowded. She had words with my father and finished up in Wittington workhouse. We used to visit when I was four or five. The residents were fenced in. I would be sent over to give her a hug and a florin (two shillings or 10p in today's money) wrapped in a piece of paper. If an adult had hugged her it was known she would be searched, and if the warders found any money it would be confiscated to pay for her keep. Who knows whether it ever was; it never went on the books.

Later the Communist Party taught me about the Speenhamland system of poor relief, and its iniquitous successor under the 1834 Poor Law Amendment Act, which forced families into the workhouse where they were separated and demeaned; but even then I thought it was horrible. I have never forgotten those visits. It was a good start to a class education.

Our house had a front room facing the street and a kitchen with a brown slop stone outside at the back. Upstairs there were two rooms for my parents, my two sisters, and my brother and me. There was no bathroom. On bath nights we had to take it in turns in the tin tub. It may seem a different world and in many ways it was. People wore clogs during the week and boots or shoes on Sunday. The best clogs were noisy but good for your feet – they kept them dry in wet Lancashire.

Clogs had steel cockers on the bottom. When these wore out we took them to be replaced. There was no leaving the clogs in the shop and going back the next day, or you would be running around in stockinged feet. You waited while the clogger hammered on the new cockers.

Preston Weavers' Memorial to the 1842 strikers

When I was a child the town's streets and pavements were still cobbled and a 'knocker-up' made a few pennies by tapping on your window in the morning with a split cane and shouting your name to wake you up. If he came back and saw no lights on, he'd give you another knock till you said, 'Aw reet' or, if you were sick or something, shouted down, 'Not going in today' (very rare). Half an hour later came clatter, clatter on the cobbles with clogs as everyone went off to work: then deadly quiet, except for the lamp-lighter who came round on a bike to extinguish the gas lamps.

Horse-drawn milk floats came down the road twice a day after the cows were milked. You took your jug down to the cart and asked for a pint or a half pint poured from the churn with a dipper. By the time the milk came in the morning, my parents were already at work; me, the youngest, left with a child-minder. A great breakfast was bread dipped in tea.

My mother was a diamond. Good cooking was usual. She baked delicious bread in the coal oven twice a week. With her working in the mill all day, then washing and ironing in the evenings, I was allowed to cook from age four or less. Pot herbs, a chopped-up mixture of vegetables left over from the weekend, were sold cheaply by greengrocers on Tuesdays and from these I would make soups, mixing my own dough for my little loaf. At the weekend I used to go shopping with Mam, and I would stand by and listen to her chatter with the other weavers we would meet.

The conversation was an obvious delight to them. At work they had to bellow words in each other's ear, or use mime language; the only way to communicate in a cotton mill with all the loom clatter. Habit made them shout even when outside the factory.

Preston, Lancashire was a peculiar place. In our first geography lessons we were told that the prevailing west wind from the Atlantic gave it the damp climate ideal for cotton manufacture. Yorkshire across the Pennines was only good for wool because the high ridge of hills ensures the rain stays in Lancashire. We were then told that Lancashire had five spinning towns and five weaving towns, and we had to memorise and repeat the Ten Towns. If you couldn't remember the names you were considered unteachable and there wasn't much point going any further. Those names were our world. Only later, introduced to the British Empire coloured in pink across the world atlas, did the Ten Towns seem a bit limited.

But Lancashire held the original large-scale industry. It imported the raw material for manufacture, and it was also the first to export its factories. In the 1930s the mill-owners shipped the looms and spinning jennies to India. Labour there was cheap, cotton was available, and soon the woven cloth was being imported. The Lancashire industrialists predated Dyson Vacuum Co. by 70 years. Many of the empty mills suddenly caught fire. They weren't set alight by redundant workers but by the owners who would claim the insurance. The payouts were never challenged; probably because the mill-owners and the insurance brokers all went to the same club, or Temple.

Needless to say thousands of skilled cotton workers went out of the mills with nothing. They walked around town with no work and no prospects. Where do skilled cotton workers go when their industry has gone? This part of the Depression was a contrived one.

The Co-op was the crucial retailer. Many Co-ops still followed the old style and tried to replicate the experience of shopping along the high street: one counter for butter, one for bacon, one for bread, etc. You developed a taste for broken biscuits and lived on the order book: Tuesday, Wednesday, Thursday, pay the bill on Friday. The biggest topic was how much the dividend ('Divi') would be. A crowd waited for it to be posted at the Co-op Centre. Its amount determined whether parents could buy their children boots or clogs.

The attack on the cotton industry stopped the longstanding militant tradition of the cotton unions. They had supported the emancipation of slaves during the US Civil War, stopping the import of raw cotton from the plantations even though this threatened their jobs. Mill towns always had a regiment of soldiers barracked to quell unrest. The local regiment would be stationed in another part of the country. You could hardly get soldiers to fire on their own folk.

My mother's side were a good stable family in this tradition. My father was more mixed up. He was a loyal NUR man, and an Irish Republican (we were not allowed to have the free mug given out to celebrate the Jubilee in 1935); but he was also a Franco supporter, and anti-culture: 'What do you want to go to the orchestra concert for? Lot of rubbish, I say.'

My father's support of Franco during the Spanish Civil War was in the good old Jesuit tradition. 'Communists are raping nuns,' he would say. I didn't believe him. A little later, I would skip Sunday Benediction and listen instead to a communist speaker in Preston market; although I wouldn't sit too close in case I was recognised. I heard about Spain, the need for a Second Front, and Stalin.

I remember that when he was heckled and accused of not knowing about class struggle the speaker removed his shirt to show the scars on his back from when he had been whipped for preaching class politics in the US southern states.

When I joined the Party, I found out that this was Pat Devine, the Lancashire communist full-timer. Preston suited the Irishman, as the town was a staging post for Dubliners heading towards London via Liverpool. (Catholic and 'Proddy' fights were big at school. I went to Dublin as a kid to leave a bed free for any one of my Irish cousins who were on strike when Dublin was the best-organised city in the world. The strikers were brickies, joiners, plasterers and painters. They didn't all come out at once, a very effective tactic.)

At the age of seven my world fell in. My mother started suffering from fainting fits and had to go to hospital. I walked with her to the bus stop. She asked for a kiss but I was too shy to give it in the street. It was the last time I saw her. She'd taught me cooking, singing, everything, but then she was no more.

I was sent away to some distant relatives while the funeral was organised. On the day of the funeral I was stung by a wasp in the garden. I attacked the wasps nest with a pitchfork. I was stung even more, but I wished I was dead.

Things went downhill from then. Father reverted to his Dublin Coombe background. We were lucky, he would say; he never had shoes as a boy, and there was no coal in winter either. Harsh lives make harsh men.

I hated everything after Mam died. I went to school and despised everyone who had a mother. With my temper, I would fight anyone. Kids used to gather in their streets and these gangs became known by their street name. Neighbourhood gangs would bring their champion to fight me. I lost once and, as the victors rejoiced, I caught the winner from behind and with my clogs kicked his legs from under him. He stopped laughing.

This went on for the next two years. During that time father grew worse. Grandfather Roberts had been an expert fisherman. He claimed he could catch fish anywhere and it seemed he did. When he died he left his fishing rods to Mike. Mike committed a misdemeanour and Father in a rage took all the fine rods and broke them across his knee. He made Mike put them in the dustbin. Mike never forgave him.

I worked the allotment we had and attended the Catholic school. The education I received there was based on rote and cane.

Then when I was nine Father brought home a lady called Agnes. I found out later that she had been in a Carmelite convent in Dolgethly in Wales but had decided to leave. Father stated that they were going to marry and they did so without any of his children being there. The next thing we knew she was living in the house as his wife.

This led to the next upset. Father said I was to call Agnes 'Mother'. I replied she was not my mother, my mother had died. My father said he would make me change my mind. There were beatings galore, but through gritted teeth I said, 'Never.' At one stage I was flogged so much Mike pulled out the kitchen knife and cried, 'Stop hitting him or I'll stab you!' Father believed he would and stopped, but my brother wasn't always to hand with the kitchen knife.

Agnes was a good cook and friendly with me. She had two lovely children, Teresa and Tony, with my father. It was all right apart from him. For my 11th birthday Father bought me a new Hercules bicycle. It was a great event, but I had to find a paper round to repay him. A newsagent hired me at 6/6d a week. I repaid Father time and time again. I was told I was costing a lot to feed.

I delivered the morning papers at 7am and the evening titles at 5pm. The round took in the posh part of town, including the halls and mansions built by the cotton-mill owners outside Preston at Broughton. It was a big round at Christmas when I could knock on the doors and say, 'Merry Christmas! Does it run t'owt?' I was given around £2 in tips. I delivered to George Formby. He was a legendary Lancashire comedian and singer on stage and film. Songs such as 'When I'm cleaning windows' and 'Leaning on a Lamp Post'. He may have been a good laugh on stage but not so funny in life. I only got as far as 'Merry Christmas' before the door was shut.

War started when I was still at school. The black-out was ordered and I made money knocking at doors and offering to white-wash their curb. That cash was mine.

I passed the exams for a scholarship to Central School. Grammars were for those who could possibly go to university. Central School was for those who could possibly be craftsmen. Religion was prominent. In a science class I raised a contradiction. 'Matter can neither be created nor destroyed,' we were told. 'But religion tells us God created the world,' I said. 'It's not for you to doubt God,' was the reply, together with six of the best. I was never keen on religion. I went to mass each morning with Agnes until the paper round came as a blessed release.

I wasn't bad at dictation, which skill proved excellent for negotiating later on. By the time I was 13 I'd had enough of the school and didn't go back for the new term. I had been given food and a basic Jesuit education. The school never asked where I was. I had simply left early.

My first job after leaving school was dismantling a factory chimney brick by brick from the top down. I went up a ladder and sat astride the chimney wall, throwing the bricks into the shaft. I was afraid of the height, but I was paid.

Father saw me joining him as a goods porter. He had me down as a brewcart boy, hitching an extra horse to the dray to pull the load up Butler Street, but the mechanical three-wheeled Scammells came in to replace horses. This led to big changes at the goods yard. Time study was introduced and the Bedeaux system, whereby a task is allotted a standard completion time, was used to cut jobs. My father was a NUR representative on negotiations and I learnt all about the evils of the system.

I heard of a job at Todkill, a traditional vehicle workshop, as an apprentice in the body shop. I applied and was taken on. The body shop made and repaired car and lorry bodies. I was first put to taking solid-tyred Leyland trucks out of store and replacing them with pneumatic tyres. The trucks were being pressed into service following the outbreak of war in 1939.

Todkill still handled horse-drawn vehicles: high-class Blackpool landaus and farm wagons (it had a contract with Preston Farmers Company). When the body shop was slack we were put in the paint shop doing rough chassis painting. The specialist painters did first class body work and varnishing, and lettering, including gold-leaf.

The factory was a craft-shop. It could build and hoop cartwheels and there was an old wheelwright on the team. There was also a bad-tempered blacksmith. I would do a bit of striking for him when his striker was on holiday. I was apprenticed under Stan Greenwood. He was a fine craftsman who produced the drawings for new body specifications. He was also a good trade unionist and a socialist to boot. He was very knowledgeable on the Second Front. From Stan I learnt much about woodwork, machinery and tools. I also learnt to be an anti-fascist.

The family had moved to New Longton, a village outside Preston. Father took a small-holding with large greenhouses and grew lettuces and tomatoes commercially. He had two thousand plants in all. We lived in the adjoining cottage. It had no sewer: the night-soil men came once a week. I would work the greenhouses for three hours in the morning before going to Todkill. I had to travel four miles to work from New Longton; sometimes by bicycle, otherwise by train. Preston was a large station then. Going home in the evenings I would catch the Preston-Southport train from platform 13. The line has now closed.

I used to stay in town sometimes after work and meet a mate. We would play cards with his family. They lived like I used to: two-up/two down. Those were good nights at cards. We played for small bits of cash, although one day my mate's dad had had a drink and attended the cattle auction. As well as the remains of the cotton industry Preston at the time was an important centre for agriculture and cattle, and it had a big commercial market: often you couldn't get by for the droves going to auction.

I don't know what he thought he was bidding for but he came away with three goats. His wife went berserk. They only had a small backyard. We had a few hands of cards that evening and my mate's dad, becoming cash-low, said he would play me for three goats. I won.

I had to take my winnings home that night: four and a half miles. I walked with the goats tied to three pieces of string. Just after midnight I was stopped by the police. Where was I going, why did I have three goats with me, and where did I get them from? Even I could not believe my story. I was asked to follow the car to Hutton police station.

When we arrived I was told to leave the goats outside but I feared they would chew through the string and escape, so I took them into the station. They had clearly been badly brought up because they promptly made a mess. One, a Billy goat, fancied the desk sergeant and jumped up full of amour.

The goats and I were thrown out with no charges against us and we reached home in the early hours where I let them on to the small-holding. I was woken in the morning by screams from my father: 'There are three bloody goats out there eating everything!' I explained that I'd won them. There was a difference of opinion but the goats stayed. I noticed that one of them was in milk. She gave nearly four pints twice a day. After that I sold all three so I made a profit, although I wasn't keen on late night cards for a bit: I wasn't sure what I would win.

With factories diverted to war-work, toys for children were scarce. I was very fond of my half-brother and sister and decided to make them a rocking ostrich for a Christmas present. I hand-carved it out of solid oak and gave it a lovely long graceful neck. Teresa had the first ride. The ostrich rocked violently, she hit her head on its neck and that was that. The only subsequent use it had was when the kids were threatened with a ride on the ostrich if they were being naughty.

Undaunted, however, I decided to replicate a rolling duck that dipped its head and flapped its wings and gave a quack. A complicated piece of machinery was needed to achieve this but I was in the right place. The blacksmith made the axles, the wheels were contracted out to a wood-turner (there not being a turner at Todkill) and the wings were painted by the sign-writer.

The prototype was so successful I set up a production line in the deserted upper mill floor and manufactured toy ducks while fire-watching. I sold them for £1 each. I did well, even after paying the workers. Perhaps I should have been a Tory businessman.

Early in the war I was told by the Guvnor that regulations designating the factory work as a reserved occupation with exemption from conscription, also forbade apprentices having Shrove Tuesday afternoon off to go pace-egging. This was an ancient custom. The apprentices' faces were blackened and they were pushed out at the factory gate to solicit money around the town.

On Shrove morning I argued with the other half dozen lads that we shouldn't let them break a centuries-old custom. They sent me to tell the Guvnor. He swore at me and said if I didn't work the afternoon I would be dealt with.

At 15 I was already seen as a troublemaker. I had led an action for a boys' shilling per week pay rise as parity with an increase given to the craftsmen. I came out of the office and persuaded the others to walk out as usual, quoting 'custard and practice'.

The next morning the Guvnor told me I was suspended without pay for three days and if I did anything more I would get the sack. It was my first private warning, and my first taste of victimisation. I dared not tell my father. He may have been a trade unionist, but he had also instructed me to keep my head down so I would get on.

For three days I spent a lot of time in the public library. I made my wages up from the duck money and managed to keep the affair secret. The men didn't support me. Stan explained that any action could be met with dismissal and a swift call-up. As such it was also the first time I came up against anti-union laws.

After that pancake day I thought it was time to move on.

# 2 Minesweeping

I turned 17 and so I decided to join the Royal Navy. As I was under 18 I had to join the Boy Service. My father disagreed but I didn't need his permission. Mike had volunteered for the Navy. He had served in the abortive Dieppe landing on a landing-craft tank and come back demoralised. He met a smashing girl, Ada, who lived in Burnley and worked in a shell-filling factory.

As Mike was under-age he asked Father for permission to marry. Father refused; he wouldn't agree to a mixed marriage. The girl was a Protestant but she was also pregnant and it was odds on that my brother would not come back from the war.

Mike went to court despite the spoken opposition and was given consent by the magistrate. Father reacted by telling them never to darken his doorstep again. I had to meet them in secret. I made the baby a cot and toys. They remained together all their lives. Mary and Joan had already never darkened my father's door, so I would also meet them secretly. If they wanted to see me they waited at the factory gate.

I asked to join a minesweeper. They were small ships and I didn't fancy the discipline likely on the larger vessels. The navy recruiting office tried to persuade me to sail on aircraft carriers where I could use my trade as a rigger or fitter, but I held out and they drafted me to Lowestoft, a major deep-sea fishing port in peacetime and now home of the Royal Naval Patrol Service.

I received word to catch a train to Port Arthur, which turned out to be a grand name for Butlins Holiday Camp in Skegness. I arrived without having to swear obedience to the King. Unlike the army there was no obligation. The Navy had always been loyal.

It was a miserable camp and bitterly cold in the holiday chalets. I was sent with a chit to get uniform. I presented myself at the stores room and a load of clothes and a kit-bag was thrown on the counter. I picked up a pair of trousers, a jersey, a pair of boots and two pairs of underwear and socks. I thanked the staff and walked out. There was a great shout: 'What do you think you're fucking doing?'

I turned around, mystified. 'You've left half your gear on my counter! Are you taking the fucking mickey? Pick it all up and clear off.' Amazed, I stuffed the rest into my kit-bag. I thought I was being given a pile of clothes from which to make a choice. It was hard to believe that I was to have more than one pair of boots and trousers.

A rough crowd mustered at Lowestoft and the Navy's discipline was not politely received. The RNPS had a fleet of requisitioned trawlers, drifters and whalers, all coal-fired by hand.

Converting these ships to minesweepers was relatively easy. Converting the men that crewed them was a different matter: there was no nick worse than life as a stoker on ships working the deep-sea fishing fields. Minesweeping owed a lot to deep sea fishing; very experienced men who hated discipline.

The Patrol Service maintained a distinct identity from the Royal Navy bases at Chatham and Portsmouth. Its Rear-Admiral melted down his family silver to create a unique badge awarded to those who had completed six months sea-time; and he awarded it, not the Admiralty at Whitehall.

We were sent on a route march every Saturday. We would set off for Oulton Broad, arrive at opening time, and gracefully break rank. Afterwards we would be driven back in trucks to about a mile from the depot where we would disembark and march into the parade ground in good step.

I was given a draft as a stoker. I was trained on Lowestoft beach by shovelling pebbles through a hole in a steel plate. After three days of this I was upgraded to a first class Stoker and ordered to my ship. I had no knowledge of how to tackle a coal furnace. It was 'hi-ho off we go', out into the North Sea.

I'm probably one of the few left who could steam an ocean-going vessel. It was hard work, but it made no difference to me. We swept for each type of mine: conventional, acoustic and magnetic. It could have been nerve-wracking but we knew, with a hull made of wood, if we hit a mine there would be nothing left of us, so equally there was nothing to worry about.

Sea mines were used extensively by the Germans to offset British naval superiority, and to disrupt the country's reliance on imports, effectively acting as an economic blockade. The British Navy mined large fields in the North Sea, the Channel and off the French coast to limit enemy shipping. Belligerent nations had to declare mined areas, but not to pin-point where each mine or line lay.

Conventional mines were tied to anchors on the sea bed by wire cables and floated at the required depth below the surface. They were packed with about five hundred pounds of explosive and had detonator horns which were crushed on impact with a ship's hull and ignited the explosives. These were augmented by magnetic devices, predominantly moored on the sea bed in shallower waters and exploded by metallic hulls passing over or near. Mines are much more destructive when exploded without contact.

When magnetic mines were first laid off the Thames Estuary, they practically shut down the London ports. Finally acoustic mines were developed. These were also laid on the bottom, and were detonated by the noise of the ship's propellers. The conventional mines were cleared by towing a hawser at the end of which was a para-vane float set to pull the line away from the sweeper. Under this was another hawser held to a fixed depth by kites. This cut the mine's mooring cables, and they floated to the surface. The bobbing mines were then fired on with rifles and sunk, or blown up.

You obviously had to stand off. I remember we fired on one that went up and exploded another near to the ship. There was a terrific bang which made my ear bleed. I didn't report it. I would have had to go for a medical and leave the sweeper. I was happy on board, but ever so often my ear bothered me; years later I found out I had a perforated ear drum which required surgery.

To find the magnetic mines two electric cables with copper tails were dropped overboard and a current pulsed through them in bursts to act as the detonator. Acoustics were dealt with by rigging a great riveting hammer over the bows of the ship, the sound waves exploding any mines ahead. Cleared areas of sea were marked by dan buoys laid out by deck winches. Clearance sweeps were only possible by day. We anchored at night or came in to harbour.

The whole process made for a lot of wires, and it was ideal for men used to handling fishing tackle. Early on I was standing on deck when a trawler-man stepped over and knocked me off my feet. I got up preparing to hit him back to be told I'd been standing in a 'bight' (a loop of wire). If it had been laid out I would have gone with it. The trawlermen had a low opinion of part-timers generally.

They had a favourite story about a Royal Naval Volunteer Reserve officer on board a big fleet sweeper. A large mine had bobbed up in a sweep and the officer was reported as asking the men to hang on while he fetched his camera for a snap. He went aft, a swell pushed the mine alongside, and it blew off the stern. The officer and his camera were never seen again. This provoked a good deal of dark laughter: 'Useless bloody people; don't know nothing.'

The RNVR supplied most officers on the sweepers. Their main task seemed to be putting men on charges. You could be charged for endless breaches of discipline. If they couldn't think of anything specific at the time it would be 'Dumb Insolence'.

Once a Commodore came aboard unexpectedly as we lay in harbour and found all hands asleep below. The entire ship was put on a charge and we were made to fill the water tanks by hand with buckets. The ship's fresh water had to be pumped from the tanks to be available for washing. It was a strenuous job.

Each of the two officers aboard the sweeper was assigned a steward. In the morning we could hear the officers call from their cabins: 'Water, steward!' We always had to be inspected by an officer before being allowed on shore. If there was the slightest blemish in our dress, a spot of polish on the inside of a shoe, we would be refused a pass.

After serving awhile on the steamer I decided to switch to one of the purpose-built, diesel-engine Motor Minesweepers ('Mickey Mouses'). I took a course learning to run a diesel-engine and was drafted to the Mediterranean. We were given 12 days embarkation leave before being posted abroad. This was unsettling. I didn't fancy spending the time with my father in Preston, but where could I go?

During the routine medical I complained of a rash and the medical officer cancelled my leave. Word went round 1,500 ratings. It was the first time it had ever happened. Instead I was put on the bread and butter party, buttering bread for the barracks.

After a few hours I'd had enough and started slapping on the butter. The leading hand was irate at my profligacy and I was made to scrape off the excess. I didn't know the score until Friday came and £5 was given to each of the catering crew. This was a fortune when pay was three shillings and sixpence a day. The unused butter had been saved and sold to the black market.

In the Mediterranean we swept a triangle between Malta, North Africa, and Pantelleria, south of Sicily, and then north up the Adriatic. I had a peculiar position of power on board ship. We had a crew of 32 but our cook had been trained on a cruiser where a dozen cooks dished up for five hundred hands. His anonymity must have protected him. At Christmas we saved up our messing allowance and bought two turkeys. As they were carved we found that they had been cooked

On the Royal Naval Patrol Service minesweeper (second from left)

with their entrails intact. They stank rotten. The cook was thrown over the side. He was lucky we were in harbour.

I decided to have a go at cooking the meal. We only had canned meat left, which was widely decried for its revolting taste, but I made some sage dumplings as accompaniment. It went down well. I began to make other easy dishes – bread pudding, meat pies, pastas.

The shout would often come from the main deck, 'Halpin, are you cooking?' The officers would insist on having my grub instead of the cook's offering. It became accepted that I would cook. I even baked when the ship wasn't at sea.

When in harbour in Malta the locals would clean the ship's dishes in the hope of taking extra food to their family. Malta was suffering from severe shortages after the long siege and if you were a labourer or dockyard matey the wages were hardly enough to feed a family. Some thought it fun to put their cigarette ends into the left over food: 'Malts will eat anything.' I remembered how it was to live on little, and said it was stopping or else. It led to our biggest mess-deck punch up, but it stopped.

My ship finished up in the Mediterranean for a long period. I had signed on 'for hostilities only'. By 1946 servicemen were being demobbed, but towards the end of the war the fascists, retreating up

Italy, had dumped mines all over the Adriatic, so there was plenty to clear and by then we were an experienced sweeper that couldn't be spared. Sailing along the north Italian coast I became quite well off. There was money to be made on the black market. It was hard in the big ports where there were frequent naval patrols. But being in a small vessel that swept everywhere, we put into unvisited, obscure little places where the ship was seen as a source for such luxuries as ground coffee.

I met a lovely girl in Trieste. Her name was Olga ('Olgetta'). She had been educated well and spoke several languages. Before the war she had worked for Lloyd Triestino, a shipping line. We became engaged to be married on 24/- a week pay. I bought her a ring which cost £150 and rings were cheap in Italy then.

Trieste, like all army centres, was run by an Allied Military Government. It pursued an anti-prostitution policy. Women walking down the street with sailors were picked up and hustled away for a compulsory medical examination. If I wasn't careful Olga would have the same treatment. When in town we had to walk apart.

I never wrote letters home. One day the ship's captain called me in. Why had I failed to communicate with my family? I said I didn't choose to. I was read the Admiralty Fleet Order by which all naval personnel had to communicate with their next of kin at least every six months. I thought of defying it but I would end up in naval gaol. (I had been there once before. It was very unpleasant: an ancient lock-up in Malta with a sunbaked yard where I had to run up and down a flight of steps with eighteen-inch risers.)

I took the paper, pen and envelope and wrote to my father. The letter had to be handed in with the envelope open. I was called up again by Skipper. 'You've only written "I am alive."' I was told it wasn't enough. I replied that I had obeyed the order. He gave up remonstrating and my letter was sealed and sent. A few weeks later I received a reply. It was the last word I had from John Joseph Halpin. In early 1947 I left the Royal Naval Patrol Service with an honourable discharge and what felt like a lifetime of experience.

# 3 Joining the party and Briggs Bodies

Back in England I rented some digs in Dagenham, Essex. 'No Irish need apply for residence' the notice in the window had said. With my name it wasn't easy but I had my discharge papers to prove that I was English.

I ended my engagement to Olga. I couldn't see me bringing her to this country in the state it was in. Work was difficult to find. It was one of the worst winters I remember, and there was no fuel. This was before North Sea gas was distributed by a national pipe network. Instead it was produced locally by coal-fired gasworks but the coal couldn't be transported because the roads were blocked by snow.

In those days most towns had municipal-owned power stations. In London these were built along the Thames: Chelsea, Battersea, Stepney, Deptford. It was not until the laying of high-voltage cables, sunk mostly under redundant canal towpaths during the 1960s, that fuel shortages were obviated.

In the winter of 1947 the crisis was a real one. I found a job at May and Baker, a well known pharmaceutical company, but I soon left under strange circumstances. I was working in chemical processing, in the Mixed Small Organic shop. There were some perks. Ethyl alcohol came off the still at 40- 45% proof. At 2am a glass of that with distilled water and ice was great. It was a good job I left.

One Friday afternoon a valve over the still leaked and while repairing the cock I got the mixture all over me. I cleaned myself up at my digs in the evening and went out for a pint.

The barman refused to serve me. 'Why not?' I asked him, 'I'm not barred.' 'Look in the mirror,' he said. I had turned a bright green all over. No amount of scrubbing would remove it. I got a drink that weekend only with my hat pulled down. I turned out at May and Baker on Monday morning and went straight to the sector manager: 'What about this? I'm all green.'

'Interesting,' he replied. 'The lab people will want to know why and will be keen to examine you. Could you go to the lab for a test?' I told him they could stick the job and walked out. I wasn't aware that I could have sued for damages.

A bloke in my digs told me there was a job going at Briggs Motor Bodies on Inspection. He was Canadian, and had worked in the motor factories in Detroit. He recommended me to the foreman. Briggs Motor Bodies was historically tied with Ford in car production: Ford manufactured the engine, transmission and frame, and Briggs built and trimmed the bodies and provided the finishing. It also did contract work for Dodge, Austin and Humber, and for the Aero aircraft engine.

The foreman at Briggs was called Leadbetter. He was a coach builder, one of the old school in the midst of 10,000 people building metal car bodies. He asked about my background and perked up when I told him I had done four years as a coach-building apprentice. He put 12 timber samples in front of me, ten of which I could name; birch, beech, English oak, American oak, chestnut, etc. I got a start in the 'knock-down' shop checking that components were meeting export regulations and that they passed quality standards. Once I had inspected and approved I handed to Ford inspectors.

During this period of Labour Government I wasn't happy with its anti-Soviet policy. I wondered if the British strategy was being determined by the United States. I decided to make up my mind and read the *Financial Times* and *Daily Worker*. The *Financial Times* was difficult to find. Owing to post-war shortages the government had restricted news print. The *FT* decided not to cut pages but restrict circulation in working-class areas such as Dagenham.

I had also joined the Amalgamated Engineering Union (AEU). Generally Briggs Bodies was a well organised factory but many of the 350 inspectors were not in the union: there was a tendency among them to see themselves as management. I decided to stand on the clock and recruit. By the time I left there was 100% union membership in the inspection department.

Meantime George Bridges was standing as the Communist candidate for Dagenham in the 1950 General Election. There were platform meetings at Dagenham Heathway every Saturday, advertised in the *Daily Worker*. One Saturday morning George was speaking outside the post office. I asked one of the *Daily Worker* sellers standing by if they needed a hand but he said, 'No, we're alright, mate.'

I walked off up the Heathway thinking it was a loony crowd. Then I heard a shout behind me, 'Hold on, mate!' It was little Sammy Brewster, a Ford worker I later knew quite well. I went back with him and we had a chat. Then they asked my address and gave me a form to complete. A day or so later I was given a doorstep interview to validate my application, and after that I was confirmed as a member of the Communist Party of Great Britain (CPGB).

Between 1939 and 1949 the Party had experienced mixed fortunes. Just before the outbreak of war many members had been sacked by anti-Communist employers; others had taken the offer of foreman's jobs. The breakthrough for anti-militants was the London Bus Workers strike in May 1937. This was led by Bill Jones, a member of the Transport and General Workers Union (TGWU) executive and one of our best industrial Communists.

Alongside Jones was the militant London Busmen's Rank and File Movement. However, with trams and underground trains running, the strike failed and the organised left was weakened. Bill Jones was thrown off the TGWU executive during a fit of anti-communism after the war which saw the adoption of the 'black circular' – a notorious document listing Communists and militants who were to be blocked from office in trade union executives and trade councils. Bill fought for years against this decision, and he was eventually re-elected to a progressive TGWU executive in a general defeat of the Deakinites. (Arthur Deakin became TGWU's general secretary in 1945 after Ernest Bevin resigned on being given office in Atlee's government. As fierce an anti-Communist as Bevin, he stocked the union's executive with like-minded officials.)

During the war the stance of class unity to defeat fascism, a position expounded by Dimitrov, was preeminent. The justness of this strategy saw unusual results, such as the arch anti-working class Churchill leading the fight. The campaign to open a second front was led by the CPGB in a series of prominent rallies, rejecting Trotskyist arguments that the war was simply an imperialist conflict.

In addition the Party had to fight the Trotskyist method of using war production to raise wages by organising strikes in key industries, arguing that such action further undermined the capacity to defeat fascism; which defeat is the first step in the class struggle. Under the Defence of the Realm Act (DORA) essential workers were directed to critical industries like arms and aircraft production.

With comrades being directed to work in these areas, DORA provided a vehicle for the growth of the Party within industry. Trade unions were represented on joint production committees in the factories, and through these Communist members were able to use their rhetorical and organisational abilities. These comrades sold the *Daily Worker* and recruited to the Party.

The issue of wages was raised at the committee meetings and reasonable rises negotiated. Briggs Bodies itself was organised by several unions – including TGWU, sheet metal, furniture trades and municipal – but the AEU was the single largest. The factory's AEU official was the Communist Claude Berridge, a member of the union's executive and later chair of the London District CPGB.

The 1948 fuel shortage, exacerbating the contraction following the move to peace production, led to factory shut downs. These were used by employers to weed out militants, severely weakening the Communist industrial base that had been built up during the war. This undermining was assisted by the Party moving its focus away from factory branches to constituency organisation.

In the general election of 1945, the re-election of Willie Gallacher and the election of Phil Piratin, for West Fife and Mile End respectively, had given the Communist Party hope of parliamentary representation and turned its efforts towards electoral work. In the 1950 General Election the Party stood 100 candidates, amounting to every leading comrade canvassing for votes.

A peculiar result of the closure of factories was that many skilled workers turned to teaching in further education colleges (which also explains the similarity between the rule books of the Amalgamated Engineering Union and NATFHE, now part of the University and College Union).

Immediately after joining the Party I went to the national congress as a delegate. Showing my Party card I noticed it was brown but saw that my co-delegates' cards were red. This annoyed me. In the AEU, craftsmen were given a green card, semi-skilled workers had red, women had light-blue and apprentices had yellow. Brown wasn't even a recognised category. Was I in a special, down-graded section of the Party? I didn't know anyone to raise this with, and secretly seething I began to debate with myself whether to leave there and then on principle.

Only years later did I have the courage to ask the Executive Secretary, Betty Reid, what a brown card meant. Brown cards, it appeared, had been issued because they had run out of red cardboard. I was glad I stayed. I kept away from the Party's Dagenham Borough organisation. In hindsight this was perhaps no bad thing. I learnt later about its then recent history. After the war a meeting of Dagenham members was called. They were told to all hand in their membership cards.

Only half were handed back: the rest were expelled for supporting the line of André Marty and Charles Tillon, both active French communists – in 1919 they had organised a mutiny of two French dreadnoughts that had been sent to the Black Sea to assist the White Russians in the Russian Civil War. Tillon later led the francs-tireurs partisans (FTP) in occupied France. The FTP was a well-armed and organised wing of the French resistance created by the French Communist Party (PCF), and later in the German occupation integrated into the broader, official Resistance. After the liberation of Paris in August 1944 the FTP nevertheless opposed giving up its arms and argued that those communists who had played the major role in resisting the Nazis militarily should now be running France politically.

However, this was resisted by the Party on the grounds that it would mean clashing with the Allies, potentially leading to the intervention of armed forces and disrupting the priority of defeating fascism. The major German counter-offensive in the Ardennes was to begin in December 1944. Dagenham could give more than just moral support to the FTP. It had a small-arms factory producing Sterling sub-machine guns and FTP plans included their acquisition.

My support for the *Daily Worker* was widely known at Briggs: I had sold the paper before I joined the Party. I now worked hard to get George Bridges elected. During the late shift on election night the manager came to the knock-down shop loudly announcing, 'Comrade Halpin, you've lost your two seats: Gallacher and Piratin are out.' He laughed. I turned round and said, 'Yes I know; but we just won China. You lose a puddle but win an ocean.' All the shop laughed. I had gained their respect, but his hatred.

There was no Party Branch at Briggs after this election defeat. At the next Congress, where I was a Special Delegate (being without a branch), it was decided to refocus efforts on industrial organisation, and the health of factory branches became a central concern again of the Communist Party.

A major factory often played a large role within trade unions and local trade councils, and Communists could influence the direction taken by these bodies. And while they discussed everyday trade union issues and supplied shop steward committees with policies on wages and conditions, the factory Party branches were not just ginger trade union groups.

They also developed and disseminated long-term strategy for their industries, and debated national and international issues. Communist delegates on political committees were able to win mass workplace support, and Communist parliamentary candidates were often people who were recognised in the local factory: myself in Dagenham, Derek Robinson in Birmingham, Sammy Barr and Jimmy Reid on Clydeside. In Sheffield all the communist candidates were engineers from Shardlows works.

The CPGB organised annual workplace conferences which I attended from the early 1960s, during Peter Kerrigan's last period as the Party's Industrial Organiser. Up to 1983 factory branches were a strong foundation of the Party, numbering 111 in 1981 and 102 in 1983, and they underpinned our work.

Most of the bigger branches formed the bedrock of opposition to anti-union legislation in the 1960s, and were the fulcrum for the massive stoppage following the arrest of five dock leaders at a picket in 1972. These activities rebutted the simplistic cries from the Eurocommunists in the 1980s that industrial comrades were only interested in their own economic livelihood.

The scathing term 'economism' was quickly refuted by the broad concerns of workplace Communists. At Briggs I found there were seven comrades including myself. I was told the factory had a branch of 260 comrades during the war but they had been weeded out with the peace: if we tried to set up a new one, we would be sacked too. When, 12 years (and many advances) later, we were eventually sacked, this comrade turned to me: 'See what I said?'

We got together a branch meeting of three comrades (the other four took some convincing). We agreed that the key task was public work. We met weekly to produce our own leaflets. Two meetings each month would be spent discussing trade union issues, and in the other two meetings we would look at wider political topics: the Greek Junta, Cyprus, South Africa, the A-bomb.

These international questions were emphasised by the Party's National Executive Committee, but just as important was the coverage given in the *Daily Worker,* and the publication, *Labour Monthly,* which included 'Notes of the Month' by Rajani Palme Dutt. These columns combined national issues with world imperialism and were a refreshing alternative to dealing with wages, conditions, sackings, trade union elections, and so forth.

Once a month one of us would open the meeting with an analysis of the latest 'Notes of the Month', and the encouragement to participate in open discussion delivered cadres who could speak confidently in public, and also countered a tendency for a few leading comrades to rule the roost.

The other, more serious, journal we read was *For a Lasting Peace, For a People's Democracy*, or *'For For'* as it was known. This was founded after World War II to replace *Inprecor*, the journal of the Communist International which had been set up to spread revolution but was disbanded during negotiations in the 1943 to construct a united front against fascism (*Inprecor's* editor at one stage was Georgi Dimitrov).

*'For For'* dealt with such issues as wars of liberation and the problems facing the People's Democracies and Socialist countries. Reading it each week I became knowledgeable on agricultural and environmental topics, learning about farming systems in Poland and Bulgaria, and the differences between state, collective, co-operative, and peasant farming. I think I knew more about the Soviet state collective arable acreage than anyone.

In many ways the issues *'For For'* raised anticipated the Green movement. (It's interesting to see Stalin as an early environmentalist. He saw the example of the US mid-west, where excessive ploughing and deforestation created a dust-bowl, with the disastrous effects on people so vividly described in Steinbeck's *The Grapes of Wrath*. With this in mind Stalin planted massive belts of trees to counter the Asian winds that blew across the steppes.)

*'For For'* also warned of the US arms race and the Schuman Plan for European industry, which as the vanguard of the Common Market (later the ECC and now the European Union), was responsible for shutting down coal mines in northern France and the rationalising (closure) of steel mills across western Europe.

We would also look at that week's Economic League leaflet. The Economic League was an employer's service that backed right-wing trade union candidates and opposed strikes and socialist governments wherever they occurred in the world. It also compiled a blacklist of militants industry by industry which was distributed to managers throughout the country.

This was, of course, seen by militants as a roll of honour, and it was somewhat humiliating if you didn't find your name on the list. The Economic League was then holding a pro-capitalism meeting outside the factory gate every Tuesday. It had a speaker called Helen Bailey who made a Page Three type splash when the weather was sunny.

The Branch would reply with a leaflet on Wednesday morning. By this time, I had become engaged to comrade Essie Guilder. We produced it together and managed to hand out 500 copies each week. I would print the leaflets at home on a flat-bed duplicator and dry them off overnight in our little gas oven. These leaflets went down reasonably well. The way you can always tell is by how many are lying on the pavement afterwards.

The big advantage we had was that the Briggs gate still had a *Daily Worker* pitch. It was manned by Arthur Messias who was there every day come hell or high water, even during shut-outs. Arthur was a toolmaker who had worked at Briggs Bodies during the war. He was not re-employed after the 1948 fuel crisis, but he was not giving up and going away.

Arthur found another job at a nearby tool factory and continued to sell the paper at Briggs, standing outside the Billiard Hall in Chequers Lane. His factory was a total craft-shop craft-shop and he was a stalwart in South Essex AEU so a half-hour later start there was fine if it meant a sale for the *Daily Worker*. He was still selling when Ford and I parted company. Without him I doubt I would have made a start politically. He had maintained his readership and gave me contacts. I sold the paper with him and handed out Party leaflets.

We think of factory branches, and put known people in leading roles, but we should reserve praise for the unknown comrades who doggedly stood at the gates and sold the *Daily Worker*. I remember that Ma Tinsley also sold the paper without fail outside the Connaught gate at the London Royal Dock. She probably introduced more dockers to socialist policies and principles than anyone. She wasn't in the Party. She was a profound Christian instead.

The *Daily Worker* was established reading in the tool room at Briggs. Every week you paid 1 shilling towards a share in the People's Press Printing Society, the readers' cooperative that owns and publishes the newspaper. Shares were (and are) sold at £1 each.

Once a week there was a draw to see who would get the £1 share as if it were the lottery. I must have won once because I still have a share card from 1953 with £5 on it. At that time my wages were £7 a week. Wally Trimble ran the share club. He was an old speedway rider and very good with engines, as I found when I bought my first Lambretta – a grey machine until it was put through Briggs Paint Shop and became black and crimson.

Gradually the Briggs factory branch developed. The remaining four comrades (who included Alex Geddes of Clyde workers fame) came over when they saw us working with confidence, and three new recruits brought the total to ten. The shop stewards committee met with us. The Briggs shop stewards committee was one joint body, even though engineering had 39 union confederations. It had good results, although its right wing organised Catholic Action and was pro-Attlee.

One of the first industrial issues involving the branch began when we were visited by Dave Kelly and Charlie Brewster, both Party full-timers from South Essex District. The BATA shoe factory in East Tilbury had a company town, and militants there had not only been sacked, but had also been evicted from their tied-cottages and made homeless. Dave and Charlie appealed to the Briggs Branch to resist the eviction. Five of us went down to the cottage in Tilbury and welded the windows and doors, in some fear as the foreman's house was at the other end of the street (this was a regular practice, arranged so a factory's foreman could observe what employees were up to when not at work).

The next day we sent out Len Lowe, a brawny Brummie, to dig a trench round the cottage to prevent entry. We left Len swinging his pick and shovel and forgot about him while attending to matters inside. Four hours later we came out again. We could still see the pick-axe as it was lifted, but no sign of Len Lowe. 'Len, what the hell are you doing?' we called. 'Digging - as you told me,' came his reply. 'But you're undermining the foundations now!' He had made the house impregnable.

We went to the Briggs shop stewards meeting the next night and raised the issue as an emergency. Most of the stewards were from the area. They were aware of BATA's anti-union stance. Coaches of union members were sent to Tilbury and a picket of all BATA shops was organised across Essex. (Halpin's lesson on slogans: I had come up with 'Black BATA's Boots', which read well, but could be heard as urging people to buy the boots and put blackening on them; not our aim.)

Eventually the union negotiating committee was allowed to meet the BATA management, who agreed to re-house the militants and make no more evictions. The *Daily Worker* covered the battle with the pictures: that always sold more papers as people wanted to show their family and mates the protest they had been in.

Labour lost office in October 1951. In its final 18 months the cold war had risen in pitch and Labour had responded, under the influence of Ernest Bevin, with pro-American foreign policies. Britain's involvement in the Korean War depleted the exchequer and led to continued attacks on wages in the wake of Hugh Gaitskell's 'austerity budget'.

I was unaware I was being inducted into such an advanced trade union organisation, where decisions were made shop by shop rather than union by union. At open shop meetings votes were taken on wages, hours, working practices, politics, and the future of the industry: one hand, one vote. Shop stewards were elected each year. The ratio was roughly one steward per hundred workers, so a shop of 300 members voted for three stewards.

Of course, some unions liked to increase their influence by having their favoured steward elected, but only if they were popular on the floor would they be elected by the shop. Union membership in the shops was determined by the shop's location within the factory or by trade. The workers in the trade shops generally represented their particular union. The trim technicians, for instance, would belong to the National Union of Vehicle Builders, and the tool makers the AEU, while in the assembly shops the Transport, Engineering and Municipal unions had a loose recruiting base. However, there were no internal union fights, although pushes by the AEU for exclusive organisation throughout the factory occasionally caused problems.

Instead the stewards had a Joint Shop Stewards Committee that elected a Chair, a Convenor, and a Negotiating Committee (or Works Committee) of seven. Those elected to the Negotiating Committee were responsible for a zone which comprised about 1,200 members and a variety of shops. Claims were put forward by the open shop meetings and agreed by the Joint Shop Stewards Committee. The Negotiating Committee would then meet the management, put the case, and wait. The management's reply came back to the Shop Stewards Committee, which would express a view. Then the negotiators would report back to their zone, and it would accept the management offer or send it back. If there was not a satisfied majority of zones the Shop Stewards Committee voted for a factory mass meeting to decide action: typically an overtime ban or a strike.

I particularly remember two of the zone leaders at Briggs – Frances Guille and Ann Davis. They were both solid trade unionists who did much to defeat the craft unions' antipathy towards women members. I used to visit Vauxhall works and the contrast with Briggs was instructive. At Vauxhall instead of a joint Shop Stewards Committee each union had a separate office and organisation.

One time, when I couldn't find the engineering and electrical people, I put my head into the next door room where the TGWU were quartered and asked if anybody had seen the AEU members. All I received was blank looks. If they had to talk to each other each union would call in its full-timer who would contact his opposite number. I believe the only time the two unions met was when they walked out of the factory on the day it was shut down. I know which approach best serves working people. Joint organisation at negotiating level is an essential condition of successful class action.

In spring 1952 the Briggs Shop Stewards Committee tabled a wage claim for 9 pence an hour: 4½ pence was offered – £4.25 for a 48-hour week. The industry was booming, so this was rejected. The Party branch decided to hold out for 9 pence. Of the 60 stewards at Briggs, seven were in the Party. We called for a lunch-time mass meeting of the full 10,000 workers. The Stewards Committee was happy to leave decisions to this meeting.

The branch members privately agreed to go for an all-out stoppage, to be moved by its secretary, after it was decided that if I didn't propose the motion it wouldn't be put by anybody else. I got up and spoke to the workforce. There were no microphones. This was when I learnt to make myself heard. I must have got my point across: the vote for a strike was carried nearly unanimously.

I was sent with shop stewards to get support for the picket from the engineering heartlands in Bristol and the mining towns in Wales, both areas renowned for their class solidarity.

We had a terrific trip to the Welsh coal pits. We arrived after dark and I spoke to an unlit crowd. As I put the class position I could see nobody for the gloom. Then I heard murmurs. As I continued speaking these murmurs spread and grew louder and stronger, until they built to great roars of approval that thundered in the night air. It was really something to hear. I stayed with Alex Tudor-Hart a coommunist surgeon and GP in Aberdare and on Saturday addressed the town's Party branch. On Sunday morning at 9.30am all the town, to the last stray cat as it seemed, went to Chapel: all, that is, apart from the Communists, who attended their branch meeting.

I came back to Dagenham to hear Claude Berridge address a mass meeting of Briggs workers. Berridge was a clever Communist and this was a speech I will always remember:

'The AEU executive committee is recommending a resumption of work, and my job on this platform is to get you back to work,' he began. 'However, if I was working for Briggs, I might say, "Why get back to work? They are making big profits. They can afford 9 pence an hour. The cost of coal is rising, the cost of rent is rising; they should pay 9 pence an hour." And I know you are correct, I know they can pay 9 pence an hour, but it's my job to get you back to work.'

Needless to say Berridge lost the vote, much to his delight. The strike lasted three weeks until we were given a better offer of 6 pence. During this strike the Joint Shop Stewards Committee had divisions. Some of the strikers had found seasonal work picking peas. A few stewards condemned them on what they saw as a point of principle: all workers should bare equal hardship. The Party took the approach that strikers working elsewhere didn't matter just as long as they respected the picket line

# 4 Communist education and work at Ford

At this time I went to my first Communist Party Holiday School for a week. The School was held in Hastings and among the tutors were Palme Dutt of *Labour Monthly*, James Klugmann, a future official historian of the CPGB and editor of *Marxism Today*, J.R. Campbell, editor of the *Daily Worker*, and party general secretary Harry Pollitt. I began to make notes of what I was hearing, but I soon realised that 'making notes' was the wrong term.

James Klugmann looked over my shoulder and said they needed structure. If I chose, during the afternoon recreation he would explain how to make efficient notes.

Of course I bristled, but James insisted that you can't fight the ruling class without having their own weapons, and that being literate was as important in negotiation as knowing a factory's technology or how a production line is organised. Also, he said, how can you report back clearly to workers without the ability to make clear notes?

So while pick-up games of football were played on the school lawns, James taught me systems of note taking which I've never forgotten. He went on to tell me about the structures needed in good speech writing.

First explain what your demands are and why, and give the position that is being set out by the employer; then explain the weaknesses of the employer's position; demonstrate how it is in the workers' interest to pursue their claim; and finally show what should be done to win the claim. James also taught me to consider management policy at plant level in Marxist terms, and showed how it was possible to harness class interest when opposing employer objectives.

The school's itinerary concerned the emerging party programme, *The British Road to Socialism* (*BRS*). It was during its drafting that I heard Palme Dutt give a lecture about advances in colonial liberation in India and Pakistan, envisaging a future of neo-imperialism.

Dutt opposed a putative clause in the *British Road* to 'give colonies their freedom', as an imperialist hand-out with no place in communist policy. He argued that it should not be a question of 'giving'. Colonies would have to consistently fight to liberate themselves, and the British Communist Party should assist this by the distribution of international funding and the support of cadres. He won support and the clause was dropped.

It was at the school that I met Essie Guilder. She was a leading comrade in the International Department. She had a son called Steve, a lovely boy of five years. Sadly she and her ex had fallen out over his custody. Steve spent weekends with his father.

When he brought him back to Essie, his father would say, 'He's a kid of five and he looks a wreck.' Essie would ask Steve what they had done together. After listening to Steve recount a list of trips and entertainments she would say, 'But I can't afford that.'

In the end I was a bit rough. At the weekly Earls Court handover I arranged for a mate of mine to take Steve for ice cream. I told his parents I wanted a word. I said that they were destroying the boy, that they were both communists and should know better, that they could hate each other but should leave Steve out of it. I made it clear that if they continued I would find a heavy way to stop it; that I wasn't going to see the boy destroyed. Things became better after that. Steve and I were good friends. When Essie and I separated he wasn't pleased, but when he turned 16 and started work he let me know he was going to call himself Halpin. I protested that he was forgetting Essie and his father, but he insisted he was proud to have lived with me throughout all my 'battles'. That made me very happy.

At Briggs I had been elected steward of 400 inspectors. I pressed for the lowest pay grade to be abolished. The inspecting line had three different pay scales: the first inspector marking up the car body snagging was on the lowest, Grade III; the second-stage inspector was on Grade II; and the top of the line approving the body for the paint shop was king on Grade I.

Giving final approval was quite a hectic job. Any undetected defects would lead to complaints from the paint shop, while holding up the bodies could lead to rows on the body line.

The argument to abolish Grade III pay was simple. If the Grade II inspector was out, Grade III moved up and was paid a daily extra. If Grade III could do Grade II's work without any extra training or experience he deserved the same rate throughout. The shop agreed a proposal to refuse to move up without a consolidated rate and backed a full walk-out if the management offered a contest. The management accepted the claim.

Disputes also arose between Briggs and Ford Communists. Con O'Keefe at Ford led a campaign arguing that since the two factories were dominated by engineering workers everybody should be in the AEU. At Briggs we argued that our joint organisation across different unions was the stronger approach.

The Ford position had followers in the motor industry where often, as at Vauxhall, two shop steward committees would be vying for membership.

The matter was brought to a head in 1952 when Ford, following the three-week pay strike at Briggs, and unable to stand further disruptions at a major supplier in which it had no say, bought Briggs Bodies. The buy-out was opposed by shop stewards on the grounds that it would kill diversity but it went ahead. After the acquisition, Briggs ended its contracts with Austin for car bodies, with Humber for fenders, and with Rolls Royce for engine casings, and concentrated on making Ford bodies.

The Ford and Briggs factory Party branches also merged and I became secretary of the amalgamated branch. Stan Weston, a great comrade from Ford, became chairman, and a close friend. Stan was from north London, proudly self-educated. He'd been a tank commander in the Guards Division of the 1st Armoured. With Doreen, his Belfast comrade, they made a fine couple.

After some sharp debate the Party pressed for a Joint Shop Stewards Committee at Ford. The Party was growing in the Shop Stewards Committee, and in the wider political context.

The Korean War was diverting steel for arms manufacture leading to a slump in car production, and lay-offs were the traditional outcome. Ford was given a contract to produce jerry cans and ammunition boxes, but the jobs per ton of sheet metal were minimal in comparison with car manufacture.

Factory Communists led a campaign advocating job-sharing and a cut in hours to keep staff in work. Shop Stewards Committees from the six major car manufacturers coined the slogan of industry-wide opposition to the Korean War: 'Steel for Cars, Not War'.

This opposition became the basis of the National Motor Combine, the official grouping of these Stewards Committees, in which the Party had considerable influence, and the names of Dick Etheridge and Derek Robinson began to become known. Although 'Steel for Cars, Not War' became a familiar cry, on the ground jingoism was the default stance.

The 'Glorious Gloucesters', lauded in the press for being surrounded and outnumbered by the Chinese army, were not easily going to lose their glamour.

We handed out anti-war leaflets at the gate, but most ended up on the pavement. This was a period of anti-Communist aggression, an environment characterised at state level by the then Labour Home Secretary, James Chuter Ede, banning the 1949 May Day demonstration.

One leading branch member at Ford was called in by the management (possibly on a police tip-off) and accused of avoiding military conscription during the war. He was Irish and therefore exempt through his state's neutrality. They claimed his references were false and sacked him. Hostility to organised workers was practically a default position.

The old Briggs Body Plant took on several hundred women to make the jerry cans and ammunition boxes. They were a good crowd and put forward excellent stewards. One night trucks from the press shop were running car body panels through the aisle next to the ammunition box area, and the doors were left open. Soon the women grew too cold to work so the doors were shut. Then the panels piled up and they had to stop the press shop before it became too dangerous.

All the stewards crammed into the manager's office. He was in a quandary – should he run the ammo-box job or the press shop? We asked which he wanted stopped and he decided it should be the box line. At the next Works Committee meeting I asked for the women to be paid. The management replied that they would not pay them until the strike ended. I had to explain that that wasn't correct: the manager had preferred that the box line should stop production and the women had obliged.

In 1952-53 the Party ran a campaign against the rearmament of Germany. It attracted wide support from the variety of social groups that had fought for Germany's disarmament.

There was a large lobby outside Parliament which brought upon us the most aggressive policing we had yet encountered. We were driven from our position and across Parliament Square by police horses, the lobbyers offering no violence.

However, the military training of certain key stewards from Briggs was obvious and a chaotic crowd was soon transformed into a tight unit. Parliament Square was then under reconstruction, and we were able to use the various ready-made weapons lying about to fight back. It was one of our best days.

I was also fighting battles at work. By this time I was on a negotiating committee that represented six unions (AEU, TGWU and GMB, plus crafts, sheet and wood machinists) so it was perhaps inevitable. There was a big issue around the Docks TGWU under Deakin.

The union's right wing was enthusiastically passing around the Black Circular that advocated the banning of Communists from union office, and had become vocal in opposing class action, and attacking the dockers' fight for higher wages, lower hours and the eradication of casual labour. The NASU, the stevedores' union, began a progressive campaign urging dockers to leave the TGWU and win with NASU.

This gave fuel to the Communists at Ford who wanted the entire workforce at the main plant to be in the AEU. They argued that the TGWU was not an engineering union; a bad argument as it had at least 5,000 members out of the 15,000 at the Dagenham plant who were in Foundry, Electrician and Engineering unions.

This fight allowed the right wing to gain an even stronger foothold in both the TGWU and AEU. The engineers led by the Party at Briggs were opposed to the principle of being anti-TGWU, and the CPGB at executive level condemned the break-away at the docks. The solution was to stay in your union and fight to change it. But many in South Essex AEU could not agree with the Party's position and I was voted off its negotiating committee.

People like Ron Todd and Bernie Passingham have since acknowledged our stand, and the help it gave to encourage change in the TGWU. With Frank Cousins elected General Secretary in 1956 the Black Circular was scrapped, and after a time Bill Jones, Jack Askins and Danny Connolly were elected to TGWU's regional and national bodies, and Peter Kerrigan gave a lead during his time as CPGB's national industrial organiser. The position within the AEU was not easy to maintain.

In 1953 the General Secretary's post came up for election. CPGB had a brilliant AEU executive committee member for the London region, Joe Scott. We decided to run him for General Secretary. The snag was that the election for General Secretary coincided with EC elections and he could only stand for one position. Unfortunately a right-winger, Cecil Hallett, won the General Secretary vote, and the right-wing maintained their position in the AEU for years. To make matters worse Joe's EC seat went to a total incompetent.

During these election campaigns I had a peculiar experience. A National Metal comrade asked for my date of birth (the National Metal

Committee was the Party's policy committee for Engineering; largely made up of AEU members, it discussed union, industry and political issues). I thought it was decent of him to ask, imagining that he wanted to send a card when my birthday came round.

I was young and naive. He wanted to find out whether I could be a rival for union office. He was wasting his time in any case. Harry Pollitt had made the point that we had many Communist trade union officers and what the Party needed now was shop-floor leaders. He got me to promise to stay in the rank and file. I agreed and never reneged on that promise.

Cecil Hallett was put on the AEU's Ford National Committee to attack the left. I had a bit of spite with him.

My union branch asked him to report back after a committee meeting. Like all branches, if you were a visitor you had to show your pence card. Cecil didn't have his card with him. He pointed to a copy of the National AEU Journal where his picture was on page two, but the members felt they needed to be firm on this rule and asked him to wait while they discussed their options. He fumed in the street until we agreed that he could be an 'outside speaker'.

The AEU executive committee was archaic. Its approved dress was striped trousers, black jacket, black shoes and either a bowler hat or dark trilby, which costume they felt became them as craftsmen. During conferences the officials could be draconian. Delegates who came in shorts were sent back to their digs to change. When you stood for election you had to put your trade on the ballot paper. Toolmakers were the crème de la crème. The other engineering craftsmen - fitters, inspectors, turners, millers - were all a lesser breed.

I managed to get elected to the AEU's TUC delegation as a fitter. If a semi-skilled worker stood he didn't have much chance. Any one down as 'unskilled' ('USK') had none. Women could stand, but prejudice against them meant that few if any were elected. The AEU had always opposed women and the unskilled being members. Only after 1939, when unions sat on the war production committees, were they taken into the membership. (In many works where it was difficult to organise, war production committees became the basis for rank and file shop stewards organisation.)

But the prejudice remained. In craft branches in the 1950s you would often hear, 'This Union's been no good since we let in unskilled and women.' Quite untrue – in my experience women in particular have been to the fore in militant committees. It was our loss when employers forced them to retire when pregnant. Something of the AEU EC attitude can be seen in the meeting procedures at their Peckham Road headquarters. Staff had to sign in and at the starting time the General Secretary came out with a ruler and drew a thick red line across the register. All those below it were late and dealt with: 'We're not paying them for not being here.' They adopted the worst capitalist practices.

Over this period we succeeded in converting the motor industry from its hire-after-Motor-Show-then-sack mentality. The Party instigated a campaign for permanent jobs. There were doubts that we could achieve much: 'What can you do? If the company doesn't want you it has the right to sack you.'

We fought hard with the same arguments made in the face of 'steel for wars', and the management agreed to cut hours and introduce a two-day week rather than instantly make lay-offs. It wasn't possible to receive unemployment benefit until you had been out of work for three days, so we arranged that the two working days were Monday and Tuesday one week, Thursday and Friday the next, enabling people to draw a dole to make the wages go a little further.

We also fought for a standard five-day week. This was not nodded through and there was plenty of grumbling: 'This will spoil my Saturday. I go to work, come out and go to the pub, see the football game, a few more in the pub, and then home. Now I'll be caught cold in the house and the wife will make me go shopping with her.' It was a battle, but we won support eventually.

I continued to go to Hastings for the Party School during the seven days holiday allowed us each year. As well as the education, it was good fun.

By then Bill Oliver had joined the Party; a great comrade, and a fine 12-string guitar player and advocate of Woody Guthrie. This was a great period for 'Wobbly' Industrial Workers of the World songs. I could sing many Irish revolutionary numbers and because we had the word-sheets the songs didn't fade out after one verse. The music livened up the bar no end and the School was in great demand.

The factory branch continued to meet weekly at a local school. Special speakers came to provide key reports: John Horner, secretary of the Fire Brigades Union; J.R. Campbell; James Klugmann ; Jack Cohen; and Sean Nolan, general secretary of the Irish communist party, to name a few.

I also remember Max Morris speaking on the importance of comprehensive education, using the experience of Anglesey, the early runner in the project, as a case-study; and hearing Arthur Horner, the miners' leader, on nationalisation and its defects.

The best, with 70 in attendance, was the great writer Tommy Jackson. He spoke about the importance of books: 'Read any books,' he would say, 'good or bad, just keep reading.' Tommy was also an excellent hedge-priest, going from town to town and delivering speeches. His collection either paid for his bed that night, or he slept rough. He had already been jailed for publicly attacking the blasphemy laws. I was glad to send him on with bottles of Guinness stowed in his pockets.

There were big rows about religion. As an ex-Catholic I knew that religion wasn't everything, but I remember a particular incident with a comrade in the press shop. They'd been having terrible injuries, including one worker who was crushed in the press and several bad smashes with the crane hauling scrap.

No-one seemed to be heeding the warnings. A set of Irish lads were blocking the election of a comrade to shop steward. He thought his first job as a Communist was to be anti-religion and sell the *Free Thinker.* After a couple of meetings I managed to convince him that his first job was to ensure people stood clear when the crane was being operated. It took a bit of canvassing, but he was elected steward and the casualties fell. Against this background the Party was gaining support in Dagenham.

Our rival was the Leyland plant at Longbridge, where Derek Robinson was now king. Derek and I were friendly at this point, albeit in a challenge to build the biggest Party branch. It was later that we clashed on methods of trade union organisation.

The Party was attacking the penetration of Britain by US capital, so it can be imagined that a dispute at Dagenham attracted more Party publicity than it would at Austin, Morris or Rover. Politically, of course, the Party Branch continued to take part in all the demonstrations that were organised against anti-proletarian and colonialist regimes – Greece, Kenya, South Africa, Cyprus, Spain, and so on. I believe we knew every embassy in London.

At this time I met Harry Pollitt when he came to speak at the South Essex District CPGB. We got on well together as old Lancashire craftsmen and he welcomed the progress we were making.

Automation was advancing in the car industry. Car body panels often had up to five separate pressings and the panels were passed by hand from press to press along the line. New consolidated presses were installed that did the job of turning body panels on the line.

Machines were brought in that performed multiple jobs at once. The Party realised it couldn't prevent this process, but argued that where automation needed less labour this should be offset by cutting overtime, shortening the working week, lengthening the one-week holiday shut-down, and raising pay, pensions and sick pay.

We had great National Motor Combine conferences on the attitude we should take to these plant changes and the counter measures that could be offered. One famous conference was held in Birmingham. All the shop stewards across the industry were there. That is, all but Ford's. Our car broke down on the way and we were three hours late. Needless to say, we were in a Ford. Big shouts of 'Dagenham Dustbins!' greeted us when we finally arrived.

We went in to work on Monday morning, called an emergency meeting with the management, and explained in no uncertain terms our considerable embarrassment. The car was brought back from the roadside where it had expired and restored to new. The stewards were also compensated. (Incidentally, the deal for Ford employees was 25% discount on new cars based on a trade-in, and that was a result of our negotiations.)

Essie and I had married in 1953, holding the party at Pat Stitt's place in Forest Hill, where we had a small flat. We went to Paris for our honeymoon, booked by Sofka Skipwith, an upper-class comrade. We stayed near Gare de l'Est. Leaning out of our window I saw lots of women walking up and down in the street below.

A little later on the stairs I passed two of the women with men on their arms. The place was obviously used as a brothel, but Saskia, being European, hadn't noticed or hadn't, perhaps, cared. Essie, however, was not pleased.

We ate at the restaurant recommended by the hotel, the Femme Nouvelle. It was run by a group of women who had lost their husbands in the Resistance. The food and wine was down to earth and tasted great. In this period the French motor industry and the French Communist Party (PCF) were particularly interesting. I asked 16 King Street (the address in Covent Garden where the Party had its central office) for an introduction to PCF and the motor unions. Harry Pollitt sent me a letter which I have still. He referred to me as a 'good industrial cadre'.

I arrived in a troubled Paris. The fight for liberation in Algeria was in full swing and a war of intimidation was being conducted against Algerian patriots. Places where Algerian Arabs congregated were raided by armed gendarmes, and whoever they found was taken away and jailed. The PCF headquarters was heavily barricaded. I presented Harry's letter and waited while they approved my credentials and checked my passport. I was then told I would have to be taken to a separate International Department.

After further processing I was driven in a Party car to an unknown address (the comrade who drove me became my courier for the rest of the trip). There I was introduced to my host, Roger Linet. I was told he was a full time officer for the General Confederation of Labour (Confederation Generale du Travail - CGT) at Renault's 18,000-strong plant at Billancourt, just north of Paris.

I was disappointed. I said that I wanted to meet a Communist, rather than a union official, only to be told by an embarrassed interpreter that Linet was a Communist: not only that but also a Resistance hero and was also on the central committee of the PCF and a Deputy in the national assembly. 'Would that do you, Comrade Halpin?' I had the impression that if my letter of introduction had been signed by anyone but Harry I would have been thrown out.

The next day we drove to Billancourt. The Party was very successful there, with a membership running into the thousands. Trade unions on the other hand were as weak as the Party was strong. Coming from a highly unionised factory I found this disturbing: a union membership of just 50% seemed a disaster.

Comrade Linet explained that the growth of trade unions in France had been different from the experience in Britain. Unions were defined as Catholic, Social Democrat or Communist, and people joined because of their politics.

What surprised me was that those workers who were not aligned to a political party didn't take membership in a union. Each union put in claims on their own behalf; sometimes they acted together, although at others they were essentially in competition. If the CGT wanted to take action it had to put a good case and appeal for support across the board. If a strike was called everyone came out, all the trade unions and the non-union workers.

I argued that people should join a union to advance their wages and conditions in common, rather than for their political beliefs. In that way the unions would be more cohesive and less likely to suffer from divisiveness.

Having said this, there was ample evidence of unified action on the floor. Opposition to the Algerian and Indochinese wars was universal and all workers would throw any military vehicles off the line. We had lunch and wine in their canteen (much better than ours) and continued the discussion about the merits of each country's system. Then I was driven back to Paris by my courier, still arguing.

My courier was very sectarian. He was introduced as a Party member, but he told me later he was also a worker Catholic priest. The church sent them into industry to work and recruit in factories. He had studied Marxism alongside theology and joined the PCF. Back at home I presented a report to the Branch attended by around 50 (Party and non-Party) interested souls.

The Party at this time was under attack from the Trotskyist newspaper *Socialist Outlook*,. The Trotskyists were anti-Soviet, and they wanted the world to change immediately. They pushed for workers to leave right-wing unions.

We attacked their arguments at branch meetings and the factory gate. Some of our leaflets went to the centre and criticisms came back accusing us of being too divisive, which we ignored. Then the branch committee was invited to meet the Party's Political Committee led by Harry Pollitt, and including Johnnie Mahon, Rajani Palme Dutt and Peter Kerrigan. After a heated debate we agreed to give their views some thought.

Harry then suggested he come down and speak at the gate. About 100 people stopped to hear him. We had been lucky to get 30 on a lunch time. Harry asked how I thought it went. 'Not great,' I said. He asked if he should come next week. 'Give it a try,' I replied.

It was an arrogant way to speak to our best orator, but I was at a phase of thinking that if you could explain to workers the theory of surplus value you would get socialism: Harry had demonstrated the workings of the capitalist economy by relating a conversation about food prices he had with some women on the bus to Dagenham. Harry's reputation was irrepressible.

The next week hundreds were listening, the third week even more, and by the fourth thousands blocked Chequers Lane to hear him. 'Was that OK, Kevin?' he asked me slyly, but he didn't rub it in.

It convinced us to change the branch's strategy to *The British Road to Socialism* rather than violent revolution. Gate meetings were now a regular occurrence. Dave Kelly, the South Essex District Secretary, would open, followed by the branch chairman, Fred Tinsley. Then I would get up

I was very conscious of any hostility when I first started speaking, whether real or imagined, and I felt afraid of making a fool of myself. I asked what I should do if someone asked a question and I didn't know the answer. The old hands told me not to worry; if someone is interested enough to ask questions then you've made it as a public speaker and the confidence will be there to think on your feet.

The next battle with King Street occurred when Dave Kelly moved away from Essex and resigned as Secretary of South Essex District of the Party.

The Party's national executive decided to replace Dave with Johnny Williamson. Johnny had been deported from the US after serving a five-year prison sentence under the anti-communist Smith Act.

The Party had campaigned for his release on the grounds that he had British status having been born in Scotland. In London we had lobbied the US embassy and organised demonstrations.

However it was a different kettle of fish when the national organiser descended on South Essex District and called for us to appoint Comrade Williamson as District Secretary. I rejected the proposition from the chair, on the grounds that Williamson had no British experience at all; and as he was, to all intents, a Yank, his appointment would contradict the Party's anti-American stance and make the Branch a laughing stock with Ford workers.

Dagenham already had an American anti-Communist priest operating with the support of Cardinal Healy. Catholic Action was a force in Dagenham, home to many Irish workers. However, the National Executive Committee rejected our arguments and Johnny Williamson was appointed.

I was hauled up to King Street again and told I would have to work with him. Together we carried out this instruction as part of democratic centralism, and I found Williamson politically astute and a good organiser.

Johnny didn't care for the state of our district premises on Ley Street in Ilford, thinking them too untidy and disorganised. He had a point, but his solution caused a clash. He was friends with the great black American singer Paul Robeson, who as a result of another of our campaigns had had his passport returned after it had been cancelled by the McCarthyites.

Paul undertook a British tour thanking comrades, and Johnny invited him to attend a Saturday function at Ley Street, which at Johnny's instigation we had cleared out, the idea being that the social would raise the cash needed for refurbishment. Johnny decided to charge £5 per ticket.

I opposed this. Yes, there were enough reasonably well-off people in Ilford who could afford £5, but to many workers on £10 a week it was a big sum, and in rural Essex £5 was a week's wage for agricultural workers. Johnny's scheme would raise cash but debar many comrades who would have loved to meet Paul. I couldn't persuade Johnny, though, so £5 it was.

During the evening Paul took me aside and said he was glad to meet the person who had opposed the event. I told him I was pleased to meet him, but explained that as a comrade I wanted equality and he was only meeting those with cash. He understood my point, but he owed Johnny and hoped to repay him by doing as required.

I told Paul that there were no hard feelings on my part, and he spoke generously about Johnny's qualities. The party premises were done up but if asked would I do the same again, I would probably have to say that I would. Did Paul agree? Without being disloyal to Johnny, he would have raised objections. Paul was a lovely man who filled a room with life.

Although the inspectors won the two-grade wage-claim without having to stop the line, walk-outs in production were not uncommon.

One dispute was similar to the spark that led to the 1857 Indian Rising, when sepoys detected animal fat on the new Enfield cartridges they were obliged to bite. The trimmers put tacks in their mouths so they could be loaded on to the hammer with more speed. Someone changed the tack vendor. The body trimmers rejected the new tacks because of their bad taste, fearing being poisoned. There was a tradition in the trade that if you changed tack supplier the trim steward would act as taster. The line was stopped until the tacks were changed again. This was one of the 289 stoppages at Ford that later went to a Parliamentary enquiry after loud campaigns in the press.

Generally, these inquiries took the view that whatever changes management proposed, the workforce should simply accept and work them - management knew best; very rarely, if indeed ever, did they conclude that the management should negotiate before bringing in any changes.

Each of the factory's shops had a manager appointed from Detroit. Whenever I was transferred to inspect on a particular line I could organise in that shop. When this was noticed the manager would insist that I be sent elsewhere. This resulted in me having an experience and knowledge of production wider than any other steward.

Inspection tried to sack me but they had little grounds. I was obeying Harry's dictum: don't be late, be the best workman.

Eventually I was given a transfer to a set-up two miles from the main plant. My shop objected. Their elected steward needed to be on call. Startling offers of self-management, no clocking-on and higher pay were rejected: how long would these conditions last if their steward was two miles away? If I was out of sight, management was told, the shop would walk out of work. I stayed, but was put on Receiving Inspection so I couldn't interfere with production.

Briggs had always negotiated directly; the national officials came in only after members had decided to take action. However the Ford tradition was very different. In the 1940s, following failure to agree procedures, there had been an occupation of the Dagenham offices. The TUC is not known to be a negotiating body, but in this case they stepped in and set up a Ford organising committee. This was the sole negotiating body and comprised national officials only; our shop stewards had to lobby outside the door.

This merging of the different cultures led to clashes, but eventually a compromise was reached. A national negotiating body of officials and convenors was established. It was weighted heavily with officials but the convenors could count on support from the shop floor. This left room for stewards and union officials to disagree; especially true in the case of the AEU, with a right-wing executive that never authorised a dispute.

Typical of the environment in which unions worked in the 1950s was the building of Ford Halewood in Liverpool. Two unions, the AEU and GMB, were each given negotiating rights, led by national officials. This ended in separate working agreements with lower rates of pay and poorer conditions than at Dagenham.

The deals were done with a third-party, Liverpool City Council, which was run by Labour but controlled by its right-wing under Tom Braddock, husband of the notorious Bessie Braddock.

The AEU stewards protested but the executive committee stuck by its guns. The situation reiterated that shop strength at Dagenham came from our joint elections, even though each steward had to apply to his own union for the credentials needed to sit on the official bodies. Significantly TGWU, TASS, and the Sheet Metal and Vehicle Builders unions were all left out at Halewood. The dominance of two unions had resulted in a bad deal for the workers.

The AEU stewards then openly rejected the agreement, as did the GMB stewards, and joined a joint campaign of protests including token hour-long stoppages and a day's national strike. Liverpool Trades Council, the hub of the city, also raised questions on the deal and insisted on receiving a delegation from the Dagenham Stewards Committee, despite opposition from Brother Braddock.

Four members were sent up: Bernie Passingham, Ron Todd, Stan Weston and myself. We stood outside the Trades Council building waiting for the session to begin, enduring meanwhile a good deal of anti-London hostility from assorted Liverpudlians, none more so than Braddock, who as he arrived had his tenured mob of heavies brush us from his path.

When the item was reached, Braddock came out on the steps and called us in. We were told we had two minutes each to make a statement. We put our heads together and agreed it was better for one of us to speak for the full eight minutes. I was to be that person.

I began by begging permission to put on the table in front of Braddock the 'Blue Book' National Agreement on Pay and Conditions. This Agreement, I went on, was designed to guarantee common rates and conditions from Southampton to Newcastle; a common Shop Stewards Committee; and a common negotiating practice.

But in defiance of this commonality, the AEU and GMB had each created a separate EC for the north-west, and delivered to its members not the National Agreement, but the Halewood Agreement.

I understood that there were many unemployed in Liverpool. We were not there to undermine workers in Liverpool. With the plant building underway, implementing the National Agreement would not undermine workers, because the jobs were already there. Rather implementing the Halewood Agreement would undermine workers, and would, by lower wages and worse conditions, undermine the National Agreement for which they had fought.

Hostile questions followed.

Was there really a national agreement? I asked Braddock to read the front page of the 'Blue Book': 'The following, rates, conditions and practices, nationally agreed...' etc. The GMB official asked where the parties to agreement appeared. I got Braddock to read out all the signatories, including the GMB and AEU.

Our delegation was asked to leave the building while the chamber debated. We waited in the street again.

After a while Braddock and his crew marched through the doors and barged past us. Then others emerged and told us that a narrow majority had rejected the Halewood Agreement. That evening big headlines in the local press accused us of attacking the unemployed in Liverpool. I believe the affair convinced Ford Motors and many national officials of their need to part company with me.

I never got the 'Blue Book' back.

# 5 The events of 1956

What with the Party, the National Motor Combine and the National Metal Committee, you would have thought my personal life meant little, but it never seemed like that. I was living in Forest Hill with Essie and Steve.

We tried to get away somewhere once a year. There was always the Party School in Hastings, and we sometimes managed to go a little further afield and discover the bad state of English boarding houses. You had to be out from 10am to 4.30pm, which was perhaps not such a bad thing, although you weren't even allowed to go back to change if you had been soaked by the rain. But there were also, now that we had won a second week's paid holiday per year, expeditions to more unfamiliar places.

One year Essie went by train to Czechoslovakia to attend a peace conference. I made her three large tarts for the journey – apple, blackcurrant and gooseberry. They justified their luggage space. The American military guards stopped the delegates' train at the West German-Czech border and the passengers were stranded for a day. The only food available to the entire party was a modest portion of fruit tart.

Britain's relationship with the Czechoslovakians was very good at this time. In 1953 Czechoslovakia had held the World Youth Festival. The same year there had been a colliery accident in Britain and Czech miners collected for a disaster fund. Unfortunately, as the Czech currency was not on the exchange market, it could not be converted into sterling and sent to the bereaved families. Lou Kenton came up with a solution. People in Britain would pay for a holiday to Czechoslovakia; they would enjoy Czechoslovakian hospitality for free, and the money would go to the Distressed Miners Fund. This was the foundation of Progressive Tours.

The next year we answered an advertisement in the *Daily Worker* and five of us went to stay with Mrs M in Donegal. We sailed to Belfast where we spent the night. In the morning Jessica (one of the wives) was happily looking forward to her breakfast only to see it being taken away by the waitress just as it arrived. She had been given the two-egg man's plate. The furore was considerable.

We had a fascinating train journey over the mountains, travelling in a small diesel railcar like two single-deck buses joined together. At the first stop the driver jumped out of his cab and went into the Station Arms. Through the window we saw him have a drink before getting back on board. As the driver again headed for the bar at the next station, me and my mate asked if we had time for a pint. 'Sure,' he said, 'just make sure you notice me leaving.' To be on the safe side we stuck to halves of Guinness. We refreshed ourselves all down the line. The driver could enjoy himself; it was a single-line working with a passing stick for the opposite direction. It was one of the world's best journeys. We spent the holiday fishing and there were some good evenings in the local dancing jigs to traditional accordion and fiddle tunes.

It turned out we were staying in an area that had been well settled by Communists. A British comrade had died the year before and been buried in a wood by a stream. His widow used to water his grave, using a hot-water bottle tied to a stick to fetch the water from the stream. 'Ah, you're too late missus,' said a passing wag one day, 'he won't be needing a hot-water bottle now.'

Whilst in Donegal I met up with Sean Nolan and Michael O'Riordan, respectively General Secretary and Chair of the Irish Workers Party, the name used by the communists in the Irish Republic. I had met the Irish at International Conferences of Empire, soon to be abandoned. Ireland then had two parties, the Irish Workers Party in the south and the Communist Party of Northern Ireland. I remember particularly the Belfast Branch; Doreen Weston having a brother who sat on the Party EC in the city. We had discussions about the divisions and the need for a united Party and a united Ireland. Belfast was not convinced.

Later a visit to John Freeman, T&G's Ireland National Secretary, raised eyebrows. Freeman was a dedicated Marxist-Leninist, although not a member of the Party because he couldn't agree with our support for a united Ireland. Meeting him in his office I saw on the wall pictures of Marx, Lenin, and King Billy.

The Irish Party tolerated me as I was secretary of the Ford branch. Ford employed 5,000 workers in its foundry, all Cork men with few exceptions. The foundry men had a militant character. Their leader, Bill Flynn, didn't speak much. I first saw him at a shop stewards meeting that was calling for a stoppage. He put his hand up and announced simply, 'Foundry will be out.' We went on to organise the picket. 'No need for foundry to picket,' he said. 'Would you scab a shop teeming with molten metal and Cork men ladling it?'

Bill had been stuck against a wall to be shot by the Black and Tans, a British auxilliary unit renowned for its brutality in the Irish War of Independence. I got this from some Cork comrades who had joined the Branch; Bill never mentioned it.

The Cork men were religious but didn't let that get in the way of a pint, a chat, and taking action. They were a target for Catholic Action and other right-wing agitators, but gave their support to the Communist-led Foundry Workers Union. The rabid anti-Communist priest shipped in by Cardinal Healy from the US was called Father Roerman. At one High Mass during a strike his sermon condemned the action as a Communist plot. Catholics should take up shillelaghs and bodily drive the Communists out of the factory. It created an uproar. However, the Cork members were not going to be led by the nose. The protests were so strong that Roerman had to be withdrawn, never to be seen again. It was a good lesson for me as well. It convinced me that we were right not to be anti-Catholic, only anti-Catholic Action.

Essie suggested we buy a Lambretta scooter. It meant I could get to work in 50 minutes rather than one and a half hours, and would avoid all the buses and pubs on the way home. In the first year it took the two of us to Italy. In 1956, Essie insisted we go to Spain. 'Franco's Spain! You must be mad,' I said. Franco was at the height of his power, leading the Falangist party and running the country with the notorious three-cornered hat-wearing national guard. I had been on anti-Franco demos in London when he was garrotting communists. But Essie was more sanguine. 'Look, we won't shout about it, although I can't see the Party objecting. In any case, we're going.' I shut up.

Essie's family originated from north Africa and were Sephardi Jews. She spoke Spanish and French and had been involved with international work during the war, interviewing and assessing foreign nationals who claimed to be Communists.

I made sure the scooter was overhauled for its trip and we set off for the two-week Ford shut-down with a co-shop steward and his wife: early English tourists to Spain. We travelled through France, putting up casually each evening, crossed the border into Catalonia without any problems (if we had flown in we would probably have been turned back by the police), and drove down to the Costa Brava.

The Catalan roads were barely surfaced and threw up clouds of dust. We could see the dejection and poverty of the country. The people were depressed. We seemed to be on some sort of schedule. It became obvious that this wasn't purely a holiday, but an opportunity to meet other people: not necessarily Communists but those in the high bourgeoisie and royalty who were planning, not the overthrow of Franco, but the state of Spain after Franco. It was only years later when I became friends with a well to do Catalan that I put two and two together. She was a most upper-class comrade, educated with Juan Carlos I. His progressive links were shown when he opposed an attempted coup in 1981. At the time I was trained as a Communist not to even ask overseas comrades their name, but to wait until they volunteered it.

In the late afternoon we pulled up at the most expensive and exclusive hotel I had ever encountered, the Hostal de La Gavina. I asked why we had stopped there. 'It would be nice, for one night, to be posh,' Essie said. We parked the bikes and walked in looking like characters from La Strada. It puzzled us at the time but now I and my mate saw why we had been told to pack a jacket and tie. Essie had bought a silk dress. After we had changed she said she had friends to meet. She'd be a couple of hours. We should have a drink or two and she'd be back for dinner. We did just that, and she was, but I was never asked to meet her friends, nor was it mentioned again. It seemed best not to ask.

We had a memorable meal on the terrace. The food was excellent. My Dagenham man, fed up with the French 'rubbish' he had eaten on the drive down, asked for roast beef and Yorkshire pudding. The dining staff did not flinch. We would be called when it was ready.

We moved on the next day to a more modest hotel in a small seaside town down the road, which cost me the same for ten days, with good food, as one night in the Hostal de La Gavina. We spent the time swimming, drinking and eating. One night Essie said she had to go to the beach. She wanted to talk to some people. I wasn't to join her but discreetly flash a torch if anyone approached. It was like being with a gang of poachers.

We came back through the Camargue. In Marseille we couldn't find anywhere to stay: an international conference on Esperanto was being held. Myself and mate wandered around the city looking for anything. We came across two women who agreed to put us up but we found we would be sharing a bed not with each other but with each of the ladies. They were good looking but our wives wouldn't have thought it a good idea. After all, there were no blokes making offers. In the end we slept under a tree in the countryside outside Marseille. The men took turns to stay awake. You never knew with these foreign devils.

It must be remembered that the political situation in Spain was not unique. Up to the 1970s, holidays abroad were not straightforward affairs: Portugal was under Salazar, Greece under the four-colonel junta, Cyprus under British military rule. In all these countries the Party gave support to Communists and progressive organisations. Solidarity was expressed at the Embassy demonstrations, and at mass rallies, where comrades pushed for the banners to come out. One of the more conspicuous campaigns was the one to free Nelson Mandela; one of the most memorable demonstrations was the Democratic Greece rally in Trafalgar Square, at which Melina Mercouri sang.

The international campaigns led to some strange meetings. One evening in the Central London Caribbean Club, after protesting at the occupation of Guyana, I met Cheddi and Janet Jagan, and Forbes Burnham. I was introduced by a great dancer called Bernice.

Cheddi and Forbes were united at the time in the Guyanese anti-colonial struggle. Britain had recently sent out the frigate HMS Bigbury Bay, a symbol of hate to all Guyanese resistance movements. I could still sing the great song, 'Go Home Bigbury Bay, We Don't Want You to Stay'. The Guyanese got rid of the British but Cheddi and Forbes were later to split under the pressure of malign influence from overseas; Forbes eventually opposed Cheddi's Marxist politics and Janet's white Jewish US background. It was another example of the classic divide and rule strategy.

Cyprus was a massive cause. The island was split into two camps: one was to comply with the Greek Cypriot population's demand for union with dictatorial Greece; the other was to campaign for an independent Cyprus led by Archbishop Makarios III. We gave our support to the communist party in Cyprus, AKEL, which also advocated independence. One of its leading organisers, Stellios Costas, was a good friend.

I was invited when one of his family married at the Camden Town Round Church. The wedding included some ancient customs. After the sacraments the bride and groom each had a scroll pinned to their heads which was signed by the opposing family. Sadly the custom of pinning on the couple gold jewels and ingots, and promises of goats and pigs and other gifts thought to be appropriate had degenerated to notes and cheques, but the hospitality felt traditionally immense. Fomenting international solidarity was frequently a good deal of fun.

At Ford we had a new industrial relations manager, Lesley Blakeman. Ford had decided that if they had to deal with unions they needed a shrewd man. Blakeman was, I believe, out of Military Intelligence, and very well briefed. We had won the shorter week and longer holidays, and now turned our attention to pensions and deferred wages. The demands were backed at shop meetings and we negotiated nationally with convenors. Our key position was a contributory pension scheme administered by a joint committee, with Ford multiplying a worker's contribution by five. We had to thank the Labour Research Department which provided plenty of advice and support. The Ford scheme we established was so successful it became a model for manual-worker private schemes throughout the industry.

The biggest dispute of this period arose from the sacking of John McLoughlin, a comrade in the River Plant tool-room. John was a deputy steward. Following discussions which failed to reach agreement, he left the manager's office and rang the bell to summon a shop meeting. The manager came out and dismissed him. The tool-room and body plant walked out in protest. A mass meeting was addressed by the right-wing AEU executive, who recommended a return to work after a sufficient demonstration of support. The executive decided that John was wrong to call a shop meeting without exhausting procedures, but it had to promise a national ballot calling for recognition of a strike after a return to work was opposed. This was lost and it went to a delayed ballot. After a vociferous anti-Communist press campaign, this ballot was also lost and John went. We lost a good comrade.

In February 1956 Khrushchev gave a speech to the 20th congress of the Communist Party of the Soviet Union attacking Stalin and the cult of personality. Foreign delegates were excluded and that part of the Congress was held in closed session. It did not even issue a statement.

News of Khrushchev's speech became known via Israel. At first we doubted it as, politically speaking, Israel was not an immaculate source. Then the Party held back from overt criticism on the basis of Stalin's role in defeating fascism. A public meeting was called at Barking Town Hall, to be addressed by Harry Pollitt. I sat on the platform as chairman. The hall was packed to the walls and the atmosphere rowdy. It seemed every Trotskyist who could make it was there. The meeting demanded that the scheduled 9.30pm close be extended, and threatened to carry on regardless. Things were becoming uproarious.

I calmed tempers by calling Harry to make his reply by 9.45pm and asked for a show of hands in support, remarking that the Spotted Dog around the corner closed at 10.30pm. As I had hoped, this steadied the audience and afterwards Harry congratulated me on dampening a fiery situation.

The Labour Party opposed the Suez War strongly. The shop stewards backed this line and called a mass meeting to encourage protest. At the appointed lunch-time I stood at Chequers Gate urging attendance at the other gate near Princess Theatre. I soon wished I hadn't bothered. Labour sent an anti-Communist MP to speak – Bessie Braddock. She only glanced at the Suez issue before launching into an attack on the Soviet Union for its response in Hungary.

But Suez had big repercussions at the works. Many reservists were called-up, and many ex-servicemen put on reserve. As the war continued petrol rationing hit the country and car sales went into recession. The production manager took unilateral action. He called on the foreman to stop three of the lines. He then asked all workers on the right-hand side of the cars to step forward, and sacked them on the spot.

The plant walked out and would not resume until the sackings were repealed, offering a three-day week and job-sharing in recognition of the downturn in demand. We could accept a reduction in earnings to keep the workforce together. The strike was solid, the AEU executive had to back it in the face of the blanket anger and indignation from its members, and the management was obliged to back down.

The unilateral manager, if I remember, was a man called Murray. If he had been successful in his action he would have been the man who turned back Dagenham to casual working. The workers' stand effectively ended the policy for good in the car industry.

Hereafter there would be no return to the unwelcome tap on the shoulder on a Friday afternoon, 'Here, don't come in Monday. Pick up your cards with your week's money, and we'll send you a letter when we need you.' For militants like me that would have meant never. As it was Murray paid the Ford penalty, and was never seen again. We asked where he was at the next Committee meeting. 'He's moved on,' was the extent of the reply. You've never worked for a harder Guvnor than Ford.

Suez didn't stop anti-Communist action, and the AEU remained stubbornly right-wing. The executive treated elections as a full-time job and its candidates, often given leave by employers, would be handed lavish expenses to secure the vote. The anti-Communist feeling was stoked in the wake of the CPSU 20th congress and the Hungarian Uprising and it led to me facing a vote of no confidence at the next Inspection shop meeting. I won it by four votes. It wasn't until years later that the women members confessed how. They put on their white inspectors coats with an arm through one sleeve only, and with their other arm in the sleeve of their overcoats managed to cast two votes at the raising of hands. They knew I would remonstrate, but they didn't want to lose their steward.

However, I lost the vote to go as a delegate to the 1956 Congress. John McLoughlin won it. Harry Pollitt was concerned because John had become a bit of a maverick since being sacked. Our Congress held in April, coming after the Soviet's 20th in February, was bitter. Members accused the EC of keeping the Party in the dark, and acting as Stalin's lackeys. After some further sharp contributions, the EC won its vote, moving criticism of, but not opposition to, the Soviet Union, and recommended that there were important lessons to be learnt and that a special congress should be convened in eaarly 1957 to treat these considerations.

On being pressed for my views on Stalin, I held in mind teachings on the role of the individual in history and reflected that Stalin would be judged on his actions in the defeat of fascism.

During the US slump he had had the foresight to subsidise the Soviet Union's biggest car factory (built on the Ford model), and his order to remove it from Stalingrad to the Ural mountains, following Germany's rapid advances at the outbreak of war, was a brilliant strategic decision. By then converted to tank production, the factory made the famous T-34. This was the most effective tank of World War II, and it was instrumental in the tremendous battles of the Russian plains, which culminated in the Red Army's decisive victory at the Kursk salient, the turning point of the war on the Eastern Front.

The CPGB's 1956 Congress overcame the immediate crisis by appointing an Inner Party Democracy (IPD) Commission, on which I sat. The central issue under debate was whether the Party should maintain its position of democratic centralism, or allow a laissez-faire process where decisions could be interrogated at all times. The majority backed the executive committee and democratic centralism, but there was a significant minority in opposition.

The minority was headed by Christopher Hill, the historian, Peter Cadogan and Malcolm McEwan, a *Daily Worker* journalist.

I fell between the two camps. If EC decisions were not binding, allowing continual public attacks and factions would lead to the eventual break-up of the Communist Party. I took the view that democratic centralism was inherent in the British trade union position. Once shop stewards had decided on action, no steward was allowed to speak against and continue opposition on the committee. Once a strike was carried by vote, no one was allowed to cross a picket line on the grounds that they were opposed to the action.

While I agreed with the principle of democratic centralism, I also held the view that the Soviet Union had become too centralised in Moscow. Quoting the provisions made during the revolutions of 1905 and 1917, which established that action in Petrograd (the centre of the Party's organisation) was only taken after consultation with Moscow, Kiev, Baku and other major industrial cities. I argued that a semi-federal EC was the answer.

Week after week we met, then split as each side considered their response. The debate was big enough to be covered in the capitalist press, which had leaked reporting from the three main figures opposed to democratic centralism – Hill, Cadogan and McEwan.

When the Commission divided I would sit in a room and handwrite my views. It was not very satisfactory. Not being a practised typist, my thoughts did not have an easy relationship with my fingers. Essie had always done a massive job typing branch leaflets, but she now refused any help because she disagreed with my proposals. In consequence I felt isolated. I repeatedly had requests from the democratic centralists to join them, but they would not adopt any of my proposals. The laissez-faire party said they would include my proposals in their report, but I would have to sign up to their anti-democratic centralist line. This I refused to do.

During one of the adjournments Emile Burns came to my small room. We knew each other a little. He had been one of my tutors at the School. I was convinced, as he was one of the pro-EC majority on the Commission, that he was there to persuade me to back them, and by this time I was well dug-in to my trench.

'The answer is I'm sticking,' I told him before he had begun to speak. 'That's the greatest thing I've ever heard,' Emile replied, 'I'm not here to persuade you to change your view. I thought you might want some references that would help you to make your case.' I nearly fell through the floor (not difficult in a ramshackle building like 16 King Street).

'Why are you doing this?' I asked, still suspiciously. 'So that you in turn are able to put up a better case against me?' His reply was memorable. 'Kevin, you must know that a full and informed debate of theoretical differences is the basis of Marxism and the only way to carry the ideology forward.'

What a beautiful comrade. I've had some rough times in the Party, but his words always straighten me out. He made me a Communist.

Forty-five years later I was in Blackpool selling the *Morning Star* with an elderly comrade. I asked her name. She was called Marca Burns. I asked if she had known Emile Burns.

'Yes, he was my father.' 'You lucky woman!' I cried. I told her this story and she jumped up and gave me a big hug.

Eventually a report went to the special congress; the democratic centralist argument, the laissez-faire opposition, and my bit. It was debated, and I believe most of those who opposed democratic centralism left the Party after putting their case. I was never able to defend my position. I was not present as a delegate. I had fallen out of favour.

Instead I was asked to be a platform steward responsible for the order of speakers, so I was able to hear everything in any case. John McLoughlin attacked the EC, particularly Andrew Rothstein, whom he accused of being a 'flagrant fucking liar' who knew about things in the Soviet Union but did not speak out. There was a tumultuous response.

There were now three shop stewards committees at the factory: one covering the Ford engine plant, foundry and assembly; one at the ex-Briggs body and paint shop; and one in the tool-room, press and trim shop. Each committee met weekly and had its own full-timer and office outside the factory.

The committees ran on a voluntary donation from members of one shilling per month. It was barely enough, so the joint committees looked at a money-raising scheme proposed by Brother Green, a leading steward in the press shop. It was suggested we hold a raffle, with a Ford car as the top prize. The proposal was to sell single tickets for half a crown, and a book of ten for £1. By offering a commission of five shillings people around the area would be encouraged to sell tickets.

I objected as the prospect of watching publicans and the like taking a cut was too like capitalism in action. I lost the vote but soon saw the benign side of the scheme's character. The committee's strike fund rose steadily upwards until we were able to vote £400 in answer to a strike appeal and the treasurer nearly had a fit.

Ford's company directors didn't care much for our cash flow. With the money to hand we could put out reports on the same day as holding the negotiations. When we went to buy a car at the employees' discounted price we were refused. After some debate, we told them we would raffle an 'Austin' instead. Horrified at the prospect, they caved in. The draw was conducted at a free-to-members Family Buffet and Dance, with the best ticket sellers also invited. The tickets themselves were spread over the whole of Essex, East London, and the Estuary, together with prominent sales at the Ford factories in Southampton and Doncaster. I think some tickets even made it to Detroit.

During 1957 and 1958 Dagenham was extended with the construction of a new Paint Trim and Assembly plant (PTA). The plant was to be run by 6,000 workers. Two thousand ex-Briggs employees were earmarked for transfer (well-organised and sympathetic to the cause), together with 2,000 from the existing Ford assembly line (largely influenced by Catholic Action and Moral Re-Armament).

At first, management wanted to hand-pick who went over, but after some skirmishing it was agreed that every worker would be transferred if their job was transferred. The remaining 2,000 were made up from new recruits. They were mostly in their early twenties, having just finished National Service. Their military training hadn't, as management hoped, made them more obedient. On the contrary, they had taken enough orders.

I was now on Receiving Inspection; checking incoming parts, and breaking down samples and sending them to the laboratory for the materials and plating to be tested whilst I checked all the dimensions. In the process I was making hard cash for the company. There were three suppliers of each component.

One of the suppliers was on a hit list. Their product was carefully examined, even taken apart and checked against the blueprints. If there was any deviation the whole batch would be rejected, the supplier called in and a lower price agreed. The supplier had little recourse as the component was often made specifically for Ford. This meant sorting through the batch and putting the defective components on the top of the pile to convince the salesman. As far as management were concerned, I had a good reputation for making favourable deals. Hard cash is always noticeable.

Inspection management got on reasonably well with me. After all, when we fought for a common inspection rate the decision was down to Personnel, not them.

When they had tried to push me out, they made it clear that they were acting under orders. They like many others respected agreements and saw that they were observed. They knew that I would never agree to rulings without the backing of my members. That said, the Chief Inspector called me aside a month before the PTA was due to open and said he had orders to take me off the job to prevent me transferring to the new plant. I assured him that moving was immaterial to me and

I'd already decided to stay put. I was an established shop steward here, but in the mix of the new factory my position would be diminished. I would be easy to sack, both he and I knew.

It was management policy to get rid of me, a known Communist agitator. Why take a chance with the new factory? He accepted my word and I continued on the line.

His surprise was obvious when my job was transferred and I went into his office and asked to go over. He refused at first, but could only comply when I went back again with the convenor and a copy of the company's agreement to move each worker with their job.

Later he said I had lost his respect by lying to him, when he had taken me at trust. I felt a bit ashamed, but said that the company had behaved in bad faith. I apologised, and told him that sometimes you had to act for the overall good. He didn't know that the Party had insisted it was essential that I move across to the new factory.

I looked forward to the move from the Briggs/Ford Body Plant with trepidation. After all, I had a lively history of management defeats, sackings, offers of jobs and promotions. During the past eight years we had built a healthy factory branch, with a membership nearing 50. Could we maintain the momentum?

Whenever I was a delegate, I had spoken at each Congress since 1951 on the industrial mandate, although for myself the Congresses of 1956 and 1957 were a disaster. In those years I was twice nominated for the CPGB national executive committee, but on neither occasion was I recommended,because I couldn't accept or support the majority report on democratic centralism.

Politically I always supported the Party's parliamentary candidates. After our defeat in 1950 we began to selectively oppose leading figures with our best people. In 1951 South Essex District decided to run Johnnie Campbell against Winston Churchill in the Woodford constituency: the Tory wartime leader facing the editor of the *Daily Worker*. We ran a good campaign but Woodford was tough. Its Tory rabble saw it as a disgrace to oppose their country's hero.

Woodford had some big houses, and canvassing some rare hazards. We would crunch up long drives and knock on the door. It would be answered by a butler, who would visibly fume when we told him we were canvassing for Campbell. The signal to let loose the dogs would be given and we would tear back down the drive, striking off the house as a 'no vote' as we went.

Public meetings also aroused great ire. We were used to standing on a street platform and hoping a few passers-by might stop to listen.

In Woodford you got attention, including being knocked off the stage by Tories in suits. We had to requisition an open-backed ex-army truck in order to speak in relative safety. The atmosphere was lively to say the least, in large part because the election was soon after the shelling of HMS Amethyst on the Yangtze by the Chinese People's Liberation Army, the action that effectively ended the era of gunboat diplomacy.

The backlash against Communists was pronounced. Harry Pollitt had been beaten up while speaking in Portsmouth. He was never well after the knocking he took. That it was an attack organised by Navy brass seemed evident; the volunteers were probably livened up by an extra tot of rum. During the campaign I was barred from the George public house in South Woodford for wearing a Campbell sticker.

In 1955 South Essex didn't stand a candidate. Instead we were drafted in to support Solly Kaye in Stepney. He was one of three Communist councillors we had in Tower Hamlets who enjoyed a healthy Jewish backing before the Jewish population moved away from the Borough.

One Sunday we were canvassing in Tredegar Square on the moral ticket against prostitution. Although the square is now occupied by the wealthy, then it was a red-light area catering for the seamen from the nearby docks.

The comrade canvassing next to me was not streetwise. A blonde in flimsy decor came to the door and he said, 'You do know this prostitution must be stopped. There are decent people living all around trying to raise their children...' The lady cut him short with a smack round the face and the door slammed shut. He was obviously not the type she was expecting. 'What happened then?' he asked me.

I improved his social education, and he moved on with a wiser degree of caution.

In the last weeks at the Briggs factory I had my first encounter with attitudes to disability. The Green Card was a government scheme to get the disabled into work. Ford claimed it had no suitable jobs. When its hand was forced it continued to raise objections.

There was a young lad on the floor who suffered from epilepsy. He was called in by the management and told he was dismissed. The general opinion of the shop stewards was that there was nothing that could be done: epilepsy was too dangerous a condition to have on a production line. I went to the management. They were intractable: 'Your own members don't want to work with him.'

I went back to the shop and pleaded. If their child had epilepsy, wouldn't they want them to be given a chance? Not on a machine line, they replied. I tried another tack. I acknowledged having a fit looked frightening, and it was natural to want to ignore frightening things, but with advice we could learn what to do and handle the matter.

This approach worked and the line agreed there would be no danger to anyone if we knew what measures to take. They could look after the lad. The management had to back down. The lad was happy and the shop was happy. It wasn't a great thing, but it was certainly something I could never have done without the Party changing me.

Workers who had organised at Ford Detroit suffered victimisation and thuggish violence. It seemed such methods were being imported. The company now led searches at the gate at the end of each shift. If any company material was found the person was summarily sacked. If this was challenged, they would be taken to court for theft. Items could be planted in the luncheon bags that we kept on a hook by our work positions. This done, the gate could be tipped-off, the bag searched, the 'theft' uncovered, the police called, and the innocent person charged. The Party urged a motto: 'Turn out your gear, and fear before you go'. I passed on this advice to the shop stewards committee.

One evening I was leaving the plant with a non-Party steward. He saw me upending my bag and rummaged through his own. At the bottom were a load of copper tips from the spot welder. We threw them out and called at the gate. Inevitably the goons drew a blank, much to their confusion.

There was another tactic. Fighting between workers resulted in both being sacked. Ford boasted that it treated each miscreant equally. But when you found out that your antagonist turned up a bit later with a better job elsewhere in the company, and when you were a Party member, or a general militant, what then?

Ford would refute any involvement with agent provocateurs. The Branch came to a decision. If threatened by a fellow worker, you were to pick up one of the 2lb hammers common in the shop, and say loudly enough for people to hear: 'I'm not fighting, you know. What's your game though? You might get really hurt.' It was a rough stance, but we were not at a garden party.

And so, with this load of experience, I went as directed to Ford's new Dagenham PTA.

# 6 Dagenham PTA

The state of the PTA when we moved was shambolic. Dates for the start of production at the new plant had been given to Detroit, so the company had to proceed, although the building itself was only half completed.

On the first day the stewards were called in by the management and told to forget their previous positions. The national agreement had to be honoured and there would be no stoppages until we had raised issues with national officials. This took a long time, and in the meantime any changes made by the company would have to be worked. Also there were to be no shop meetings without management approval. This meant no protests or opposition to increasing line speeds. These measures were, of course, welcomed by the right-wing executive committees of the T&G, AEU and GMB.

It wasn't long before issues arose in the untried factory. The new system of moving the cars on skids rather than trolleys was untested. In one incident, a car stuck on the line but the next moved on regardless, trapping the legs of the operator. Conveyers ran over gangways and several cars fell to the floor. These dangerous conditions triggered a stoppage. The management called in the stewards and demanded a resumption of production.

We told them we couldn't have a meeting without permission. The management granted us permission. We told them that we didn't represent the views of management, but of the shop, and asked how shop grievances were being addressed. If we were threatened with disciplinary action for holding unauthorised shop meetings on the premises, we made it clear that we would meet off the premises, which would mean extended lunch and tea breaks. We were beginning to rebuild our strength.

Because the new paint shop was not finished at the time of the move, a number of Briggs stewards were not present for the annual election of convenor and deputy, positions sought by me and Bill Francis, a good comrade. We both lost.

The new convenor was a right-winger, and his deputy a member of Catholic Action. They developed a close relationship with the management, but not with their members.

The new PTA manager was a disturbing thug from a rugby changing room whose only refinement was in the arts of bullying, which he practised by walking around the factory and intimidating workers. After a run of stoppages he came up to me on the floor. 'Halpin, what's going on in this factory?' he bellowed. I looked up.

'It's Mr Halpin, Mr Rees, and I don't know what you're talking about. You should be talking to the convenor.' 'Fred Brown doesn't know what's happening. It's you and your crew who are behind these rows,' he replied.

I told him that he had made a name for himself by opening the plant without testing the line. He puffed himself up as some creatures do to appear threatening, shouted at me for a bit, then walked off.

Later on this manager took some of us into the new luxurious boardroom. For the wall he had chosen three pictures of geese flying against a wintry sunset. He asked what I thought. I told him they were nice. If you told an artist his pictures were nice you would have to step back. The personnel officer with his French wife knew it was an insult. After a brief hanging the flying geese were replaced.

We worked hard to put the factory in order, suspending nets below the gangways, installing stays on the skids to prevent the cars closing, and controlling the line speed with Rheostats. The paint shop was well behind schedule. The wiring was a problem, and often had to be redone. Some of the more militant electricians happily accepted this as 'more days, more dollars'. Since many were comrades, the manager eventually asked me to have a word. 'If things don't get any better tell them they'll all be sacked.'

As chair of South Essex District I was able to call a meeting outside the factory. I knew there were differences among comrades, so I didn't want to cause any resentment. I briefly explained the management position, and left them to it. They finished the job.

With the paint shop running there were another five stewards, plus two on the night shift. The new convenor insisted on accusing members of stopping work without reason.

The paint shop was strong and it wasn't long before there was a vote for a Total Shop Stewards Works Committee. I was elected convenor of this and Bill Francis was made Chair. It showed that the factory was still militant.

At the Dagenham PTA there were three car models running on three lines. Ford wanted unionisation of the lines to be organised vertically throughout the factory, so that each line could be treated as an autonomous unit. The stewards saw that if sales of one car model were declining, management could impose new practices on that line without fear of interrupting production on the other two. We resisted this and organised in one shop over the three lines, so that if, for instance, the trim shop was in dispute, trimming on all cars could be stopped.

The convenor's job was heavy. If during a dispute one of the shops went out, the whole plant was often hit. The management would send down a summons and demand a resumption with the threat of a lock-out. The convenor had to weigh whether the grievance was sufficient. Locked out members could be resentful at losing money by the actions of another section.

Oddly, it seemed to me, members on the day-shift would complain bitterly about a night-shift that had had itself locked-out. I couldn't see how it affected them. Bill Francis was ruefully cynical. Shift-work helped bed-hopping. Someone must have been caught out. It appeared to be the only explanation.

When Christmas 1959 came round the manager sent for me and the deputy convenor and handed us a parcel each. We opened them at our desks. It was a bottle of single malt for me, and a blended for the deputy. The Ford pecking order applied to the stewards. We raffled the bottles with the stipulation that the winners took the bottle back to their shop.

Although production was going well the management begrudged a Christmas party and tried to buy us off with a half-hour earlier stoppage. The floor thought this was rubbish. At the lunch break the lines were stopped, the cars pushed back and our pipe band played. What can you do in the face of a pipe band?

The PTA pipe band included a member who used to say that the convenor was like a laird who had his own piper and who would often lead our team on political demonstrations. With him playing at the front our progress was impressive, but attendance with his instrument did have a drawback – the custom of taking your piper to 'wet the pipes' which would be observed afterwards. I remember a particularly long evening that started at a Scottish 'Youngers' pub.

Our piper struck up and, while at first the music was welcomed, the novelty soon wore off and he was told to pack it in. There was a short protest and we were thrown out. We visited 'Youngers' pubs from Trafalgar Square to Whitechapel. The evening ended at the Black Bull and I last saw our piper playing his way down Whitechapel High Street at 11pm.

Ford's pay system was different from the rest of the motor industry. This led to a long debate with Derek Robinson and other comrades. They favoured piecework, which is a gang-based system where any bonus is based on the difference between the time allowed for a job and the time taken to complete it. So if a gang member was off sick the bonus was shared between fewer people. We countered this and said that a measured day rate for each individual worker was more equitable. We argued for a national agreement because a united fight for national wage rates helped weaker factories, whereas they - wrongly in my view - claimed that piecework gave more control over wages.

In addition to the national agreement, Ford introduced discretionary merit money of up to 9 pence an hour. This was privately agreed with the individual. Stewards couldn't negotiate it. During a quiet period we held a shop meeting and asked who had put in unsuccessfully for merit money. We produced a list of names and put this to local management who refused to discuss it.

We went back to the shop and members showed their objections by deciding to be uncooperative over requests for overtime. When management asked why, the stewards shrugged their shoulders and said we couldn't discuss that with them. The end result of all this was nothing: the stewards were still denied negotiating powers over merit money.

However, during one meeting the local manager asked to be excused. On his desk he had left a list of all those who had been recommended for merit money. The stewards were bad-mannered enough to have a look. In this game you get so used to reading upside down it's sometimes difficult to read straight.

After the 1959 General Election was called, South Essex District decided to run a campaign in Dagenham and convened to pick a Party candidate. I was chosen on the basis of my working in the motor industry. I stood against the incumbent Labour MP, John Parker, a mild, Toynbeeish man. My agent was Percy Denny.

Percy had a good track record. He was sacked by Ford for militancy pre-1939 and blacklisted. He could only get a job doing an insurance round. By God, I could speak a bit, but he could really canvass.

Women would often answer the door to our knock. They would say, 'I can't vote for you, it would be a sin.' Percy would step in. 'Now look here, I can see you're a Catholic. Do you go to confession? Well, you must commit sins. Give our man a vote and confess it next time you go.' His audacity took my breath away, and created some sinners, I believe.

We had called a march for one Saturday. Only ten people turned up. 'Not much good,' I said. But Percy was not to be defeated. 'Ten placards make a poster parade,' he said. Percy told me that, under the Corrupt and Illegal Practices Act, once the election had been called I couldn't buy anybody a drink when in the pub after a day on the stump.

The Act was introduced as one of the Chartist demands when lavish election parties were held in licensed premises and votes were bought with free drink. Earlier Hogarth pictured the scene. Percy advised me to spend the money saved when it was necessary, after the votes had been counted, for then any supporters would really need a drink. He was also responsible for pushing the Party's policy of touring the constituency afterwards with a loudspeaker and thanking the electorate for their vote, no matter how small it had been.

The issues on which I ran were clear: opposition to NATO and its anti-socialist aims and threat to peace, and opposition to any extension of the Schuman Pact; and an advocacy of arms cuts, social housing, comprehensive schools, and the take-over of the motor and aircraft industries. It was a busy campaign, attracting backing from all areas in Essex and there was a real district spirit at hand.

The campaign also led to the factory branch growing in size, a trend noticed in other areas where the Party had fielded a candidate; Derek 'Austin' Robinson in Birmingham, for example, and Jimmy Reid in Clydebank. There were ten Communist Party candidates in all, if I remember correctly.

In the PTA pressure was growing for an increase in wages. The negotiating machinery was a TUC set-up filled with national officials from the Confed. The Confed was a representative body of 39 engineering unions. It was opposed by the Engineering Employers Federation, which in the 1920s had locked out every engineer until the unions accepted the York Memorandum, decreeing no stoppage of labour until the grievance had been subject to a protracted approval procedure ending with a vote at the annual York Conference of engineering unions. The Memorandum was eventually defeated after a long campaign.

Factory convenors were only recognised within their particular union, not jointly. Therefore we had to wait in the street for a report back. After a series of negotiations a successful wage claim was announced at the expense of both the morning and afternoon tea break. Of course this agreement wasn't subject to the indignity of the members' endorsement.

All 350 members of the Dagenham Joint Stewards Committee rejected the agreement but the management insisted on implementing it. No tea service went out the first day. On the second day the lads brought in their own drinks. The management threatened that the first person to walk off for tea would be disciplined, but it was difficult to discipline the entire shift of 3,000 in the PTA.

A mass meeting was addressed by Claude Berridge. He said the deal had been the only a way to get a wage increase which met with howls of disapproval. He quoted Shakespeare: 'This above all: to thine own self be true.' As chairman of the meeting I then stood to oppose. I too quoted Shakespeare:

'He which hath no stomach to this fight,
Let him depart; his passport shall be made,
And crowns for convoy put into his purse;
We would not die in that man's company
That fears his fellowship to die with us.'

This brought the house down, and Claude retreated. Afterwards he good-humouredly ribbed me about the incident. Quoting Shakespeare can be dangerous, he reflected, because he will always supply your opponent with a counter-quote. The officials had to return to the negotiating table grinding their teeth and give back the cash and reclaim the tea breaks. In the end the wage increase was won by an overtime ban and work to rule.

It's evident that the leading Ford stewards were more unpopular with national trade union officials than they were with management, even though the 2,000 new employees at the plant were mainly T&G or AEU members acting under right-wing executives. They had the choice between these two unions. The factory was recruited on the basis of 100% union membership, and in one or two cases failure to join led to stoppages. The issue spawned lengthy discussions. To anyone who said enforced recruitment was against his will, I would reply that he could go ahead and work on the line. The members exercised freedom, and they wouldn't work with someone who wanted to take benefits with no commitment.

I never believed in a 'closed shop', which meant you had previously to be in a union to get a job. This came from the old craft philosophy to keep labour scarce. Surplus labour was forced to travel, with union branches giving sustenance and lodging under rule; hence the term 'journeyman', the name given to those who came out of an apprenticeship for which there was no job available. This control tried to limit the number of craftsmen and benefit wages through scarcity.

Craft wages were aligned to that of a Coventry toolmakers' differential won in 1916. This was a bad deal: it didn't fight for higher wages, but if another section was given a rise the craftsmen had a percentage, say 10%, of the gain. The attitude which for years refused to recruit non-craft members, semi-skilled workers or women stopped engineering unions moving into the new production industries. This finally ended between 1939 and 1945 and the presence of the new entrants began to flush out the old craft attitude.

Meantime I continued with my education. I was given a place on a month's School at Hastings. The first week we had a general history class; the second week we read Marx and Lenin on the role of the individual in history; the third we looked at history and Marxism; and the last was concerned with International Socialism and the way ahead. I managed to get the whole month off work to attend the School: I had a good team in the District and a doctor's certificate.

In the last week I received a phone call from an unnamed friend who said he would like to meet up with me in the local pub. It seemed strange so I mentioned it to the School chair. This happened to be James Klugmann, a perfect person to give his opinion on the matter, having been undercover with the SOE in Yugoslavia. He advised caution and thought I should return home. I was shipped out of Hastings in the back of a van lying under a tarpaulin. Safely in London I saw the certificate out and returned to work on Monday. I never got to the bottom of this, and have speculated that the mysterious caller was either Special Branch or a Ford investigator.

During this period I changed my Lambretta scooter for a Jawa model with a bristling 175cc cross-country engine. I decided to take it back to Czechoslovakia. We had a three-day run to Prague. There I was able to put the scooter in for a service at the Jawa shop.

I had arranged through the Party to visit the Skoda car plant. It had been nationalised in 1945. I met up with the trade unions. They were well organised. The Party was strong within the membership. The unions were supporters of the Government and there were not many strikes, if any at all. I was introduced to the manager of the Skoda plant, an engineer, who showed me around the factory. Coming from the newly built Dagenham PTA I looked about in horror. Car bodies were being pushed from shop to shop on wheels, rather than running on moving conveyors. It took a gang of eight to navigate them over the cobbled yards between shops. I said that to increase productivity they could easily concrete over the yards. The suggestion was not well received.

The work on the car line was a joke. Their system was to stop the conveyer while the gang worked on the body. I don't know how many cars an hour they turned out but it wasn't the 34-36 we were producing in Dagenham.

At Ford the lines started at 8am and 1pm. If you were half a minute late you were working out of station and had to slave to get back. You had to shout for a relief if you wanted the toilet. If you went too often you were hauled into the manager's office and could be in for a reprimand. If the line stopped during working time a hooter blasted and a red light flashed where the off button had been pressed. All the managers whizzed to the place. The reason for the stop had to be good. Switching off was a major crime. There would be an inquest and if there was found to be insufficient reason, a dismissal.

There were no stacker trucks at Skoda. Throughout the factory, components were pushed around in barrows and then stacked. I explained that, with their engineering skills, they could build stacker trucks if they didn't have the cash to buy from abroad. I received looks of consternation.

I toured the factory all day and afterwards had a big debate with the Skoda team. The stewards wanted greater productivity and I argued that trade union economics saw that when there were more cars made, more profits were produced, and higher wages were justified. Just installing concrete tread-ways would save 75% of pushing, and making half a dozen stacker trucks would enable a good amount of palleting. But the management was aghast and my arguments fell on stony ground. I left with a large fine vase, but not good wishes from the engineer.

After Prague we drove around the country. One day we stopped in Pilsen. We were meant to be moving on but the beer was so good we had to stay the night. We spent a week in the Tatras mountains, 3000 metres up by funicular railway. As we couldn't take the scooter we asked where we could leave it. We were advised to see the police station. The police were happy to lock it up and very friendly to a westerner who had bought one of their products. It was the first time the scooter had been detained.

There was a pool at the mountain hotel where we stayed. After a few beers I jumped in. I wish I hadn't. It was fed by mountain streams and colder than ice.

Back at the Ford PTA I explained how Skoda worked to the stewards. They couldn't understand me. It was as though I was speaking a foreign language.

I was working at Dagenham PTA when one day I was given a message: 'Two women are waiting at the gate for you to finish work. They say they are your sisters, Joan and Mary.' They said they had seen me on TV during a strike meeting. I remembered Joan used to write while I was serving in the Mediterranean: 'When are you coming back? Don't forget that you have somewhere to stay.'

Her letters used to make me feel fed up. The Med was so full of mines that very few Patrol Service crew were ever released. When I was finally discharged and back in London I knocked on Joan's door. It was Saturday lunchtime. She opened it. 'Oh, we are just going out. There's a good cafe down the road. See you later.' I didn't wait in the cafe and I didn't return to the house. Now, when I came out of Ford on my scooter and saw them both at the gate, I carried straight on.

Then my step-sister, Teresa, telephoned me at the shop stewards office whilst I had the plant out on strike. Father was dying. She asked me pleadingly if I could come to see him. I felt an obligation towards her, whom I had helped to raise.

The next day was Saturday. I agreed to drive up. It was a long run on the scooter. I arrived in Preston Penwortham at 7pm that evening and saw him. There was no death-bed reconciliation of the kind you read in novels. I detested him and he felt likewise about me. I didn't stay but got on the scooter and drove back to London. I had to prepare for a strike meeting that I was to chair on Monday. It was the last time I saw my family.

I had a few drinks in a pub as I headed south. Later I was pulled over by a pair of motor-cycle cops. I admitted I'd had a few. I'd just been to see a dying father. They said I would have to stay off the road and asked me to follow them carefully. I thought I was being taken to spend a night in the cells. Instead we pulled up at a pub: 'It's best if you stay here,' they said. They came in with me while I booked a bed for the night. I thanked them and offered them a drink. They declined.

Writing about Halpin's non-family I ask myself if I would do the same now. Of course I would. That's what made me who I am. I had a family with the Party.

It's funny how things change. My Boris grew up and decided at 16 that he wanted to be trained as a chef. Anita thought he should go to university. After a debate I said, 'He lives in the East End but he's not on drugs, he doesn't have a police record, and he wants to be trained. We're lucky.' So he applied to Walthamstow College to do a three-year City and Guild catering diploma. He was accepted (he was asked what were seasonal fruit and vegetables to buy in April, to which he replied that the question was out of date but he hoped the college wasn't). Luckily he came from a house used to cooking a variety of foods, a great advantage over those applicants who grew up in families where a lack of cash often leads to ready-cooked dishes.

He passed the course, and began work when he left, and married Jerusa. And now they have a family and the two children ask if they have any great-grandparents, or great-aunts or uncles, and I can only give vague answers. It seems strange to them with their extended relations on their mother's side. Perhaps they will read this when they are older and realise what a funny person their Kev was.

At the PTA we were given constant warnings that we were conducting illicit shop meetings, but as car sales were flourishing management had no incentive to attack us. With every battle we had, the personnel manager, Lesley Blakeman, became wiser. In fact, if you want a career in personnel I think it's a good idea to be given some left-wing opposition. Blakeman was so well-trained that he became Ford's UK Personnel Director.

The factory manager moved on, his place taken by the lower factory manager. Ford were so status-conscious that over a weekend his office was made smaller, a thinner carpet laid, and the easy chairs replaced with less comfortable examples. I remember his face when we observed that he had rather come down in the world.

I was offered the convenor's office but turned it down because I preferred to be on the shop floor. It was like being on the bridge of a ship. We had an enormous log-book which noted a wide variety of facts and data, and kept me up to date with what had been happening on the night shift, and the night shift with the day.

Round the desk I had sitting the works committee. This consisted of two right-wingers, two Communists and one loyal supporter. As an ex-Catholic I would sometimes tease the right-wingers: 'Have you attended Mass for your Holidays of Obligation? I expect you to live up to your faith, you know. As a Communist I scrupulously attend my Party branch.'

One day the bullying manager caught me walking around holding a stack of *Daily Workers*. 'I've totally caught you distributing and selling papers on the premises without approval,' he said. 'You had better come up to my office.' 'I'm not distributing them,' I replied, staying where I was, 'I have them for the study of typography. I get sent them and I'm required to give a report on printing deterioration. And you haven't seen me selling anything.' 'Have them then, bastard,' he said, and walked away muttering.

In 1962 demand at the factory fell off, particularly for the oldest model on the line, the Ford Anglia. New processes and increased line speeds were enforced on the trimmers finishing the car. Bill Francis, chair of the trim stewards committee, called a joint trimmers meeting without consultation. As soon as management heard of this they sent for Bill and me. They told Bill he was dismissed with immediate effect as he had been repeatedly warned about holding shop meetings on the premises. Bill said that changes without consultation made ad hoc meetings mandatory, but no discussion was allowed. Then the management turned to me: 'Mr Halpin?' I replied there was no alternative but to call the factory together at lunchtime.

I had in my pocket a letter from AEU officials which urged stewards to keep to the 'no meetings without permission' rule, but which failed to understand that if this rule was enforced our members couldn't respond to changes and would have to work them. The result of the mass meeting was a total stoppage of the PTA. The Joint Stewards Committee convened and got the body plant out (although in doing so the chair was sacked). The chassis foundry was shaky, but would try. The Party then held a national meeting, which called for all Ford factories to come out in support. The National Motor Combine also met and recommended all-out strikes across the Ford plants.

The outstanding feature of car production at the time was that productivity could be gained by updating machinery in the mechanical and press shops but that this increased productivity had to go to the 'car-end' processes in the PTA, which were all manual. Management might try to consolidate the gain by increasing line speeds, but this physical pressure on PTA workers was met with resistance, disputes, and calls for action.

However, we were under great pressure from the CPGB to get all shops out in solidarity. In hindsight we should have concentrated on keeping the PTA on strike. If no finished cars were being produced, the PTA had a chance of winning this dispute on its own without being distracted by any of the tensions possible in maintaining a total stoppage. The PTA had counted practically 6,000 through the turnstiles in favour of strike action. There were only 20 against. But with a majority of the Ford and National Motor Combines backing strikes the Dagenham Foundry and Engine plant went back to work. At this point 700 workers in the PTA were sacked. I was one of them.

National union officials had already been called in. They had been holding off the balloted strike action while they conducted further negotiations. Now they ended the strike and were left to negotiate the summary dismissal of 11% of the PTA's workforce.

After long discussions 700 sacked was reduced to 300. There was no negotiated resumption and all the stewards were still on the other side of the gate. The 400 workers who were given their jobs back were issued with a brutal warning: any more objections to changing practices and they would be out of the gate again. Manufacturing output didn't count; the company wasn't producing cars, only victimised militants.

After further negotiations another 250 workers were taken back. It became evident that each person was being screened. Another call for action was held off by officials. By this stage we were officially arguing victimisation. Union officials, with only a few exceptions, maintained it was a national redundancy.

After two months there remained 17 workers whom Ford refused to re-employ, principally the leading stewards at the PTA. The management claimed that we had worked against the company quoting statements that 'Communist Candidate Halpin' had made about US control of factories and the need for nationalisation.

The fact that there had been screening of the workers was made obvious in a peculiar anomaly. One of the 17 had no track record of militancy. We remembered that he had refused to join the union until we threatened a stoppage. His manager clearly saw him as a source of trouble. A final ballot on action was lost due to the disillusionment of the work force. The organisation at Dagenham was so weakened that a strike called from outside the gate was near impossible.

Trotskyists came to Dagenham and argued that everyone at Ford should stand up and oppose the sackings. The CPGB Industrial Sub-Committee met and decided that any militants who got back should keep their heads down.

It was more important to rebuild trade unions from within the factory than have another defeat so soon. We carried this to the stewards meetings. It was hard luck for the 17 who the management refused to have back. The case put up against us by the media was relentless. We were hunted men.

This continued throughout the autumn and hard winter of 1962-63. The CPGB could only advise Communists in the Motor Combine what to fight for in the stewards committees. We picketed the gates and leafleted constantly, urging backing of the shop stewards' position and continued membership of unions. It was rough sitting together all week arguing the Party line. Some comrades were not convinced and joined the Trotskyists. We sent speakers throughout the country, visiting shop stewards, factory branches, district committees, regional offices.

After a few months I received a call from Ford to present myself at the gate and pick up my tools. I was escorted to the tool store and shown to my gear. I never knew I had so many expensive tools. The storekeeper winked as he handed the boxes to me. I took them away, heartened that the working class will still looks after its own. I refused to pick up my cards or dismissal notice, but they were sent to me by a special delivery.

We were receiving cash from the strike fund, and when we were 70 to feed we were given a good tip from the T&G regional office. We should buy food at the wholesale markets: meat from Smithfield, fruit and vegetables from Covent Garden, fish from Billingsgate The father of one of our comrades owned a pub in old Billingsgate; The Mermaid I think it was called. We bought in bulk when the markets opened at 5am and met back at the pub where we roasted some of the haul on a shovel over the fire in the public bar. Then we went back to the stewards' office to share the food out.

Militant market stewards also sent us food. Many mornings we opened the boxes from Billingsgate expecting cod and hake, the cheap fish at that point, but the boxes had been marked incorrectly and inside we would find salmon, halibut and Dublin Bay prawns, all of which were then caught wild and very expensive.

On occasion we discovered game in the meat boxes. The trouble was not many people knew how to cook the food: they were more used to cod and chips from the chippie. I had a funny job of writing recipes to go with the butchered portions, improving Essex cuisine by leaps and bounds. It got me the title 'Halibut Halpin', but it kept up morale.

The Ford shop stewards committee continued to meet weekly but the management would only recognise the negotiating committee of TUC national officials. After a short time I stepped down with the other victimised stewards.

By now the unions had accepted we were victimised; even the AEU's right-wing executive paid out Victimised Workers pay under pressure from Reg Birch, the new communist executive member. It was less than half the Ford wage, but we were some of the very few members to be paid victimisation money in our union's history. The Party factory branch suffered badly but carried on. The majority had seen the wisdom: lose a battle, not the war. It was a set-back, but the survival of trade unions at Ford proved the Party correct.

At one of the last negotiations on our case I wandered out of the hotel where we were meeting, and to gather my thoughts went into a pub where convenors lobbied national officials during recesses. To my surprise I found a group of them drinking with Mr Lesley Blakeman, the architect of my demise. What was I to do?

Raving would surely give him too much satisfaction. One of the convenors was at the bar and bought me a pint. I returned the round next time and asked the convenors what Blakeman was drinking. I wasn't going to let him give his colleagues a laugh about a humiliated Halpin. He sipped the pint with an ashen face.

# 7 Blacklisted and Ship Repair

Then began a very rough period. The relationship for which I left Essie broke up. For a while I lived in furnished rooms in Kilburn. It was a bit bleak.

Thankfully, good comrades and friends Ron and Barbara Champion (she had been chief sub on the *Daily Worker*), offered me a garden flat in West Hampstead. It did up nicely.

I started looking for work. Skilled engineers were in short supply. Often convenors or stewards would tell me of jobs and be surprised that the black list operated.

As a typical example, I was offered work planning plates at a printer. I was told it was losing its only engineer. The management didn't want production to stop: could I turn up tomorrow?

I was taken to see a West Indian man who was doing the job. For domestic reasons he had to go back to Jamaica urgently. I promised the foreman I would be on the door at 8am the next morning. When I got back home there was a telegram waiting for me. I was no longer needed, the job had been filled. So it went on.

Eventually I decided to save demoralisation and only apply for three jobs a week.

As a hobby I began to learn about architecture. I would visit cathedrals on my scooter, taking in the local Georgian houses at the same time. I found Rochester Cathedral the most interesting. It contains all the orders of English medieval design in its nave, so it is rich ground for a student – 'Never Eat Dirty Potatoes': Norman, Early English, Decorated, Perpendicular.

I combined this study with an interest in pub games. It was a good combination as old pubs could often be found close to the precincts of the cathedrals.

They were untouched, still at that time traditional houses resistant to the trend for luring custom in with 'pub grubbe'. You could buy a plate of food, but it had no aspirations to modernity: cold meats, lumps of cheese, pickled walnuts.

The games I discovered were various: ring-board, table skittles, alley skittles, bar billiards, bagatelle, shove ha'penny. The strangest I came across was in a pub in Hertford. Standing in a corner of the bar I was surprised to hear the locals intermittently shout 'Heads!' while ducking for cover.

It turned out they were playing Ringing the Bull. A giant bull's copper nose ring was hung on a chain, which was thrown at a hook on an upright. When it missed, the ring swung on its chain in great indiscriminate arcs. I don't think the game would have survived Health and Safety regulations.

I wrote a pamphlet for the Party titled *What's Wrong at Ford?* It was the first time I came across professional sub-editors, who pruned it to leave only the words that were needed.

It was the Champions who worked on it. Barbara had been well trained by the great Allen Hutt, the person responsible for the *Daily Worker's* prize-winning design.

I was still busy with Party campaigns. I gave a report on the importance of not giving up trade unionism to the Dagenham Trades Council. At that point the Council was in the political centre and sympathetic to the victimised.

On the basis of my report I was offered a job. Since the terms included me dropping union membership I declined. Picking up a paper the next day I read the headline: 'Communist Halpin leaving Union for a Job'.

I telephoned the editor and asked for an apology. He was abusive. 'Do I believe a Communist, or my reporter? Shove off, Halpin.' I arranged for the Party lawyer and distinguished members of the Trades Council (two Mayors and several members of Essex County Council) to vouch for my position.

That afternoon the editor rang back apologising. I told him he had had his chance and it was now in the hands of my legal representative. I gave the same reply to his subsequent calls. The lawyer, a good comrade, settled for a published apology in the same place on the front page, and several hundred pounds in damages. The cash went into the Party funds.

I carried on looking for jobs that weren't there; weren't there for me, at any rate. I went to a leading diesel-injector firm. The notice board announced there were vacancies for a skilled inspector, assemblers, grinders, and in the heat treatment shop. I walked into an empty recruitment office and applied for the inspector job.

I had experience checking their diesel pumps when on receiving inspection at Ford. The woman in the office was delighted at my application form. Not many had my experience and were available. She asked me to wait while she took the form to another room for processing. She came back, puzzled. There was no vacancy in inspection. I changed the application to assembly.

She returned even more confused, so I changed my application again, this time to be a grinder. She came back again. There were no vacancies in grinding. I asked if this was the only office, and said I thought I was the only person in it, unless there were people I couldn't see coming in through the window.

Where was she taking my forms? Two doors down. 'Oh, but Mr Halpin, you can't go in there...' I didn't knock and surprised the personnel man. He told me there were jobs left in heat treatment. It was dirty work, he said, not what I was used to. I told him I'd take it.

'It's night-shift.' OK. 'You won't get moved on to days.' OK. Then he leaned back in his chair and told me that, in point of fact, he couldn't employ me as the company did a lot of trade with Ford and they knew all about me.

He then asked if I could explain exactly what had happened at Ford. I couldn't decide if he was trying to improve his knowledge, or wanted to dine out on this rejection of Halpin, the well-known militant. Either way, I decided I didn't want a job lecturing in personnel management and said goodbye.

A couple of days later as I was walking home the Party Industrial Organiser Peter Kerrigan pulled up in the road and asked me how it was going. I said that it was no good, I was fed up. 'These things happen, comrade,' he replied, 'I've known militants who have been out much longer. Just stick to it, and whatever you do, stay in engineering. You've been victimised by Ford, but don't be victimised from the industry. It seems hard, but this is what being a communist is all about.'

I had given up the fight for my job at Ford. Some of the 17 wanted to organise a victimised workers body, but I didn't want the conflict. There came a time when it was important to move on.

Reminding workers how good it used to be does no good for stewards in the factory trying to pick up the pieces. Equally workers can look at victimised members and think: 'They were militant and were sacked; we had better keep our heads down.'

It was hard working publicly as the Communist parliamentary candidate in Dagenham. Ford workers would tell me how bad things were compared to when we were in the factory. I always said 'different days, different people', remembering Marx and Plekhanov's theories on the role of the individual in history. Individuals don't make history, but can be there to seize the chance of circumstances. Saying this would give their view of the situation some perspective.

I have since always opposed victimised workers' organisations. Coming from a strong base and losing is enough to suggest to working people they can never win. In fact I think that employers should pay the people they have smashed to go round the country on display: their presence alone says the worker loses.

I was called in by the manager at the Labour Exchange. I knew him from when we paired up to draw four days unemployment during the two-day weeks at Ford. He offered me coffee, which I thought unusual treatment for someone signing on for a long time.

We began to chat about my employment prospects. He suggested I change my career path. Maybe I could take up hairdressing. I could be given some financial backing to train and enter at a high level. For a moment I saw myself in a little shop on Curzon Street, barber to gentlemen. But then I remembered what Kerrigan had said. I thanked the Exchange manager for his suggestion, but something would turn up. I liked being an engineer.

I was kept occupied at the Party branch and with the parliamentary campaign. I had plenty of time for it. I would also visit galleries and museums. I wasn't rich but I discovered ways to make savings. I would scooter down to the Westons cider shop and by filling a 4.5 gallon barrel (a 'pin') I could buy my drink at 10p a pint.

I was also busy pushing comrades in organised engineering to pressure for a job. I was aware that I would not get a start until a stewards committee insisted and threatened action. I was fed up with convenors telling me there were vacancies at their factory and their puzzlement when I didn't get a start. I determined that if ever I did get a start, wherever I worked, tackling victimisation would be a priority.

At least I knew exactly why I was out of work. During negotiations Ford had declared: 'We have nothing against Mr Halpin's work or qualifications; his time-keeping record is first-class. We are dismissing him because he is hostile to Ford Motor Company. His public statements as parliamentary candidate for the Communist Party are there to prove it.'

There was also my hostility to the Halewood agreement, and to low wage offers with increased work-loads. I had a good work reference that I could never use. I was on the blacklist kept by the Economic League as a dangerous man to employ.

Eventually comrades in London ship repair (Arthur Wells, Bill Robb and George Anthony) told me there was a job at one of Harland and Wolff's repair yards. The news came on a down day for me but young Ann Champion, then aged 14, urged me to give it a go, so I went down to Surrey dock to see the foreman.

Unlike dockers who were now registered, ship repair workers were still casual and had to sign on daily at Silvertown labour exchange. If a ship repair worker went on holiday he still had to sign for work on the casual register each day in the town where he was staying.

However there was a boarding house in Scotland miles from anywhere where you didn't need to sign on as the house was outside the stipulated mileage from the nearest labour exchange. I believe that it was run by Mrs Mackenzie. So when you went to a certain lady at the Silvertown exchange and said you were going on holiday she would say, 'I suppose you're staying at Mrs Mackenzie's,' and sign-off a non-attendance pass.

Mrs Mackenzie must have occupied a very large and well-run house and welcomed the loyalty of many casual workers over the years. The labour exchange lady would receive gifts from holiday-makers at Christmas; chocolates, sherry, gin; but not flowers, for the sake of discretion.

Harland and Wolff ran an engineering vacancy list. Employers in a casual industry periodically applied for skilled men and I was on the register. There was no great interview procedure, no forms to complete. If you didn't suit you were sent away. The previous driller and marker-out had drilled through the machine bed without realising it and been dismissed. The yard depended on the marker-out and radial driller, along with the other dozen or so tool men who provided engineering equipment what kept 200 men working, hand-sharpening drills up to four inches in diameter.

I was lucky. The foreman stated that he didn't think drilling would be a problem to me, but what about marking? How would I mark out 27 holes in a pitch circle of 25 inches diameter? Often you would have to acquire the accuracy by trial and error, but having come from Inspection I was able to give a simple formula based on a table of constants multiplied by the diameter. I got a start.

I went in on Monday and was given charge of a radial drill big enough to frighten an ex-inspector to death. Coddy (generic name for the yard's charge hand; private name, Peter Cresswell) gave me some plain plates to drill.

He showed me how to do 'holding-down bolts' and then I was off. For the first couple of days I was very anxious that Harland's management would lay their hands on a black-list. I jumped every time the foreman's phone rang, thinking the upstairs office had rumbled me. I kept my head down and didn't speak to anyone. I let my smart toolbox do my speaking for me.

After working at the yard for a few days Harry on the machine next to me said 'Hey, why do you jump when the phone rings?' I was aggressive, and asked what it had to do with him. 'It looks like you've broken out of jail,' he said. The steward, Bert, came over. 'Leave the bloke alone, Harry, OK?' 'OK, Bert,' said Harry.

The next day Harry said the sweetest thing I'd ever heard. 'Look, Kevin Halpin, we know who you are and that you've had a bad deal after Ford; but we look after our own in Ship Repair. The day before you arrived, the shop had a meeting. We were told all about your Ford story, and we decided that if you didn't get a start we wouldn't work.'

I looked at him and thanked him. Then I went for a walk around the yard so he wouldn't know quite how affected I was.

Having your class back you in that way is better than any honours, or medals, or cash. Sometimes in the ups and downs of trade union life you get a bit despondent. At those times I remember the lads at Harland and Wolff.

A few days later Bert said that when I wanted to be a shop steward he would resign and the lads would elect me. I told him that I wasn't intent on replacing him. He knew the industry and had served his time in ship repair. I came from a different game. I would love to represent his members, of course, but give it time. I had a lot still to learn. Certainly, there was a lot that was new.

The engineering trade at Harland was different to what I was used to at Ford. For a start I never had to hand-sharpen drill tools at Ford. Here it was only you, the drill and a grindstone. They were a good crowd though and gave help when it was needed. Our Coddy was one of the best. His desk was right next to my drill. I couldn't go wrong.

In the meantime I was still putting myself about as the candidate for Dagenham, raising the politics of our Party over issues like South Africa, Vietnam and Tory scare-tactics.

I moved my union branch from Dagenham to the great AEU craft branch called 'Tower Hamlets' (a name it had held long before the

Addressing a meeting organised by South Essex District of the Communist Party

newly-formed united Borough took it in 1965), and also sat on a very active Stepney Trades Council.

One weekend I had to stand in for the Stepney and Bethnal Green delegate to the London Federation of Trades Councils monthly conference. On Saturday the statutory meeting was held.

I knew that most of the people attending would have raised the Ford victimisations at council meetings. I walked in to a greatly embarrassed silence. The chair asked me to go outside. He came out and said he was sorry, but as a Communist the model rules imposed by the TUC barred me from being a delegate.

He was a sympathiser, however, and said that if I retreated today he would raise a Special Rules Revision Meeting to overturn the 'Black Circular'. The following month I was welcomed back to the Federation with a round of applause. I was delighted to be breaking the bans and proscriptions on militants and Communists. This weakened the influence of the Black Circular and began a great period in the trades council movement.

I settled in to ship repair. The lads at Harland and Wolff also found a berth for Taffy (Bill) Francis. Although Taffy hadn't done much engineering outside motors, they got him a job with General Steam Navigation, overhauling the pleasure steamer Daffodil. In season, this was doing the cockney outings down the Thames to Southend and round the Kent coast to Margate. His yard was about four miles downstream from Surrey Dock.

One of the outside fitters at Harland had worked on the Daffodil, so Taffy was able to explain to me what needed doing and I would talk it over with my fitter, taking his instructions back to Taffy by scooter during lunch. It worked OK, ship engineering by courier.

Later I went on the Daffodil for a Sunday outing. I listened to the engine. It sounded fine. In those days, however, there were no concerns about being adrift without power. Even with a four-knot ebb tide under the keel, there were plenty of tugboats working the river to overhaul you and give a tow.

There were 4,500 people working in the dry docks at this time. The London docks derived from the canals built to enable sailing ships to come up the Thames in a straight line, under sail if the wind was right or otherwise by a land tow. The canals became wharfs; then in the 1800s the non-tidal docks were built.

Berths were charged by the day or tide, and were not cheap. This was handy for ship repair because there was great pressure to catch a tide as demurrage would be incurred if a ship was forced to prolong its stay.

A ship eager to sail before the next tide would negotiate a 10pm job. We would be paid overtime, but if we knew we could complete the repair within the time we would do a 'job and knock'; going for a long lunch break while leaving a noisy machine running to make it sound like we were hard at work, or we would knuckle down and get to leave the yard early.

The term for this ploy was 'hoppy hoppy out', which came from the days of sail, when the bowsprit of a moored ship would sometimes poke over the dock wall and a sailor could go ashore early by taking a shoot from it down a rope.

Hiring and firing was still the main employment practice. Only a few were permanent men; they were called the 'Royals'. There were no women in the yards. The only ship work they did was cleaning on passenger liners; a dying breed as flying took over.

The graving docks in which we worked were based on designs perfected before the advent of pumps. Originally craft would be moved in at high water and a lock gate floated to the entrance. As the tide retreated the dock emptied and was then sealed. This worked only on tidal waters with at least a 25-foot drop of water. The Romans must have used the method for their galleys. One graving dock, the

Orchard, by the river Lea, was very old; built before the introduction of pumps, it appeared. It should have been researched. I suppose it has been filled in now.

Harland and Wolff was a peculiar place to work. I was there before the Thames Barrier was constructed, so at neap tide the river came over the shop floor and we would be forced to retreat to the local pub. There we would often be put to work by the landlord filling sandbags to save his cellar from flood; for free beer, of course.

The yard was very traditional, with long memories handed down the generations. I was told to watch the storekeeper. I didn't know why, unless it was because like all storekeepers he would give out old tools and hoard the new ones (when the yard closed they just emptied all the good gear into a skip while he stood aside weeping).

After a bit I asked why I was watching him. I was told that as a youngster he had scabbed during the General Strike.

We worked exclusively on Port of London Authority craft. The PLA had a large service fleet of tugs, huge dredgers, and immense floating cranes capable of lifting steam locomotives. It wouldn't want a bolt to go when swinging one of those across a deck so its inspectors were tighter than Lloyds of London.

Perhaps the best job we had came when Winston Churchill died. His coffin was taken on the Havengore from the Tower to festival pier. My shop had the job of creating a highly polished bier. Overtime was unlimited. There was working all night with no check on hours. It was a great financial week.

One of the lads observed that dying and getting us the job was the only good thing Churchill had done in his entire life.

A boiler-maker at the yard came up to me and said, 'You're a Communist, did you know Harry Pollitt worked here? Oh yes, he used to come every morning for a job. Foreman would come out and go 'You, you, you, and you – but not you, Pollitt'.'

Harry had a good reputation as a plater. Plating was the top job in ship construction; they were the highest paid craftsmen. The blacklisting continued until the platers had had enough.

On that morning the Foreman came out of the gate and picked his hands; as usual, Harry was not among them. 'What about Pollitt?' the platers asked. 'Not having him.' 'Well, we're not going in without him, and we'll ask your boiler-makers what they think about it. We reckon they would be happy to join us out here.' The boiler-makers were permanent workers.

The Foreman hurried in to see the manager. A few moments later he came out again. 'Right: so it's you, you, you, you, and you, Pollitt.' There was a good tradition in the yards.

Harry Pollitt was well-known all along the river. He had been in the front line of the action to prevent the Jolly George shipping arms to the White counter-revolutionary army after the October Revolution.

The dockers unloaded the hold, and the munitions were still on the quay when the ship eventually left port. Harry was well up the black-list.

Most of the ship repair yards in London had connections to the shipping lines: Russell & Co were linked with Blue Star, Green & Silley Weir with P&O, Harland and Wolff with City Line. Many of the apprentice engineers in the repair yard went to sea as ship's engineers. It was an occupation that appeared to lead to drinking. After retirement the old hands loved instructing the new apprentices. Before lunch they were brilliant, demonstrating complex theoretical positions with a piece of chalk on the wall.

Trade unionists gave the apprentices particular attention. They might be employed by the firm but we trained them and gave them trade union politics.

On Wednesday afternoons the Harland and Wolff apprentices had Social Studies. I was responsible for their cultural education, taking about six youngsters around London. Sir John Soane's Museum was a good start.

We would look at Hogarth's 'Industry and Idleness' series, showing the apprentices starting out together and ending with one going to the gallows and the other sniveller becoming the mayor of London; we'd laugh to speculate which of them would be which.

The next week we would go to the Courtauld Gallery. Then we would save up and go to Greenwich. Then pick a good play at the Old Vic, or watch a ballet at the Royal Festival Hall.

Afterwards on those evenings we would go to Bertorelli's for a meal, a real favourite. Once, to their loud amusement, the Italian waitress congratulated me on my 'lovely sons'.

It was a good period. Very few apprentices in my care didn't end up with class politics.

It was a funny industry. A mad manager had a campaign against casual tea-making. On one occasion he caught a cup being brewed out of hours. He asked the blacksmith's striker, who was standing nearby, whose tea it was. 'It's Brooke Bonds',' he was told.

The levity of the reply drove the manager's fixation to an extreme pitch and he sacked the striker on the spot. Three days later the manager went up to the blacksmith and asked him why there was no more dredger chain.

'You've sacked my striker,' said the smith. The manager called over a mate. 'Here's your striker.' 'I'm afraid not. We always pick our own strikers.' Eventually the manager had to find the striker he'd sacked and ask him back. The striker said he would see the week out and be back in on Monday. They paid him for that week.

Once we had a visit from the managers at Harland and Wolff's yard in Belfast. I fell down laughing. They all had bowler hats, black jackets, and striped trousers; one or two even carried umbrellas, like typical Orangemen.

I became a steward. It was different from Ford.

We had a series of dock cranes to repair. Our estimator agreed a price with the owners. Then I cheekily asked how we would stand if we couldn't make the job pay by delivering on time. I was expecting a reply along the lines of 'hard luck', but instead I was told there was a guaranteed 'fall back' rate.

The yard had a shop stewards AEU committee which supported all the progressive international motions on Cyprus and South Africa which were then being debated.

There was also a Party Branch which met regularly, and which sold the *Morning Star* (formerly the *Daily Worker*) and distributed leaflets in all the shops alongside the dry docks.

I soon became aware of craft-consciousness in the yards. There was a crafts confederation which held wage negotiations and joint meetings on major issues.

At one point it agreed a complete stoppage. I asked what I should do. They told me to shut my tool-box and tell the mate to lock it in the crib. Then I asked what of the mates and labourers – would they be voting? I was surprised to hear that they would just stay at home and be told when the strike was over. They had no say at all, even though their wages were linked to the craft's.

Coming from Ford where all workers had a vote regardless, I argued the point, but they were adamant. In the end they grew tired of my persistence and threw me off the steward's committee. I had to fight to get back.I hadn't realised that I was in the sectarian craft world. When I left Dagenham AEU to join Tower Hamlets, I learnt that my new union branch had not long agreed to take in women and the unskilled.

The Communist Party local councillor, Peter Roach, couldn't at first get in; not because he was a Communist but because the branch was full. According to their rule it could only have 500 sitting members. If it was full you had to wait for a death.

I was accepted as a great favour. The secretary announced because of my past I would also be given a low number – 69. I was mystified about the meaning of this until I attended my first meeting. Putting my hand up to speak

I was told by the Chair to wait for my number. Number three spoke, then 16, then 24, and so on until 69 was reached.

The craft branch was proudly rigid, right from the start: an apprentice applying for a card had to be endorsed by two members, both of whom had to have worked with the applicant and could swear he was skilled at his trade.

# 8 Tower Hamlets and anti-union laws

The Communist Party was particularly strong in Tower Hamlets. It was a good place for politics with banches in the docks, lighterage, ship repair, and clothing shops (including the famous Rosner factory on Commercial Road). The Party had a Borough Committee representing 1,000 members, and the Borough itself had three prominent Communist councillors.

Solly Kaye led the way, standing for the Party in the Stepney constituency in each General Election from 1955 until the constituency was abolished in 1974. He had been raised as a furrier, a traditional Jewish trade. I was familiar with Solly, having been sent into Stepney to support his campaigns when South Essex didn't have a parliamentary candidate. He was an excellent public speaker. With Solly were Peter Roche and Barney Borman. Barney was recognisable during elections for his idiosyncratic canvassing style. He would single out houses and advance on them with a loud-hailer. 'Mrs Speigel, you remember me, it's Barney. I got your front door mended. Come out now, and give me a vote.' Peter Roche was a market-trader, quieter than the others but a grafter. It was a big loss when he moved to Australia.

Tower Hamlets council was largely characterised by Labour and Catholics. Irish dockers had long been in the area. It's said that the Labour Party in Stepney was set up as a cover for Irish Republican supporters who reputedly used it for running guns to the resistance. This influence was centred at the Church of St Mary and St Michael. The local MP went to every service there.

The lightermen and tugboat men were a rough lot, but intellectual and well-read. I made the observation to a comrade, who explained that waiting for a tug while swinging on a buoy gave plenty of time for reading. The Watermen, Lightermen, Tugmen and Bargemen's Union was one of the most political in the country.

The peculiarity of Tower Hamlets was its building workers who were active under the rank and file London Joint Sites Committee where Lou Lewis was Secretary. The building sites and exhibition industry were very well organised. The close links to building gave Tower Hamlets Trades Council its base as the docks closed.

Building sites were still dangerous places. The scaffolders' union branch met in a pub called the Scarsdale on Prescott Street. There was never a time when I visited the pub that I didn't contribute for the family of a scaffolder who had died or been maimed in a fall.

I was on the Communist Party's Tower Hamlets Borough Committee when we lost our secretary. Solly was under attack as treasurer for letting Council work distract him from his Party responsibilities. In the end the secretary walked out, leaving comrades aghast. Who will do the job? I was so fed up I volunteered. I told my comrade from ship repair, Ted Crook, that he was Treasurer.

Being secretary was quite an education. We occupied premises opposite the Mann and Crossman Brewery. I didn't start all that well, calling a meeting for Friday evening, forgetting that it was the eve of the Jewish Sabbath. I also had to negotiate Jewish jokes. They were invariably excellent, but took about ten minutes to arrive at the punchline. Then someone had a better one. A meeting would be set for 7.30pm, but wouldn't get down to official business until 8.15pm. We must have been the only Communist committee which changed the standing orders to call time on Jewish jokes. I was accused of anti-Semitism. I revised it to, 'No jokes of any nature'.

The seamen's national Communist Party branch also met in Tower Hamlets, at 46 Burdett Road, the house of Diana and Jim Cameron, an International Brigader. It was near to the cafe opposite Mile End tube from where recruits set off to Spain (the cafe is now an estate agent). During the seamen's national strike opposing flags of convenience, John Prescott would attend these meetings.

Years later we met again when we spoke on the same platform during the P&O dispute at Dover. By then he had advanced up the ranks of the Labour Party. I asked him if he remembered the evenings at Burdett Road, and drinking in the pub opposite after the meeting had closed. Prescott said he hadn't been there; he didn't know what I was on about.

The problem of the Borough was that it comprised Stepney, Bethnal Green and Poplar, but most resources were concentrated on Stepney. By comparison the branches were dead in Bethnal Green and Poplar. Ted and I decided to reinvigorate these wards. We got them going with Saturday loudspeaker meetings from Ted Crook's van. Ted insisted we couldn't speak from inside the van, even in pouring rain. 'They won't like you sitting in the dry while they're outside getting wet,' he would say, although it led often to a very wet Halpin.

We took the loud-speaker out to the markets and asked comrades to turn up and sell the *Daily Worker*. It was hard work but worth it. Gradually Party branches in Bethnal Green and Poplar began to be re-established.

The Party in Tower Hamlets suffered a set-back in 1967. Israel's Six-Day War was generally supported by the Jewish residents. Once when canvassing, if you saw the Mezzuzah scroll in emblem by the door you could hope for a vote as representing the party that opposed fascism and was associated to the Soviet Union, the first nation to support Israel.

This changed as the Soviet Union and the CPGB opposed Israeli aggression. The position accounted for a drastic loss of support. We argued ideology on the doorstep but couldn't overcome the sentimental pull to the Jewish nation. During this period we lost our three councillors and many readers of the *Daily Worker*. It was a very hard time, and it appeared only Marxists in the Jewish community stayed loyal. They had to resist enormous pressure from their families, even though we were a party that couldn't open our premises on Friday evenings. After Solly left Stepney I stepped into his shoes as parliamentary candidate for Stepney and Poplar, but I found them hard shoes to fill.

Nationally the Party was active in the promotion of peace, opposing the apartheid government in South Africa, and providing international support for socialist countries. Ireland was on the horizon, but at this point the IRA was still the official resistance: the split that led to the Provisionals had not occurred.

The CPGB was still advocating class struggle, supporting the Labour Party where necessary but also standing candidates on alternative policies whenever possible. But some of the positions on class were developing following the increased study of Gramsci's writings, initiating a debate on intellectualism and plural politics.

In the course of this debate the proposal to change the name of the *Daily Worker* to the *Morning Star* was put forward by its editor, George Matthews, and supported by the CPGB Executive under the General Secretary, John Gollan. The change wasn't automatic as the paper enjoyed autonomy from the CPGB in the shape of its shareholders, who had to approve the vote at their AGM. The argument from Matthews and Gollan was that ever since 1951 and the adoption of the Party programme, *The British Road to Socialism,* we were no longer a party relying exclusively on the working-class, but also the middle stratum of society. The change of name represented this new approach and would broaden the paper's readership.

I saw the change as figuratively diminishing the role of the working-class in the Party. I argued that if a product was known it had an identity and reputation, and we would be wasting a lot of time explaining it was the same product under a different name. After all, one of the key positions of the advertising industry was establishing the brand name. The *Daily Worker* had been founded in 1930 and made its name as an antifascist paper, which reputation had survived the Korean War and the Cold War. To change the name now would be a disaster. It seemed to represent a shift away from the CPGB as a working-class party. My branch put aside democratic centralism and spoke firmly against throughout the debate.

The name change was voted upon at the People's Press Printing Society shareholders meeting. I spoke and voted against, joining leading Communists in opposition, but the vote was carried and the change went ahead. There was no disciplinary action; that would have undermined the paper's separate identity from the CPGB.

However, there was once again a black mark against me: I was unreliable. I feel that at the subsequent Congress it cost me a place on the EC, even though I was notorious as a victimised comrade and well-known as a parliamentary candidate, and Chair of the South Essex District with 1,200 members. Such is life, but in hindsight I believe that I was correct and the *Daily Worker*'s change of name was the start of the slide towards Eurocommunism.

Soon after being elected secretary of the ship repair Party branch I was approached by a leading anti-apartheid campaigner. He was in the Party but working unrecognised at a time when the South African Government was using secret service assassins to eliminate opponents. He asked me to meet a South African in the remote Royal Standard pub in North Woolwich. The need to keep the meeting confidential was impressed on me. I was to mention it to no-one, not even the Party EC.

Arriving at the appointed time, we were introduced without giving names, and over pints at a quiet table the South African explained what he wanted. There was a ship bound for Cape Town secretly carrying goods for the resistance. This ship was lying disabled in the Red Sea having run her main-shaft bearings and the skipper did not want to put in to any of the ports along the coast for fear of discovery. Could

I find a team that could sail for the Red Sea and cast new bearings on board? They would be paid well, but there could be no known comrades, or anyone who would look on it as anything other than a normal job (repair teams would take ship to damaged vessels, so this in itself was not unusual).

I agreed to help. I told a reliable comrade at the yard that there was a job going and asked if he could gather any volunteers in the normal way, but not to put his name up for the job. This done, I never enquired further to maintain a disinterested attitude. It seemed he got a team together because after a time I received word that the job was completed and the ship had sailed.

I was in a Communist Party that was responsible for assisting many colonial countries to become ex-colonies. One of the traditions of this struggle was that of 'need to know'. If you didn't have to know who you were helping, and it wasn't essential that you knew names, you were trained never to ask. Gossip could be the end of successful clandestine operations.

It wasn't until after the Mandela victory that the South African Communist Party was able to send openly a fraternal delegate to Britain. I was introduced to him. Before his name was mentioned I said, 'But I know you already, I'm sure; we've met before.' 'Yes,' he said, 'we have met. Do you remember where?' I smiled. 'It was a long time ago. I don't remember where it was.' But I knew it was at the Royal Standard, North Woolwich. I told him my name for the first time, and found he was Ronnie Kasrils, a prominent member of the ANC's 'Spear of the Nation' military wing, and the then Deputy Minister of Defence in the ANC government. It doesn't, perhaps, take too much to guess what was aboard the stranded ship.

The 1964 General Election coincided with my start at Harland and Wolff. I stood again in Dagenham. Paddy Grimes was my agent. Paddy was a marvellous Irish personality. He had worked in the Party branch at the Cooperative Society on Leman Street in Stepney, at a time when the whole of the area's Cooperative Wholesale Society was led from that address.

I remembered the ban on buying drinks, so for progressive reasons Paddy got them in. However when the poll closed I headed into the Travellers Arms, opposite the Dagenham Civic Centre, and thanked my support while the count progressed. Concerns that I would miss the call were unfounded, and I remembered a bottle of Scotch for those comrades working as counting agents.

Overall, working the Dagenham streets was dispiriting. I grew weary of people from Ford telling me how bad things were there now the unions had been defeated. It became depressing. I decided that it was in everyone's interest for me to leave Dagenham behind. We had everything going there and still lost. Turning up and canvassing only seemed to reiterate that defeat. It was much better to move on and start again elsewhere. When Dagenham was called I had received 1070 votes, 2.11% of the total cast. I spent a further week taking the loud-speaker round thanking people for their votes, and continued on South Essex District CPGB and as Dagenham 5 AEU Chair until 1966, by which time I was well established in ship repair.

I was being kept busy down at the river. The Ship Repair Branch supported every call and as it had enough clout to mobilise the support of shop stewards and members, demos and marches were big affairs. After the hiccup over voting rights in the yard, I had been restored as steward at Harland and Wolff No. 2, Surrey Dock.

Then in 1966 the stewards committee was confronted with the Labour government restricting trade union rights with an incomes policy. The CPGB saw it as a deliberate curtailing of union activity. Labour had been emboldened by the TUC, which throughout the first half of the decade had been pushing for caps on worker's pay; the cry being, make industry more productive, increase competitive exports. It was in effect class collaboration.

This policy of wage restraint had been defeated. Local and national negotiations forced employers to concede in the face of strike action from a strong rank and file. Between 1960 and 1970 prices rose by 54% and wages by 97%, resulting in company profits on output falling from 25% to 12%. This was a set-back for capitalism and very often termed by latter-day New Labour speech-writers as the 'Bad Old Days'. The question is, bad for whom? Not for the workers who appreciated and joined the trade unions that fought for and gave a better life. Between 1960 and 1984 trade union membership increased from 7 million to its peak of 12.5 million.

But the defeat of employers over incomes generated a great impetus to curb trade unions and led to demands for stronger legislative programmes as a way to prevent advances. One of the key players was Sir John Donovan, a leading Tory figure responsible for the pamphlet 'Giant's Strength'. This was published in June 1958 by the Inns of Court Conservative and Unionist Society and proposed a raft of restrictions on trade union activities. How neutral legal people are can be assessed

Tower Hamlets' CP candidates, Kevin is bottom row second right, Solly Kaye third from right

by the fact that under Labour Donovan was in a position to enact his policies by his appointment as head of the Industrial Relations Court, directing its attention to anti-union laws. Then in 1965 the government set up a Royal Commission under Donovan to 'consider relations between managements and employees and the role of trade unions and employers' associations in promoting the interests of their members.... with particular reference to the law affecting the activities of these bodies.'

The Prices and Incomes Bill, introduced in February 1966, had one great weakness. Its restriction on incomes for working people set a norm for trade union negotiators, but there were no restrictions on dividends or profits, both of which had been increased as a result of greater productivity. The TUC's acquiescence in this was rejected by large sections of working people, particularly those involved in direct negotiating, which included dockworkers, coalminers, engineers, and furniture-makers.

If you have trade union officials agreeing to collaborate on prices and incomes, the next step is to ensure there are restrictions on militancy. This was the sell to trade union leaders, who went a long way with it. Seeing the limits on unofficial strikes giving them a return to their power, union leaders, in common with capitalists and government, opposed the democracy attained by their members, who defended the right to decide for themselves what wages they would work for.

Workers wanted to maintain a decent bargain: if profits rose, why shouldn't wages? This question was fundamental, but denied by TUC General Council members, often from the House of Lords, where they were sitting as thanks for favours received.

The Communist Party saw the need for resistance. Bill Dunn had become the CPGB's Industrial Organiser for London District, working full time. Bill had a great industrial background. He was a welder employed by various industries across the Midlands. Bill, together with Bert Ramelson and Julie Jacobs, fellow members in the industrial department, called a meeting of comrades. We decided to set up a national body to unite against Lord Donovan's proposals which were now being adopted by the Labour Party, as the Prices and Incomes Bill clearly showed.

It was useless giving this over to national convenors such as Dick Etheridge, Jack Adams or Arthur Wells, who it was felt would be too busy to really galvanise the campaign. Instead it was agreed that it should be fronted by Jim Hiles and me. Jim Hiles was a builder with the Joint Sites Committee, a rank and file secretary in the London exhibition industry (traditionally strong), and one of the best comrades I knew. The initial meeting at Conway Hall comprised the strongest sections from the Party's industrial base, including Lou Lewis; Arthur Wells and Ted Crook from engineering; Bill Neary from Harris Lebus, the furniture makers; Derek Fullick from ASLEF, and George Anthony and myself from Ship Repair. Joining the table were Tommy Durkin and Margaret Witham from the London Trades Council.

The result of this meeting was a joint organisation to co-ordinate trade union opposition to Lord Donovan: the Liaison Committee for the Defence of Trade Unions (LCDTU). As the pro-Labour TUC didn't want to rock the boat, we had to push to be recognised as an official opposition by the General Council.

It's funny now to relate that the National Union of Mineworkers (NUM) under Joe Gormley was amongst the right-wing, and its particular right-wing was most heavily represented in Yorkshire, Lancashire and Durham; areas which were at the same time the heaviest regions for overall membership and extracted tonnage. The situation was so bad that our comrade Frank Watters was allocated by the Communist Party to work at turning Yorkshire miners around.

The break-through was compounded by a changeover at the Yorkshire NUM which meant Arthur Scargill emerged as a leading voice. Watters had success, and later his daughter, son-in-law and his grand-children played a big role in the re-establishment process of the CPB and the Young Communist League.

The second principle in question was whether LCDTU should be a rank and file organisation. Leftists argued that it should aspire to this to counter the right-wing TUC leadership, and were united in carrying forward their pessimistic outlook that all union executives had been and would continue to be supporters of capitalism, and that therefore there was no place for them in the LCDTU.

The Party countered that it recognised the need for a strong rank and file organisation, but the Committee could also win progressive union executives. The LCDTU's constitution always stated that we wanted a representative body. This wasn't a walk-in position. We consistently had to argue that we could win officials and win executives; and that we would need to do so to succeed and in the course of time change the direction of trade unions.

One of the first jobs I did after being elected to the LCDTU was to address a meeting of progressive lawyers and students arranged by Michael (Micky) Seifert at Oxford. It was a good meeting of about 40, held at the University. I don't know under what guise we were sitting; probably the Oxford choral society, or whistle-blowers, or hand-bell ringers. I was introduced and the first words I said were, 'Anti-union legislation is to lawyers what the pox is to pox doctors: they don't like it, but they make a living from it.' This was met with a great gasp of incredulity, but I went on to give my opinion why. Good comrades such as Micky and John Hendy have practices that prove my predictions were correct, but fortunately the cash hasn't changed their principled opposition from a justice and class position. They have been instrumental in the fight to defeat these laws.

We called for a London conference and sent out circulars for delegates. The Conference was held on December 3 1966 in the main hall of Friends House. The response to our circulars had been enormous and Friends House was besieged by delegates and others. Our only demand was that delegates should be issued with credentials and letters from the secretaries of their branches to avoid bogus attendees. The Conference was stewarded by shop committees from Ship Repair, Kent Miners, Joint Building Sites, London Airport Exhibition Workers (a hard bunch) and ASLEF from Waterloo, Euston and Kings Cross. In the end 671 delegates were counted into the hall.

We agreed that Bill Jones would be in the Chair. Bill was well-known as a London bus leader; he was also really capable, and with a lovely cockney sense of humour. I would open for the LCDTU and reply to discussion on its behalf.

We could tell that the Conference was going to be united, but with sharp differences. It began with Bill announcing the vote on the LCDTU 'Declaration of Purpose', which included solidarity with those who took action against points in Donovan and any anti-union measures that the Labour Government threatened to enact.

The Trotskyists wanted to have the right to amend, but we hadn't the type of organisation for this and argued that the items in the Declaration were justified by its previous endorsement: it had been drawn up by committee and issued to all the supporting organisations and leading stewards committees for approval prior to the Conference. The Declaration was adopted by the Conference with an overwhelming majority.

The next shout was whether LCDTU should be wholly a rank and file organisation. Bill again made clear that we were having no amendments to the clauses allowing union executives as members. Again this annoyed the Trotskyists, who tried to storm the platform. Not only were they met with vocal opposition from the majority of the Hall, but the first rows as the Conference floor dashed to defend the stage and stop disorder.

In the course of my experience I have found many comrades and friends who claimed to make sure they sat on the front rows to defend the platform; but I have never in all my days heard anyone say that they would get up and defend the disruption. I would thank those who backed unity and would ask the opposition whether, if the Conference had ended in disorder, it would have benefited the working class or the class enemy. I think anyone examining the LCDTU would answer that employers would have applauded its disruption. It would have made as big a headline in the Sunday papers as I did in the Trotskyist: 'Halpin the Stalinist'. We went on to build support and take the Declaration around the country. There was no anti-Labour policy as such; rather criticism aimed to change its and the TUC's direction. At first we met with little success.

Meantime the legal arm of capital had been busy. The Lords decision in the Rookes v Barnard case was a set back for unions. Rookes had left his union, and other union members in refusing to continue working with him were judged to have 'intimidated' him. This effectively spelled the end of the closed shop and bypassed the protections of the 1906 Trades Disputes Act.

These paralleled damages given in 1901 against the Rail Servants Union in favour of Taff Vale Railway Company for financial losses during a strike. Compensation was awarded on the basis that the railwaymen had a contract with the Company which they broke by striking. That this was unequal (any dismissed worker's claim of breach of contract by employers would never be upheld as it was agreed that managers had the right to sack) is something that those who profess to be enacting fair laws do not consider. After all, that is class politics.

I attended meetings of stewards all over Britain as part of LCDTU's campaign for strong trade unionism. We began to win the support of many areas, and indeed of union executives, but government opposition to free unions continued. Eventually in 1968, to augment an already hostile press, the Donovan Commission Report was published. I was due to speak against the Report in London on the day it came out. I had to analyse it quickly. The lads in the shop at Harland No. 2 let me sit under the stairs while they covered for me. 'Do your work,' they said. Talk about solidarity. Thanks to them I was well briefed and delivered a good speech that night which got terrific support.

Barbara Castle had become Minister of Labour and in January 1969 her White Paper, In Place of Strife, sought to put unions and management on the same side. She preached this to the trade unions but unfortunately not to the managers. The Paper recommended penal sanctions for unofficial strikes, cooling-off periods of 28 days, and the right of the Secretary of State to call a strike ballot herself. It was met with massive opposition from trade unions and there was an upsurge in LCDTU activity. As the Paper was being introduced to the House, Parliament was already being lobbied. The subsequent mass-meeting at Central Hall was addressed by Labour MPs Stan Orme, Christopher Price, Joan Evans and Norman Atkinson, who all urged action to strengthen their hand in the Parliamentary Labour Party.

When the Bill was put to Parliament 62 Labour MPs abstained but it was carried 224 to 64. But on March 26 at the Labour National Executive it was defeated by 16 hands to 5. James Callaghan was reported to have been one of the 16.

An overflow meeting organised by LCDTU on April 12 1969 had 1700 delegates, with Trades Council members and even some of the TUC National Executive attending. This called for 1 May to be a day of national protest action. The biggest demand, however, was for a recall of the TUC. This was successful and the TUC gathered at Fairfield Hall in Croydon. A massive lobby was organised by the LCDTU. I opened up with the megaphone and was, I thought, doing rather well. Then a policeman approached. There had been complaints about the noise from local shopkeepers. Please could I keep it down? I turned off the amplifier, drank half a bottle of lemonade to grease my throat, and carried on. After a short while the policeman came back. It was better with the megaphone, he said, much quieter altogether

It was always important at public mass meetings to introduce yourself to the local constabulary. The beat officer would turn up in his usual way. 'Hallo, hallo, hallo; what's this then?' 'Are you going to be in charge today?' we would ask, 'Otherwise, could you summon whoever is and in the meantime we'll make a note of your number.' Along would come his sergeant, and then his superior, with whom we would go through the same process, until eventually the Officer would present himself and we would officially notify him of what we were doing. Well, Jim Hiles would do this while I carried on speaking, not missing any delegates as they entered the Conference. It was a good way of dealing with the situation, and we would always write an appreciative letter to the Old Bill afterwards.

The TUC Conference uniformly opposed In Place of Strife. In June I was due to speak against the Paper at a Saturday Conference organised by the Scottish Liaison Committee in Glasgow. I arrived on Friday night to the news that Barbara Castle's proposals had been withdrawn from Parliament.

In high spirits we had a quick meeting to mark the victory, then broke up to celebrate. Archie McAlpine, organiser of TASS in Scotland, took me for a day's cruise around the public houses that dotted the lochs north of the city to give me an education in single malts. I applied myself assiduously to my studies and learnt quickly. By the evening I had declared Glenmorangie as my particular favourite.

# 9 Docklands Action, Trades Council, TUC

I still had plenty of Party activity to occupy me in Tower Hamlets. Ted Crook and I would always attend the CPGB Borough Committee. Coming straight from Harland and Wolff we would arrive looking like muck. As we both lived outside the borough we would have to sit in the pub until the meeting began at 7.30pm, which probably didn't help much.

Ted was 'salt of the earth'. His mate, Jean French, and he got on well. He was Secretary of Sutton AEU and she was Secretary of Battersea AEU. People used to joke that they couldn't marry until they could merge the branches.

Jean had many virtues. She was a leading steward in a factory that manufactured switch gears, and one of the CPGB Women's Committee who preferred to argue on industrial and class positions. She would say, 'The employers are the enemy not men.' Of course there was prejudice against women, not least in the AEU (on whose National Committee she sat), but Jean was for rooting this out and concentrating on the class struggle. Along with Ann Davis, an old mate from Ford, she successfully battled the chauvinism.

One of the best meetings I can remember addressing was convened by Jean at her factory to oppose anti-union laws. Out of 400 employees, 380 had stayed after work to listen. Jean was adored. I basked in her glory afterwards in the pub. Then I had to get up and sing.

The Conservatives had taken control of the GLC in 1967. Horace Cutler, a real Tory, was given the chairmanship of the Housing Committee. This was during the great period of social housing, when the GLC was the biggest landlord in London. Tenants were now to be means-tested. You were poor, and then you had to prove that you were poor. The poorest would receive a rebate and the rest pay more. It was supposed to be clever but it didn't work.

The tenants organised a rent strike and mass demonstrations. Women were prominent in the campaign. On one occasion outside Stratford court they blocked the main Romford Road. People didn't think they could get away with it for long. Charlie Goodman (an International Brigader) went back to have a look later in the day. The women hadn't moved: neither had any traffic in or out of the East End. Some of the slogans were robust: 'Horace Cutler, you can wait. We don't want your rent rebate. Stick it up your 'two and eight' '. Eventually a compromise was reached, but the widespread movement ensured a Tory defeat at the next GLC election. Cutler was not happy.

The period of Cutler and his attack on GLC housing was significant and the resistance to it was part of a working-class fight-back after the legislative attacks on their freedom to organise.

At this time the dock closures began. First to go were London Dock at Wapping and St Katherine's Dock just upstream at Tower Bridge. The development of containerisation meant a ship could be loaded and emptied by a single crane rather than hundreds of hand-working dockers. The CPGB and comrades in the docks opposed the containers as it shifted cargo to new deep-water ocean terminals, and encouraged the use of lorries for onward shipment, with the consequent congestion of roads. We felt the answer to containerisation was the LASH (Lighter Aboard Ship) loading system, where cargo is loaded at the docks into lighters which are then towed to the mother ship and stowed by deck-cranes. Docks and quays would be maintained and Britain's extensive canal network could also be put to use. This suggestion was opposed by the road lobby and the scheme buried. The dock closures continued inexorably.

My trade union branch at this time was involved in support of a variety of actions, including the picket of Barclays Bank because of its pro-Verwoerd policy in South Africa, and the picket of pubs that had a no-Blacks bar policy, there being no law banning discrimination. We also showed up in support of every industrial dispute bar one: when dockers and Smithfield porters came out in support of Enoch Powell's 'rivers of blood' speech.

Ship Repair members rejected calls for solidarity and crossed the picket line, and the Party held a protest meeting addressed by Danny Lyons and Jack Dash. The lightermen, led by Harry Watson, also rejected the dockers' call. Come to think of it, when did anyone ever see a black docker or porter?

When people shout about the sanctity of picket lines, I'm always proud to say that I crossed as a Communist and anti-racist. It was a bad time for our class, and it probably contributed to the dockers' demoralisation and acceptance of closures. This was abetted by the offer of redundancy money, a wedge of cash unseen and unheard of to soften the blow. One of our leading orators took the money. 'No names, no pack drill' but I never spoke to him again as I held the view that accepting redundancy undermined opposition to closures. I had an argument with him and he quoted his age: 'Kevin, when you get to my age you will do the same.' I never did.

One leading docker took redundancy from the Pool of London. He was then taken on and made redundant from two more sites. The employers must have been pleased with him.

With the closures came communities deprived of upwards of 20,000 wage-earners. The question after defeat was what was going to happen to the vast areas of former docks. It was possible to be given planning permission to build blocks of offices on former docks without even owning the land. This permission was then hawked to the highest bidder. Communists took the line that the land should be returned to the local people, who had suffered from a lack of facilities by living tooth and jowl with the docks. They should now enjoy open spaces, and new housing and schools.

We opposed derelict land being turned over to private property dealers, and the settlement of businesses which would give nothing to the communities that had survived. Five boroughs had large areas of former dock-land; Greenwich, Newham, Tower Hamlets, Southwark and Woolwich. Each was run by a Labour council and we pressurised them to redevelop the land with these principles in mind.

I was then Chair of Stepney Trades Council. Our secretary was Dan Jones, the son of Labour stalwart Elwyn Jones QC, a prosecutor at Nuremberg (an experience which made him very handy on the campaign against German Re-Armament), and latterly Labour MP for West Ham and Attorney-General.

Dan was himself an excellent secretary and a great organiser. We decided to canvass tenants who had been politically active since the 1968 Rent Strike and soon grew into a large network across all five boroughs committed to the rights and welfare of local communities being dispossessed by the dock closures.

Our burgeoning organisation was named Joint Docklands Action Group by an active priest from St Mary's and St Michael's Church in Stepney. Our priest was a solid supporter and a very effective propagandist, particularly on Sunday mornings, when he said he could reach 800 people through the various services he gave. He claimed in comparison that the local C of E church only had a Sunday attendance of 100. In Tower Hamlets we also had strong links with the Methodist Chapel in Cable Street, and could hold meetings at St George's Church in Shadwell. There was one nonconformist church on Bigland Street that imposed a condition before we could use it as a venue. It had to have 50 people at Christmas Eve evensong. Needless to say the Action Group provided the required parishioners, although they sang off a different hymn-sheet.

I became chair of the Joint Docklands Action Group (the single body of each Borough's Action Committee), and when the government formed a Dockland body, the Docklands Joint Committee, I attended statutory meetings as JDAG's representative. I was the only rank and file delegate at County Hall meetings. The rest were financiers, builders and supermarket executives, apart from the TUC Assistant General Secretary, Norman Willis, who had a seat next to me and would ask which way we should vote.

As the Joint Docklands Action Group became recognised by the five Borough councils and the GLC, grants were awarded and permanent offices found in Tower Hamlets. A team of three staff was recruited, with pay and conditions aligned to those of local government.

Marj Mayo, Nick Sharman and Heather Newham did a terrific job unpicking planning applications, lobbying Parliament, and working to influence the council meetings which endlessly discussed fanciful schemes. I remember JDAG opposed the planning permission for a floating hotel in Wapping only to find that the applicants didn't even own the ship, which was at that moment steaming with cargo in the Far East.

Applications to build heliports were coming in at a breathless rate. At this time helicopters were only allowed to fly in to London along the Thames, so flight companies coveted the acres of derelict dock land. These heliports were opposed by JDAG as they were obviously only for City use: I don't think any people in Tower Hamlets used helicopters.

We held a series of meetings to protest at this undemocratic use of land. We had considerable success and many applications were rejected because of the disturbance the heliports would bring to neighbouring estates.

During one protest meeting a woman stood up and said we shouldn't oppose the heliports. Her reasoning brought the house down. The closure of shops would lead to an emergency and we would need helicopters to airlift food into the East End. The point was real.

Tower Hamlets Council was busily closing down shops in a further effort to unsettle communities and pave the way for the bright new future it had imagined.

David Sainsbury agreed with the people who protested at the lack of shops after the closure of Watney Street Market in Shadwell and promised a Sainsbury's store on the site. He honoured his promise, and when the store closed for a bigger one at the Watney's Brewery site on Whitechapel Road he kept his word by laying on free transport to bus people in Shadwell to and from the new shop.

After the closure of the Royal Docks an application was made for the construction of an airport. JDAG objected on the grounds of the immense noise and irritation it would bring to local people. However, there was seen to be an overwhelming need to extend Heathrow, and a new airport would meet some of the demand.

We argued on the Docklands Joint Committee for the use of the Thames Estuary instead. Maplin Sands, traditionally used by the Woolwich Arsenal, had just closed as a gun-testing sight. We met opposition from environmentalists who were concerned to keep it as a bird sanctuary, although I don't think exploding shells had done a lot for birdlife. We made the case that nobody lived at Maplin and an airport would provide many jobs in an area suffering with the closure of Chatham Docks.

We proposed building a new rail line to take passengers in and out of London. We also argued that extending Heathrow would have a severe effect on local housing, and the necessary Underground extension would block up the system at great cost. Clearly our proposals were rejected, but the problem with Heathrow remains as it swallows more and more land and is fed with more and more transport initiatives. We did succeed to some degree with City Airport at Royal Dock, restricting its traffic to smaller, quieter aircraft, and preventing late night flights.

JDAG was closely involved in the debate on the extension of public transport in East London. This was a long term issue. There was only one Underground line serving the area; the old line from Whitechapel to New Cross, running under the Thames through Brunel's tunnel.

When I first travelled from South London to Dagenham, steam goods trains were still using the line as a link to the Southern Region. When one passed in the Thames tunnel the noise, smoke and steam was like something out of Fanny by Gaslight – something you could do without.

The railway was so old my nearest station, Shadwell, had a staircase of 100 steps from the Platforms; no lift or escalator, though as a concession a bench was put halfway so weary climbers could rest.

The class position was clear: we wanted lifts. Contrast this with west London, where the wealthy were delivered to their shops and houses by automatic lifts and escalators. At Sloane Square well-heeled dowagers rose to the surface on an escalator with only fourteen steps. The policy in east London was to close Shadwell station. Our campaigns managed to keep it open until the line was redeveloped and lifts installed in the early 1990s.

Debate focused on a transport network for the new Docklands. The Docklands Committee asked for tenders. Transport attracts more cranks, schemers, pipe-dreamers, and utopians than most issues. It was a full-time job for Marj and Nick just reading through them all. The proposals included overhead suspension systems, tramways, monorails, and hydraulic self-propulsion; anything that could be imagined.

We argued that there should not be a separate system from the tried and proved London Underground train. This was agreed at all the five Borough meetings. But developers insisted that any new rail line should run cheaper, modern stock.

The office of the Joint Docklands Action Group produced a brilliant paper on future population and use projections, showing that the plans for small, light carriages would be inadequate. But the Docklands Light Railway was built. At first it had no link with the tube, ending at the bottom of Lehman Street. The only thing there was the Brown Bear public house; not a bad pub as it went, but, like a lot of dock pubs, there more was on sale than liquor. Since then government has had to extend the Underground system and increase the capacity of the DLR, at vast extra cost. Perhaps they should have listened more closely in the first place.

There were also victories for JDAG, however. One was the prevention of dumping in the disused docks. London Dock, the closest to houses, was being used as a tip for waste fruit and vegetables from the London markets. We questioned the practise, to be told that it would be alright covered over with a top filling. Prior to the Green Environs campaign we proved that the methane produced would be unstable and dangerous. From then on only building hard-core was allowed to be dumped in the former docks.

Dock closures meant the rundown of the Port of London Authority. The PLA's prestigious Tower Hill headquarters was cleared out. JDAG investigated its resources and noted that a series of famous and highly expensive paintings had been bought to hang in the boardroom. When visiting the office we found the walls were bare. We asked what had happened to the canvases; after all, they were public assets. Our questions were resisted.

A short while later the pictures turned up at the house of the PLA's Chairman. He denied all allegations of theft and eventually returned them to the government department with a letter explaining that he had been moved to hold on to them for safe-keeping.

The PLA offered many perks. The meals they gave to dignitaries on the St Katherine steam yacht were legendary. She was a lovely vessel, powered by the last of the Triple Expansion engines. Ted Crook was one of the few fitters who could set the valves on this type of engine. I never found out how to do it.

Stepney Trades Council fought to combine with those in Bethnal Green and Poplar, the other wards in Tower Hamlets. Bethnal Green was happy to unite but Poplar resisted because, it became clear, they were nodding dogs for Labour and the TUC right-wing, and uncomfortable with Stepney's Communist membership and militant tradition.

Eventually we convinced the TUC that to have the two Councils in one borough was a nonsense and a united Tower Hamlets Trades Council was formed, which I was happy to chair.

However, the TUC revised the structure of the trade councils. It wiped out areas where the Communist Party had influence, and pushed for a federal structure under the control of regional trade union officers in the hope of further curbing rank and file militancy.

The Party opposed this move, arguing that it undermined the autonomy of individual Councils and made them subservient to regional trade unions often controlled by right-wing executives. For instance, T&G hadn't then removed the Black Circular banning Communists from standing for office. The AEU executive was also stubbornly right-wing, and as for the GMB....

However we couldn't convince the TUC General Council and the trade councils had the new structure thrust upon them. We debated what to do next: fight to repeal the decision or try to win over the Federations for progressive policies.

We decided to move in and win. Communists led the left into making something of the new structures, and created a progressive united movement, with the new County Associations leading the campaign in the regions.

In this period regional trade councils elected their own officers independently; only later did the TUC vet applicants. Most of the progressive causes were backed at regional level, where the majority were on the left, and some were Communists.

I sat on the South East Region Trade Union Council. The left managed to win the twelve seats on the Council for this region, and others elsewhere. We elected all the officers, but the TUC stepped in to approve the secretary, largely because they paid the post's full-time wages. To date the favoured nominee of South East Region's rank and file has been approved on each occasion.

The situation improved further when the Greater London Trades Council was established, not least because finally this saw the end of the Black Circular. Jack Dromey (elected secretary of the South East Region TUC after our secretary vanished in the Adriatic) made it a body to be recognised.

The GLTC was a good successor to the old London Trades Council led by Julie Jacobs, which had been pulled apart in a witch hunt by TUC lords; the final blow coming when in defiance of the ban imposed by Chuter Ede, the London Trades Council called for a May Day Trafalgar Square protest against the Korean War, which resulted in a battle for the right to walk into Trafalgar Square for the closing rally.

Julie later became the CPGB's influential Deputy Industrial Organiser alongside Bert Ramelson. Julie's knowledge of union rules was highly detailed. At meetings Bert would propose a solution which then had to be withdrawn when Julie would draw attention to a particular rule it breached. The end of the black circular was a breakthrough in London. Margaret Witham and her husband Ron; Tommy Durkin, a rank and file Communist from the building sites who along with Jack Dromey also sat on Brent Trades Council and Law Centre; and Harriet Harman, were all liberated by its demise.

Jimmy Knapp had come down from Scotland to work for the NUR in London. We wanted him to succeed and thought the presidency of South East Region Trades Union Council would give him a good base. The incumbent, a right-wing boiler-maker (yes, there were some) stated he was undecided whether or not to stand for re-election on account of his age. He obviously hoped that members would urge him to continue. I stood up, moved a vote of thanks for his good work, and nominated Jimmy Knapp.

The nomination was swiftly backed and Jimmy became a great political President, working very well with Jack Dromey, and giving himself the platform to run for NUR General Secretary. Jimmy went on to become one of the team that established a progressive NUR leadership after its conference moved a vote of no confidence in its General Secretary, Sid Weighell, after Weighell ignored the NUR delegation's mandated candidate during elections for Labour's National Executive Committee and voted for a right-winger of his own choice instead.

The South East TUC supported every dispute in the 1960s and 1970s, however apparently minor. This support was not just on paper, we also mobilised action. We backed the mass pickets at Grunwick, the photo processing plant in Willesden. Its staff, which included many Asian women, had walked out over bad pay and conditions, and the non-recognition of trade unions. It was a vicious fight. Industries from around the country were represented at the picket.

The miners led by Arthur Scargill came down the M1. White collar workers turned out in support. Mary Davis, a lecturer, had her leg broken by a policeman. We did not win the strike, but it helped to convince Asian workers that they would not fight alone. In those early days we also came out in solidarity with the squatters who occupied an empty Centre Point to protest at the homeless left on the streets, and the staff at Garners Steak House who revolted at their appalling pay and the victimisation of union members.

I went as part of the Greater London Trades Council delegation to the Annual Conference of Trades Councils. We noted that the day was full of motions that addressed points such as hunting with dogs, unrestricted railway crossings, and tied cottages. While entirely commendable in themselves, we thought they didn't challenge the policy which often lay at the root of the problems.

However all motions were given equal time on the floor. Comrades objected that with 200 motions in a two-day Conference there was no time for a serious debate on items such as anti-union laws and incomes policy. The issue came to a head at a Swansea conference. The chair, Terry Parry (secretary of the FBU and a fine socialist), insisted all items should again be given equal treatment over three minutes.

Several of the London delegation, which included Jack Dromey, Margaret Witham, Tommy Durkin and myself, moved a challenge to the agenda and won the vote. Terry Parry, however, was forced to stick to the agenda by George Woodcock, the TUC General Secretary, so we moved 'the Chair out of the chair', a standing order challenge that required a two-thirds majority. The count gave us over two-thirds and the Conference stood adjourned.

At the restart Woodcock stepped in. We must withdraw the motion or he would close the Conference. He gave us half an hour to decide.

We went into a huddle and decided if delegates were sent home without their delegation fee we would be isolated. We accepted Woodcock's ruling. That evening Margaret approached Terry, who complained about the challenge though he sympathised with the sentiment. He agreed that before future Conferences he chaired he would meet us to read over the agenda and decide the key motions. During the sessions he would then ensure that the minor votes were quickly recorded (hastened along with our help) to leave time for a proper debate of the major issues. This became, and still are, the modus operandi for conferences until the standing orders changed. Terry Parry was subsequently President of the TUC Conference.

Unions at the Conference gave welcoming dinners that always invited the President or General Secretary. They both had to divide themselves quite thinly over the week. One year, when the Conference was in Brighton, Terry was at the AEU dinner at the Old Ship Hotel. Unlike Amicus which invited everyone, the AEU was very formal. I attended as a delegate despite being a leader of the union's left-wing. After the soup course, Terry asked me to join him at the top table (it was as formal as that) because he was bored and wanted to have a decent conversation. It was amusing to observe the consternation of the right-wing massed around the table as they struggled to courteously accept this thorn in their side sitting with them.

It was also interesting to watch the AEU's General Secretary, John Boyd, a much-honoured man, avail himself of the Old Ship's wine cellar, which was very good. I wondered at his thirst for the finest vintages as he came from a Scottish Presbytarian background with Rechabite (temperance) traditions. Obviously I didn't see him on a good night.

Equally extraordinary was the dinner held in Glasgow when Gavin Laird laid on a Scottish banquet to celebrate the Conference being held in his home city. A Baron of Beef was piped into the room by a dozen Highlanders.

Gavin came out of the Branch at the giant Singer Sewing Machine factory, having been as good as raised by the Party. His mother remained a Communist long after he went right wing. It is reported that she was proud of her son becoming AEU General Secretary, but not proud of the politics that secured him the dignity.

We used to play a parlour game at the AEU dinner. During the aperitifs the left delegates entered into a competition to note whose

Television footage of Kevin speaking in defence of trade union rights

Industrial Relations Manager had been invited. If your company's manager wasn't there you couldn't be working for a kosher firm. At the Union's peak we counted 35 from all the key engineering employers.

The AEU sent 32 delegates to the TUC Conferences; two from each region. The delegation was split between left and right-wingers: if your side had 14 votes on the first motion that was the way it went for the rest of the agenda. The left delegation was a tight ship. It was a battle every day, so we had to be disciplined.

The EC would watch the left delegates closely and it had a crafty tactic of introducing issues on which a decision hadn't been taken. These unexpected issues were voted on by a method called 'pass the pad'. A pad was passed through the Conference as a register. If a name wasn't down for two consecutive motions the absentee would be obliged to offer an explanation, and if this was considered inadequate the miscreant would be sent home.

Of course the pad was passed when a left-wing delegate was absent, so if someone wanted to go out for refreshment they gave notice and we would call them back. (This was particularly useful for LCDTU activists. By custom the Committee had a Monday lobby and lunchtime meeting with leading left speakers. Not much happened on Monday; it was Mayor and Corporation day.) Otherwise your vote was tied and the General Secretary would observe to ensure you hadn't broken your delegate's mandate. I remember at one Conference an AEU left delegate from Hull voted the other way. There followed a delegation meeting where we attempted to excuse the action as a mistake. The General Secretary was firm. The delegate did not have a mandate to vote that way. His delegation fee was cancelled, the TUC Executive was informed, and he was sent home.

The AEU left grouping had great assistance from the TASS delegation, whose left wing was led by Ken Gill. I remember at one TUC waiting for the meeting of the General Council to decide the following year's President. Ken Gill had been had been due for the job on 'buggins's turn'; your place moved round the General Council table when a member retired and as new members joined, and eventually finished up at the top. The appointment was usually automatic but we were concerned that the TUC right-wing would set aside precedent and reject a Communist. But Ken was respected so he proudly made it.

In its heyday engineering had a loose integration of engineers, draughtsmen, technicians, and sheet metal and construction workers, all of which, with the exception of the AEU, had a Communist leadership. Attempts to unite the autonomous four sections into a single Union failed. TASS wouldn't agree to the election of officers, whereas the AEU left had made it a cornerstone of policy.

The contrast between left and right delegations was often exposed. I remember queuing for coffee next to a right-wing delegate who was out of a job and saying to him 'I expect your friends have looked after you, though,' only to be told he hadn't been out of his digs throughout the Conference because he was trying to pay debts. This gave me a shock, for the left-wing was different.

At the first left meeting of the Conference we would ask if there was anybody 'out of collar'. If any were (and as militants they were likely to be unemployed for a bit) we would make sure he would be bought drinks from the 'whip' without having to put in any cash himself. I remember one new delegate protesting that he didn't want charity but he was told there was nothing he could do. This was the unwritten agreement of the left. It was not made for him personally but was the general rule. None of us knew in that team of militants when it would be our turn. It was great when I told this to the right-winger. I think he believed he had backed the wrong side.

Of course at all the TUC conferences there was a reliance on the AEU providing a base of support for the General Council's right-wing politics, although the AEU executive did have some bright periods. The left won Jimmy Airlie from the Clyde shipyards for the Scottish Executive, and Roger Butler won the EC's London seat. Roger came out of the long struggles at Trico Windscreen Wipers, among other disputes. He was the protégé of Regional Officer Len Choulerton, and also a strong member of LCDTU where he had earned his spurs.

The best decision of the TUC was the 1982 vote for unilateralism after Ronald Reagan announced production of the neutron bomb. This was led by Ron Todd and seconded by Ray Buckton of ASLEF. The set-back was the EEPTU Secretary Frank Chapple pleasing the nuclear power companies by moving a fuel policy that gave a central role to nuclear energy.

The ETU before its merger with PTU was a case of a left wing union, recognised as powerful and hated by employers, whose leadership was ousted. They were attacked particularly by the right wing at TUC level. An idea of ETU's power can be seen in its battle with Ford Motor Company over Ford's resistance to closed shop recognition. A TUC committee could gain limited negotiations but not 100% recognition. ETU pressed for an agreement: if one was not forthcoming the electricians would walk out and Ford would be stopped. Management backed down and the TUC committee jumped on the bandwagon and had the same rights conceded to it.

The attack on the ETU started after the death in a car accident of Wally Stevens, its brilliant General Secretary. Maybe there were problems finding his successor. The chair, Frank Fawkes, continued but some of the left leaders back-tracked. It is worth speculating whether, if the ETU model had been repeated throughout the trade union movement, it would have gone from strength to strength.

Much later, AEU's proposed amalgamation with the right wing EEPTU was met with opposition from the *Engineering Gazette*. The *Gazette* was the organised left of rank and file members. It was distributed in factories by shop stewards and it was the mainstay of resistance to the right-wing AEU Executive, and the basis of the later defeat of Ken Jackson.) The EEPTU organised scabbing for Murdoch at Wapping and had been expelled from the TUC. The amalgamation with AEU enabled it to look decent and get back into the TUC. The EC members backed by the *Gazette* sold the merger promising AEU democracy would continue (crucially, the election of officials and the national committee). Unfortunately those taken to be upstanding men forsook these principles, concluded the merger, and quickly took early retirement.

Needless to say I never had the opportunity to speak at the TUC. Speeches had to be submitted to the General Secretary for approval: nothing that I wanted to say was ever approved.

There was only one time I got unity on the floor. It was during a Conference at Blackpool. The LCDTU had a demo outside on the Monday morning. Traditionally we occupied the blind-end street next to the Winter Gardens.

I met supporters in the after-lunch bar in the Gardens, then went back into the Conference and discovered I had lost my wallet. I went round to the police station. The desk sergeant said I couldn't have been pick-pocketed as the pickers work in teams and there had been no other incidents all day. I walked back to the Conference and told some of my mates. I had lost £150, a lot of cash in those days.

The delegation took a collection. I was astounded; everyone was generous, the right-wing, the General Secretary, and the President. I worried about the attitude of the police. Had they taken the opportunity to compound the misfortune of an irritating agitator? I decided not. There had never been a problem at any of the demos I had organised in Blackpool. My motto, 'What we bring to the demo, we take home tonight', was always well-received by the police.

Later that week I was again sitting in the bar in the Winter Gardens. An instinct told me to shove my hand down the back of the bench cushions. There was my wallet, intact after four days. For a moment I thought about giving the money to the *Morning Star*, but then I wrote a note to everyone telling them of a negative collection; they were to take out what they had put in. Since it was a Friday, with cash running short, it made their day, and established that Communists were straight.

Incidentally there was one occasion when 'take home what you bring' was clearly demonstrated as a truth to Lancashire Constabulary. After an anti-Thatcher demo one of my delegation became uproariously drunk, was found incapable on Blackpool promenade by some policemen, and taken into custody.

I went down to the nick to petition for his freedom, but he had already been charged. He was conditionally released into my care on the provision he was kept off the streets and removed from Blackpool by the next train. This was accomplished without incident, but he was censured at the next Committee.

During the 1960s I remained living in West Hampstead, in the Champion's flat. Barbara Champion had bought six hens out of pity (they were bedraggled) and they had a coop in the back garden. One Saturday evening me and a mate, John B, were enjoying a drink. It was warm enough to have the back door open.

As I was in the kitchen six Rhode Island Reds paid us a visit. John said, 'I swear I just saw six hens go past.' I laughed and said we were in West Hampstead not the countryside. He resentfully took more water with his Scotch until I put him out of his misery. I used to buy feed for the hens on Portobello Road when, aside from the antiques, the market also sold livestock stuffs, including hay for the last remaining dray horses.

It was a good crew in West Hampstead. I got to know Desmond MacNamara, death mask and puppet-maker, and a very learned man. He was a good friend of Brendan Behan. Brendan used to turn up in a cab without funds saying, 'God will provide'. It wasn't quite God who provided, but he was worth his fare.

I remember once attending an Irish political social. I didn't know what it was in aid of. I made a bet with the others that we still wouldn't know at the end of the night. Before the collection someone stood up and said 'Well, we all know what we are here for, I hope everyone can dig deep,' and sat down again. I won the bet.

We lived in a flat in Earls Court or, if you were a snob, South Kensington. It had been a serviced house. If you pressed a button in a bedroom a flag waved in the kitchen.

The bathroom was on the first floor landing, down a flight of winding stairs. A piano couldn't go any further up so I think it was the only flat in London with a piano in the bathroom. When the Sunday Times published an article about a ship-repair rough and an educated lady it was obvious who they were because it carried a picture.

We used to hold social evenings on Saturdays. One night Eve, Claire's daughter, was making up a dress to go out in, but she was only 15 and a hopeless seamstress. After a few G&Ts the professionalism of the visiting East End ladies who had come with my ship repair workmates took over and it finished up a lovely dress.

This was the period of Rachmanism in rented housing. Sitting tenants with protection against high rent increases were driven out of their homes and replaced with new tenants whose rent could be raised at will. Heavies would knock at doors, frightening people to leave. They did the same with us and gave us notice, but we arranged a reception for them. Our heavies were a lot heavier than theirs; we even got a bit of cash off them.

In the wake of the dock closures people living in rented buildings in Tower Hamlets were increasingly under threat. This was countered by a squatter's movement and many old rough Stepney dwellings were occupied, but the Rachmanites used coarse methods. They would break open the door, throw the people out, and replace them with guard dogs. These dogs were rumoured to be utterly rapacious; trained to go for the throat on sight. If tenants had managed to keep some keys, they were too frightened to even enter and retrieve their goods. The police said installing dogs was 'legally allowed'.

At a meeting of the Tower Hamlets AEU branch I argued we should protest about this to the council and police. A little fellow at the back of the room asked what the problem was. The dogs could be led away, he said. If someone could kick in the door, he would handle the rest. It sounded dubious.

However, as purported leader of the protests I was duty bound to lead; so after providing the self-proclaimed dog-charmer with string, Guinness and Irish whiskey, we ambled down to one of the guarded houses on Turner Street, accompanied by several people, who I think were friends, interested in seeing Halpin savaged by a wild dog.

The beasts caught our scent as we arrived at the door and started howling like Hounds of the Baskervilles. The signs were ominous. However I took courage and booted the door. Immediately two enormous and irate canines launched themselves at me, apparently intent on taking my face off. But just then my partner, the little fellow, stepped in.

The animals backed away. He spoke to them. They stopped barking and listened. Then, coaxed by his flattery and endearments, they allowed him to tie the string around their necks and they were led away in mute obedience.

I was proclaimed a hero and taken to the local pub where I saw off several pints. Over the next few weeks we repeated this at squats all over the area, and the Rachmanites suffered the Great Dog Loss. I believe the little fellow started a security firm of his own with the dogs he had bewitched.

While roaming about on my scooter during my enforced sabbatical, looking at architecture, I had admired the Georgian style. Stepney Council was now determined to demolish whole streets of Georgian town housing and replace them with blocks of flats, so I decided to pick a relic to save and chose a derelict house in Cable Street, overlooking the Hawksmoor church, St Georges in the East.

I purchased it through an agent but had to pay cash to a bloke in a white Rolls Royce sitting in the car park of a bed and breakfast hotel in Forest Gate. When I bought the house there wasn't one unbroken pain of glass in its window frames. To receive a grant from the Georgian Society most of the features had to be given genuine period replacements. I would round up some mates and a truck from the docks, and with the promise of a few pints get them to deliver what I dug out of other houses under demolition.

The houses next to St Anne's Church in Limehouse were typical. From these I would rescue eleven and a half inch wide pine floor boards; 200 years old and they still smelt of resin when cut. They were only planed on the top side and levelled where they came across the joists with an adze.

Luckily I was in an industry where shipwrights passed their apprenticeship by making a tapered mast from square using a line screwed into each end and adzing it down, so I was taught how to level boards. Terraces of Georgian houses built back in the 1770s had everything made in sets, the builders receiving a single order for a street of houses, so the post and hand-rail from the stairs at Limehouse fitted Cable Street perfectly.

I got a building worker called Tim to work weekends for me. I used to knock up a mortar mixture of sand and cement for him first thing, then go off to the London meetings I had to attend. I once asked Tim for a lunchtime drink. 'I work or drink,' he replied. 'If you want the work done, I'll drink after we finish.'

Being an optimist I put up window boxes. The neighbours were sceptical that they would last long: the kids would tear up the plants the same day. After all, the school behind the house taught disturbed children. I was knocking up the boxes when the kids came past. 'What you doing, Mister?' 'Putting flowers in that people say you will tear up.' I asked them what colour flowers they would like planted. After a week's debate they made their choices. The plants stayed in for as long as I remember.

I was also told to watch my tools, otherwise the kids would nick them. I was putting up a cast iron railing retrieved from the Oriental Street demolition. It had a granite base and the rails were set in lead. I would embed two rails then line them up with a spirit-level. Some kids walked by. 'What you doing, Mister?'

I showed them how the level worked. They obviously spread the word because more came by a little later, jumping about and clamouring for a try. I showed the level to about 30 children over the next few hours. They must have been bunking off school to come and have a look. Then someone stole it. I told them they had let me down. I wouldn't talk to them for all their protestations. Instead I went for a pint. When I returned the level was on the doorstep.

It was great to interest 'hopeless' kids, and they were always friendly, although in school their headmaster spent all day hollering at them. I met him, and a couple of suits who were child psychiatrists, in the pub one evening and got chatting about working with children. They had heard I'd collected an open-air classroom.

I told them about my apprentices. They asked me if I had considered teaching. I laughed and told them I had left school at 13, but they said there was a job for me in the school if I was able to interest the children. I had to explain that where I worked was crucial for my politics. But it was nice to be asked.

This reconstruction job kept me busy. My partner Claire was a diamond. She would come over at the end of the day and clear up all the mess. I'd never known such a worker. When it was all finished I had even found a door-pull circa 1778. I found the date from a farthing embedded in the surrounding plaster. It was a tradition for plasterers to leave a dated coin in their work, but they would only spare a farthing.

# 10 Saltley Gates and the Pentonville Five

In 1970 Harland and Wolff No. 2 was shut down with the closure of Surrey Dock. I went on the register for casual outside-fitters and found work with Badgers on the Isle of Dogs. They had a site with a dry dock at Thermopylae Gate, named after the famous tea clipper which was the first to enter the lock. (Whilst at Harland and Wolff the firm had the job of refurbishing Cutty Sark. One or two of the sail-winches needed repairs. The foreman said if they needed to look a bit roughened with Atlantic weather it was best to give the job to Halpin.)

I had to get a stable job in a shop. A fitter was needed at the Graving Dock Company on Preston's Road opposite the Gun public house, but he had to be able to 'mill'. This was with machinery I had never used before. Milling was different to fitting, and the craft trades did not mix easily. So I had to be a fitter miller to get the job.

Two old-timers had come out of the mothballed EMI factory in west London and set up their own steel milling works (every day the toolgrinder from EMI called in with cutting tools to keep their work top notch). They were old mates of the convenor at EMI whom I knew, Frank Stanley, later London secretary of the CPGB, and they hired me on a temporary contract, giving me a course in milling.

I worked on some of the jobs they had in hand and learnt to stay in the game. I must have qualified as they asked me to stay on with proper pay.

After a while I had a start at the Graving Dock Company. The charge hand, an awkward sod (he would refuse fitters who couldn't steel mill) but a member of my union branch, gave me a job on the mill. I looked at the cutting tools and saw they were all chipped and rubbish compared to those turned out by the grinders at EMI.

I threw the tools on the floor of the shop, called Coddy over, and said I couldn't work with them. I even threatened to take them to the AEU branch and name him. I wasn't put on that machine again.

A swing bridge separated the yard from the Queens pub, but the beer there was one penny a pint cheaper than in the Gun, which was on the lock itself. The down side was that if a ship came through at lunch time you could be trapped and arrive back late, although sometimes you would be excused if you pleaded a 'bridger'.

One year I worked all winter on the lock's sluice gates, replacing the brass slider strips. It was a rough, cold job, but I had to be precise.

We had a fridge and an oven in the shop so I would cook each day for the dozen or so workers. The foremen in the yard could smell the food but only the shop ate. At Christmas a delegation used to go to the butchers to decide on turkey, goose or duck. It was a serious business.

In 1971 the LCDTU gave its support to the Upper Clyde Shipbuilders' sit-in opposing closures. The Upper Clyde Shipbuilders were always prominent on the LCDTU. They were organised by Jimmy Airlie, a Communist and former Orangeman, not unusual in Scottish Marxist terms. As soon as they decided on a sit-in, Jim Hiles circulated an appeal for solidarity funds.

Public support was widespread. There were factory collections across industries, mass meetings of support, and members travelled across the country to support the picket line. The two Jimmies, Airlie and Reid, were charismatic leaders and speakers, and they had an excellent team of stewards who organised throughout Britain. The strike became a crusade. It demonstrated that it was possible to win support from broad, non-unionised sections of society.

I remember that students at the Royal College of Art organised a Solidarity Students Social, with the two Jimmies speaking. It was a roaring night. We closed at about 2am and the beer made everyone inclined to lock up and count the cash in the morning. But the Treasurer of the Upper Clyde Shipbuilders Strike Committee intervened. Money was falling off the tables everywhere. As it was workers' money he thought we owed it them to stay, count it up and take it away. It took a long time and we counted thousands of pounds. It's often the supporting members who make sure the ship is kept tightly.

This Students Social was a great show of solidarity and not an isolated case. Similar events were happening all over the country. Neither was LCDTU's support for Upper Clyde unique. The Committee included shop stewards from building sites, coal mines, the railway, clothing and furniture manufacturers, and printers, to name but some. Disputes were built into its fabric.

LCDTU's support of the miner's pay strike in 1972 was in keeping with its class position. The Government used its restrictions on picketing introduced after Donovan to push through scab coal trucks at

Saltley Gate, a coke plant in Birmingham. A large police presence had swept the pickets aside. It was decided to counter with a mass action.

We did the rounds calling for a solidarity demonstration. The location was ideal with the motor factories, organised and militant, within marching distance. Their leaders were all LCDTU backers: Derek Robinson was among many who had helped form the Committee. The Communist Party was also influential through having Branches at all the major plants.

The greater part of Birmingham's engineering base came out in support. Leyland's tractor and transmission factory was the nearest to Saltley. Its convenor, Arthur Harper, an ex-paratrooper and comrade from my motor industry days, was instrumental in organising the action, and his entire membership joined the march.

That morning the police were cock-a-hoop as their numbers had again cleared the miners from the plant gates and allowed the coal trucks to sweep through. Then they turned and lifted their eyes and looked and saw on the crest of the hill a banner, and swelling behind it a vast body of people who flooded irresistibly

down the slope to join the miners and occupy the road in solidarity. The police could do nothing; they simply retired, absolutely overwhelmed. The defeat of the Midlands Constabulary, reckoned at 1000 strong, by tens of thousands of workers was historic. It was a great working-class victory.

The National Incomes Policy Committee had to breach its guidelines and rule a wage increase for miners. As a face-saver the NIPC said the miners were a special case. This, to its credit, was never accepted by the National Union of Mineworkers as it would have bolstered the prestige of the NIPC and strengthened its rejection of other claims. Saltley Gate was one of the victories that made the miners a class enemy for the bosses, and a strategy to destroy the industry was devised by the ruling class and implemented by the Thatcher administration. The miners' defeat of the incomes restriction policy, one of the key planks of the 1970 Heath government, gave an impetus to wage claims and inaugurated one of the few periods in which living standards actually increased. The wage demands were higher than just cost of living rises, which are, at their best, defensive.

The year 1972 was a busy one for LCDTU. In February a conference was held to oppose the National Industrial Relations Court, set up with the power of injunction to stifle industrial action; followed by another in June against the Industrial Relations Act which banned non-balloted strikes and introduced cooling-off periods. These measures, of course, gave employers the time to defeat a strike by finding alternate production facilities and recruiting scabs. Any talk of industrial relations strategy being equal was condemned. When was there ever a ballot on wage caps, or sackings by employers?

This was the message of the June Declaration, which pledged action if anyone in breach of the Act was jailed. Right wing commentators tried to portray this position as one determined by ultra-left union executives. This was rubbish. The position was wholly rank and file. A total of 1,235 credited delegates attended the June conference. The Declaration was carried unanimously. Betty Crawford, convenor at Ferranti electronics and LCDTU Treasurer, took the traditional Conference collection and raised thousands of pounds.

Then the London dockers took action. The issue was the transfer of container processing to Chobham Farm in Stratford. The dockers objected that the work was being done by unauthorised labour on lower wages, undermining the National Dock Labour Scheme. The National Industrial Relations Court ruled against the objection and sent a tipstaff to arrest three dock leaders, Bernie Steer, Vic Turner and Derek Watkins, for contempt. The day before the threatened arrests 35,000 dockers in ports across the country went on strike.

The Official Solicitor suddenly ruled there was insufficient evidence to convict and the arrest warrants were held back. The picketing of Chobham Farm went on. The common union for dock workers and container drivers was the TGWU. The drivers continued to work the depot and drove past angry picket lines.

The NIRC and the Government decided to have another go. On Friday 21 July Steer, Turner and Watkins, together with fellow dock stewards Conny Clancy and Tony Merrick, were arrested and taken to Pentonville Prison.

As soon as they heard the news the rest of the docks walked out in solidarity. I went down to Pentonville with a large crowd to be told by the dockers to leave it to them, they could handle it. We rejected this as it wasn't solving the problem.

The CPGB called a meeting of leading trade union activists at King Street. We crowded in and were addressed by the General Secretary John Gollan. We were told to press for the LCDTU's call of national strike action.

We had the good fortune to have a major print dispute happening at the same time in London. For several weeks the SOGAT members at

Solidarity in print, Briant workers produced posters for the Pentonville 5

Briant Colour in Old Kent Road had successfully held a sit-in at their factory to resist closure. The LCDTU had been backing the workers. I was in touch with leading stewards led by Bill Freeman, convenor and leading LCDTU member. The Briant factory printed all the high quality posters for the dockers' dispute. Their most famous poster was of the Pentonville Five, naming them (Conny Clancy, Tony Merrick, Bernie Steer, Vic Turner and Derek Watkins) and behind bars.

The whole of the printing industry was holding a solidarity mass meeting for Briant workers at Clerkenwell Green. Jim Hiles, Bill Neary, myself, and others decided to go to that meeting and call for a march up the road to Pentonville.

The intention was to march to the prison directly the speeches had ended. However, immediately after the last speaker had sat down Bill Freeman was up and introducing a street theatre group. They weren't bad but they were enjoying the audience of 2,000 people more than the audience was enjoying the entertainment, and there was a consequent drift to the pubs. I asked Bill if we could cut it. He agreed so I moved a vote of 'Thanks to the Theatre Group' (a bit unkind but there was a bigger cause at stake) and managed to divert the crowd towards the jailed dockers.

After the demonstration outside Pentonville we met up with dockers' leaders and agreed we would march on to Fleet Street, picket the Sunday titles and stop the presses. The idea that no one would have a poisonous paper on Sunday morning would alert trade unionists of the need for action.

The Fleet Street electricians needed little prompting: even though they were under a notoriously right-wing ETU leadership, they were angry and powerful enough to resist executive control. Mike Hicks at SOGAT, and Ann Field, leader of the National Society of Operative Printers and Assistants, followed this by bringing out their members in unison and the print shops fell silent.

On Sunday I had a phone call from Derek Fullick, leader of Waterloo Station ASLEF. There was a meeting that evening. I should get to the Rose of Denmark, round the back of Waterloo station. I saw Derek at the bar and asked where the meeting was. 'Right here,' he said. 'Get up on the stage: all the pub are members or family.' He called the bar to order and I called for a stoppage. A unanimous 'hear, hear!' came back. I asked Derek what happened next. 'There are no trains from Waterloo from tomorrow,' he said.

My telephone rang at about 4am on Monday morning. I had always believed it was tapped. When I lifted the earpiece this time I heard a voice: 'Why are they using the phone this early in the bloody morning?' Then the line was connected and Eric Rechnitz, the drivers' leader, came on. The ruling class wanted to know what the LCDTU was planning. Eric wanted my loudspeaker gear to address container drivers at the Royal Docks. We needed a car to take us there. Luckily Bill Edon, a friend and comrade, had just bought a new Triumph, although he was at first a bit dubious about such a trip, fearing our wheels would be turned over by disgruntled lorry drivers.

That morning I had a decommissioned wooden stage delivered to my house on Cable Street to be filleted for the restoration. Time was pressing so it had to be left in the road. Eric, Bill and I arrived at the Connaught pub close to the Royal Docks. The first to speak was a dockers' leader. He was given a rough reception from the drivers. Eric then called for me to say some words. I didn't usually speak without notes, but this time I was completely unrehearsed.

There was a bit of rumbling from the crowd as I climbed to the top of a pile of dumped asphalt (the traditional speaker's podium in the docks). I decided to give it to the drivers straight. I said that the dockers were not as glorified as sometimes presented – I had worked in

Engineers lobby Blackpool Labour conference against pay restraint, Kevin on far right

ship repair, and had experience of stoppages as a steward, and they could be an overbearing lot.

I said that after the five arrests I had asked the dockers if we should keep all members out, but was told that it was none of our business, the dockers could win any dispute on their own. Such arrogance that the disdainful dockers had! This admitted, I asked the drivers to ignore it, although it was hard when all in the union were falling out. Like a family we should settle things amongst ourselves, not give an excuse for the police to be called in. The jailing of trade unionists, above any other issue, was an attack on us all, every working person. I ended by asking for a vote in support of a solidarity picket.

It was going to be hard. I got some 'hear-hears' and applause, mainly because I wasn't a pro-docker sentimentalist. The vote was put and it was carried. I was in shock. The press had prepared headlines: 'Drivers turn down dockers'. It would have had a bad effect on solidarity. But now even the drivers supported the dockers. It gave the campaign a significant boost. I went home to free Cable Street of timber. It wasn't mine, I told the Old Bill, but I would take it in. OK, he said.

All that Monday reports of stoppages came in to the *Morning Star.* Stenographers were constantly taking down the messages. Each place that came out I could name and knew the comrade responsible.

I was asked to go to Scotland to talk to Raymond McDonald, Regional Secretary of the TGWU. The structure of the TGWU was changing but the Regional Secretary was still king. Raymond said he would bring out TGWU in Scotland. It was a big call.

How would he do it? Was there a meeting of officials to get agreement? He just pointed to the phone and said that would do. I said what about democracy, people having a say? 'Do we want to talk about democracy,' Raymond replied, 'or stop all Scotland T&G?' I quickly decided that stopping Scotland T&G was the reason I was there. Sometime in the future we could have the democracy debate. Raymond's action was as good as his word: Scotland stopped. He must have had enormous power.

Meantime the rest of Britain's rail, buses, airports, mines, engineering and shipping stopped work. In line with our strategy to not just be rank and file, a meeting of the TUC was called. The Amalgamated Union of Engineering Workers moved a vote for a General Strike. The motion was successful, for the first time since 1926. The strike was to begin on Monday 31 July.

Immediately the NIRC was convened. It stated it was not influenced by pressure from the TUC, but the Official Solicitor again had to come out from behind his desk. He attended Pentonville Prison with an instruction to release the five dock stewards. They were freed to a jubilant crowd that cheered the actions of the LCDTU. They were cheering themselves and all the others who in a decisive expression of class solidarity had won a memorable victory. Jail for contempt of the Industrial Relations Court was never tried again.

But the legal battle against trade unions continued. Building workers had a national strike over wages and dangerous working conditions. Union activists Des Warren and Ricky Tomlinson were arrested and charged under the 1875 Conspiracy and Protection of Property Act. During a picket in Shrewsbury, Des Warren, addressing a meeting on work safety, had said the building site was not fit for burning. He was accused of inciting arson.

The trial was drawn out but both Warren and Tomlinson were found guilty and the judge sentenced them to three and two years respectively. Unfortunately the case didn't have the same impact as the Pentonville Five. LCDTU convened a well-attended conference but an official dispute wasn't called by UCATT and TGWU.

The unions went to appeal against the sentences. Labour came into government but refused to release the prisoners. Conspiracy is the hardest charge to refute. You don't have to do anything, just be accused of talking about doing something.

There was an LCDTU picket outside Home Secretary Roy Jenkins's house over Christmas 1974. I remember the family setting off one afternoon. Jenkins swept past us, unreachable within his cocoon of police constables. His wife and daughter and son stayed behind and listened and agreed with us, but Jenkins never turned.

Ship repair at Graving Dock Preston Road shut down. I was given redundancy pay. My mates in the shop laughed that as I was late every day (well, I had to buy the shop's lunch) I would get less due to time-keeping deductions. It turned out that the yard's computer hadn't been set up to deduct lateness so I got away with it. The only time I was early was when I was speaking at the docks during election campaigns. The timekeeper had such a shock he nearly fell out of his office window.

I was left to find another job. There was no chance at the Mint, where many ex-ship repair workers had found work: it was being run down and I was on the blacklist. From comrades I heard of a job at London Underground working on the lifts and escalators. I was well received by the convenor and had an interview but was rejected. The convenor said he couldn't understand it.

I tried again with the same result. I found out that the convenor was a Party member who had gone round telling everyone that the Chair of the LCDTU was going to start. It was hardly a good reference. I used the time to bring the house on Cable Street up to the standards required by the Georgian Society.

After a while I got word to try London Underground again, this time at its Acton works, where all the trains were overhauled. Of 1,200 members, 400 of them were engineers, so it would suit me.

I was given a strict interview. Bill Taylor was there as chairman of Engineering at the works. I was asked how I would line up a set of bearings. I went into how shipping main-shaft bearings were set using plates and lights that were shone through a small hole in the centre of the plate. They started shaking their heads and asked why I didn't just use a spirit level. I answered that the bearings were too far apart and that ships rocked on the water. The interview finished. They were convinced I was a craftsman. I got a start.

The first week I had to remove obsolete doors from a set of carriages (called 'cars' by the Underground workers). One door was proving reluctant so I kicked it out. The window smashed. I expected a sacking but the foreman told me I was 'getting the feel of the job'.

There was very good organisation. Alongside Bill Taylor (a Dublin agitator) was Don Cook as convenor. Don Cook had been the last occupant of the St Pancras Tenants Association sit-in. I remember taking two coaches-full from Ford to give back-up. With Bill and Don you were sure of a job; militants were not allowed to be rejected.

I was put into the Heavy Repair shop. I was given six 50-foot girders and told we were building a vacuum cleaner. This would be attached to a drive car. The resulting train would run through the tunnels cleaning as it went. It was based on a model built in Montreal for the city's own tube system. That one blew up in an explosion of fine dust. It wasn't really my game but I got on with it, working with Peter Cudmore as a team.

Peter was Secretary of the AEU Barnes Branch. Endless drawings had to be consulted to make the chassis. It was all hot riveted. I worked on this project for four years. It was some job. You had to concentrate. Having worked in ship repair was a big help. You were used to heavy work. The other advantage was that it killed the right wing slur that Bill and Don were packing Acton Rail with their unskilled comrades.

I soon learnt that our vacuum cleaner was badly needed. Asbestos from the train brakes lined the Underground tunnels. Women (and it was exclusively women) worked at night cleaning the tunnels by hand. They were known as 'fluffers'. The other big job was cleaning under escalators. Those cleaners were cut back to save cash, but this had serious consequences in the catastrophic Kings Cross fire, I'm sure.

I stood for steward in Heavy Repair and was defeated by one vote. The works included body makers, electricians and sheet metal workers. All had their separate unions. One or two of the Sheeties had worked at Briggs Bodies when I was inspecting there. They still remembered their jobs I had rejected.

The AEU had quarterly meetings after work in the canteen. These had good agendas, both practical and political. At the first I attended I was introduced as the LCDTU Chairman and endorsed to join Bill and Don as a Liaison Committee delegate from Heavy Repair. The Lift and Escalator and Signal workshops also sent delegates.

I worked unobtrusively and held a steady job. It was quiet, but anti-union laws were operating. There was, though, still a space for resistance. As well as banning unballoted strikes, the 1972 Industrial Relations Act allowed the sequestering of union funds if notice of strike action was not given seven days in advance. The LCDTU Conference had decided to defy the law when it arose.

Come rally, LCDTU banner on trade union rights demonstration

Workers undertook a spontaneous stoppage at an obscure factory in Surrey owned by Con Mech. The Amalgamated Union of Engineering Workers recognised the strike and it faced a fine of £100,000 for each day it continued.

As chair of the LCDTU I called for a lobby of the AUEW headquarters on Peckham Road to urge the executive not to back down and to fight sequestration by stopping work across AUEW's membership. Hughie Scanlon, the left-supported President, came out and took me and Bernard Panter aside (Bernard had been first Treasurer of the LCDTU and was old mates with Hughie from Manchester).

Hughie said the executive was split down the middle on defying the law or calling off the strike. He had the casting vote. He said he would like to talk to his union members at lunchtime round the back of the building. We agreed to vet the attendees, and I was put in the chair. When everyone had assembled Hughie asked if he cast a vote to order a complete stoppage whether the order would be successful.

The meeting considered, and stated that members would obey the instruction to stop work. The executive met again, Hughie Scanlon encouraging other EC members with the news that the rank and file would support an all-out stoppage, and the vote was won; the only time all of engineering had been due to stop across all industries.

We went back to work. Two days later all convenors received the letter stating that action had been called by AUEW for 12pm that day. A meeting of Acton works was held in the canteen at 11am. Bill called it to order and Don read out the letter. Someone asked for a vote but they were told we would simply carry out the instruction. That was what they had agreed when they joined the union. The meeting agreed a 12 o'clock walkout.

This was happening throughout Britain. I went back to the shop stewards office (by then I had been elected steward). At 11.50am I was sent for by Personnel. They informed us that the Official Solicitor had yet again intervened. The sequestration of funds was cancelled: could we get a resumption? Most of the members had already clocked-out, I told them. We couldn't get them back that day.

The AUEW still lost £400,000. The Labour Party made election promises to repay the money, but it never did. Hughie Scanlon earned himself a bad name for a while, although he finished up in the House of Lords. He went down in history as being the right man, in the right place, at the right time. He was able to develop an advantageous situation: by advocating and agitating the LCDTU had prepared members for action. I've forgotten how the Con Mech dispute ended, but I know that the members and not the judges made the decision.

# 11 Interviews, elections and Acton Rails

I was becoming known. A sacked Ford convenor, chair of the LCD-TU, leader of national stoppages: I was getting a good name from bad press. I was invited to an early evening television programme on current affairs and grilled by (ex-Communist) Lew Gardner. I had watched trade unionists facing hostile interviewers.

Once at Briggs Bodies during a strike the convenor, Jack Mitchell, had been interviewed in the street by a reporter with a camera. The reporter, a notorious scourge of militants, harangued Jack and shouted at him: it was a Red plot, he was pushing people into strikes, ruining lives. This of course led to a heated response. After Jack had walked off I held back and saw the reporter ask the same questions to the camera, but this time calmly, to be cut in later for the news broadcast to show Jack raving without provocation.

I resolved to be prepared and to make my case with studied clarity. I wrote down headings on the palm of my hand: high profitability of factories; wages compared to governor's salary; the right to sack is fine, but the right to strike is wrong; I was proud to be a Communist with our class policies and the members had voted me in. I wanted to step aside from the interviewer.

I was met at the door of the studio and taken to the hospitality suite. The usher showed me the bar. Having seen Brendan Behan come to grief by appearing on television drunk I decided not to have any alcohol. Instead I conspicuously drank large glasses of ginger ale after downing a single scotch to give me the smell of booze. Lew Gardner seemed happy to see me knocking it back. The interview was filled with the usual hostility and antagonism. They were the predictable questions. Did I enjoy the misery strikes caused? Was I a Communist? Did I believe in communism? I had the answers.

Later in the pub round the back of the studio Lew and all his retinue were putting their backs into it. I went up to him. 'You know I'm a Communist. Why ask me and appear shocked? After all, you were a *Daily Worker* reporter; although you made a mess of the Briggs Body

Strike report. I was one of the people who went to see Johnny Campbell and have you taken off the story.' Lew hotly denied this, anxious not to be diminished in the sight of his followers.

Within a fortnight I was invited on to the same show. It happened to be January 25th, Burns Night. The television crew behaved badly. There was a Burns Night recital by a lovely woman holding a large bunch of red roses. As they filmed only her head and shoulders the viewers couldn't see that water from the flowers ran down her dress, provoking a stream of schoolboy jokes and much laughter. It was the same kind of interview for me as the last time, and then I was asked back to the pub.

All this so Lew could deny the *Daily Worker* story and give the name of another reporter. But I had dug out the evidence and read it to him. Lew congratulated me on being a thorough bastard and asked me for a meal. Haggis and neeps' seemed a good idea. Lew rang around the good restaurants. None of them served haggis. It seemed that wealthy Scots in London didn't celebrate Burns Night, only the Feast of St Andrew. Eventually he found haggis at the Savoy. We turned up and as it was on expenses I ordered a dozen oysters and a good bottle of Chablis to start. With the haggis I called for a Pomerol. Lew was surprised. I think he was quite sure I would be out of place in the Savoy. I arrived home by cab, just about. For all that, Lew was still a friend, at least whenever we met at the odd event.

I was also invited to a Depth interview by Woodrow Wyatt, at that time one of the nastiest anti-communists alive. This interview was held at Wyatt's palatial home in St John's Wood. I rang the bell at the gate and was shown in to Wyatt by a fashionable Japanese house-boy. It was a posh house. I bet it cost a fortune for the TV company to hire it from Wyatt. He asked me what I would like to drink. I said a pint of bitter. The houseboy was sent off to fetch it. Presently he reappeared to confirm there was no bitter in the house. What else would I like? To rattle Wyatt I said I always expected to be able to give people what they asked for. Wyatt had to send out for a bitter, moaning all the while about how it would be a dear pint because of the extra time this was adding to the clock.

The crew enjoyed all this and told me they would make sure they filmed my best side as they were earning overtime. It was a good interview, all about how I was opposing a law brought in by a democratically elected government: I couldn't do this in Russia. I replied that it wasn't that you couldn't strike in Russia; you didn't need to because the workers owned the factories: how he must welcome that. I was only given the one pint.

As chair of LCDTU I was often sent to speak around the country. On one occasion I went to Oxford for a weekend forum on industrial relations and the economy. It was run by the Public Relations Society and stuffed with prestigious gurus from the scene. In the bar I ran into an official I knew from the Furniture Workers Union. He was a good comrade, and on Ford's national negotiating body. In his company was Lesley Blakeman, my old Ford opponent. He hardly knew which way to turn but found it in himself to ask if I would like a drink. 'Of course,' I said, 'you owe me one from the Ford convenor's pub-round.' Even though he was responsible for black-listing me and keeping me unemployed for two years I played it cool, as Communists do.

The opening Oxford session was held the following morning and began with introductions. I stuck out like a bare brick among all the managers from British Gas, the Post Office, the Coal Board and other towering heights of British industry. They were well aware that Blakeman had made his reputation in the sacking of Ford Communists led by Kevin Halpin, later chairmain of the LCDTU.

In the second session of the morning Mr Blakeman spoke at length on how strikes were undermining the economy and how militants were leading honest workers astray. To finish, he produced a letter that he said he had received that week from a friend in Canada. This friend wanted to buy a British car but all these strikes meant that he couldn't be sure it would be delivered. The whole performance was met with tremendous applause and loud approbation for his attacks on the unions at Ford.

I put my hand up, to the consternation of the chair, who thought I was going to rave at Blakeman. But I only asked one question. When did he receive the letter from Canada? Last Thursday, he said. I stood up and said that while Lesley Blakeman and I had disagreements I had never doubted his honesty until now. That my partner, Claire, was Canadian and she had not had letters from her family for the past three months owing to a postal strike.

The audience howled, none of them but a bit amused to see such an idol smashed. Blakeman blustered, went red in the face, and looked as if he could have shot me. I sat down and the chair called the meeting closed for lunch.

Blakeman dashed out shouting 'Get in the car!' to his wife. She was due to open the afternoon session (she was a Professor of Labour

Relations), but she left abruptly amid a pile of gravel from her husband's car wheels, never to be seen at the Conference again.

At the beginning of the afternoon session the chair advised the meeting there would be a change to the scheduled list of speakers. I innocently asked what had happened to the billed opener. She had had to pull out for domestic reasons. Blakeman's cohorts rocked with laughter again. I couldn't have hurt him more if I had stabbed him.

When I lived in Forest Hill the flat below was occupied by Ruth Kalman. She was a very petite lady, youngish (gentlemen don't guess at ages), and German. She had lived in Paris. I suppose her parents had left Germany in the 1930s.

Ruth was in London as a correspondent for the Allgemeiner Deutscher Nachrichtendienst (ADN), the news agency of the German Democratic Republic. She was the only person of any status from the non-recognised GDR then living in Britain, and she represented its Government unofficially. She reported on the first CND march to Aldermaston. She came on it with me and the Briggs banner and was very impressed. I gave her much information on the British labour movement that Essie approved.

Through Ruth I became interested in the GDR and I was pleased to receive an invitation years later to visit the country. It came through the London Trades Council, which supported recognition of the GDR. This position was in opposition to the General Council of the TUC, which was not only right-wing on domestic issues, but also welcomed the influence of the United States in international matters and appeared to have its foreign policy written by the Pentagon.

I travelled with Scottish, Welsh and English delegates. I represented London. We had to fly to West Berlin and take the U-Bahn to the East, crossing the border at Friedrichstrasse station where we were welcomed by GDR comrades. Above ground the difference between the two sides of the city was sharp. The West had everything; shopping arcades, department stores, neon lights; all subsidised to make the contrast with the East a propaganda victory. We were shown around the new suburbs and hospitals constructed for East Berlin's workers, and saw where they had sieved through the bombed ruins of famous buildings and meticulously rebuilt them.

We were taken to a brown coal open-cast mine outside the city and met the trade unions. They spoke of life pensions, schools, housing and hospitals. I went up in one of the coal dredge lines, mammoth machines that scooped up six cubic metres at a time. It was operated by a jolly, confident lady. I asked if she was married. Yes, with kids in school. What did her husband do? She pointed to a man sweeping the yard below us. He was happy, she said; he had no ambitions.

We went to the Berlin Wall. It was explained logically that the West would use an open border to bleed the economy of the East. This was accepted by the delegates.

The Regional Council of Dresden invited us to watch a ballet at the Opera House. This was a great honour as seats were generally overbooked. The ballet was Swan Lake and it was very well danced. Perhaps not as memorable as the time I saw the Bolshoi with Galina Ulanova as principle, but good nonetheless. Asked how we enjoyed the performance by the Regional Chairwoman, our Scottish delegate made a remark that I stopped the interpreter from translating: 'I didnae think Communists would teach workers to believe in fairies!' The highs and lows of delegations.

The 1970s saw me with a triple role as secretary of Tower Hamlets CPGB, chair of the Tower Hamlets Trades Council and chair of the Joint Docklands Action Group, and I was making sure all our policies were mutual. I was living two doors down from Dan Jones in Tower Hamlets. Dan is famous for his works of primitive, East End-based art but he also worked hard for young people in the Borough.

I remember Dan painting LCDTU demos, darting in and out to ask whose banner was this, and whose that, needing their names for his highly realistic paintings. One had the Tower of London in the background. I complained that I couldn't see myself. Dan said his sketches were made from my platform, so he could have the Tower in the background or me. He chose the Tower as it has been there longer and gave a better sense of place. When the painting was finished he had a hanging at the Royal Academy and then presented it to me.

Another canvas was of a stoppage during the dockers' dispute. He discussed where it should go. I suggested he give it to the TUC to remind them that there is a class struggle and insist it hang outside the General Council chamber. It's still there, by the door.

Dan and I organised an under-11 football league for the local children, played on Bigland Green. The pub next door, The Australian, had a friendly landlord. But the council stepped in and banned us from playing – we were told that the Green was not a designated play area. Instead dogs used it as an open toilet. The Communist Party, the trades council and the churches, together with JDAG decided to organise a festival in protest. There was a wire fence around the Green and Dan suggested covering it with large panels which could be painted by the youngsters. Materials were easily found, provided by some hard-nut families engaged in unconventional business practices: wood boards, paints, brushes. Football matches with a six-foot ball were also organised. These were great fun, until Comrade Bob Boyton, to everyone's astonishment, managed to lose the ball on the way home.

The festival was stewarded by volunteer hard-men who were noted with respect in Wapping. I remember someone who was running around was grabbed by the stewards and brought to me. 'Is he OK?' I was asked. 'Yes.' 'Well, tell him not to provoke attention.' 'OK.'

With Dan I came to know these people well. They opposed socialism because there would be no rich to rob. I said they wouldn't rob old ladies. This was taken the wrong way and I was lifted up and threatened until the matter was clarified. They thought I had said they would rob old ladies. They explained their philosophy. I spent one third of my life at work. If they were unlucky they would spend a third of their life in prison. What was the difference?

It was their party when I had my trip on the Daffodil: an invitation you couldn't refuse. They took over the whole of one deck. On the next deck up, Leman Street nick was having a fling. Both the gangsters and the police were in the same industry, I suppose.

The running down of the docks left local youngsters needing to earn money. There were a few who worked a racket at the Prospect of Whitby, the riverside pub. It was then a trendy place; no-one who lived around drank in there. People drove to the pub in expensive cars. The ten-year-olds would approach the driver: 'Look after your car, mister?' 'No thanks, be alright,' was the invariable reply. 'Well, we will stop kids scratching it with a brick.' Then one with a brick would come into view, to be shouted at to keep away by the others. The bloke would hesitate and the kids would offer protection for a quid. They would usually pay up. It saved a re-spray. They were tough kids but class-conscious in a way.

The area was largely feared by the middle classes. West End stores wouldn't deliver to the East End. It was enough that they passed through on their way to Greenwich. There were no mortgages because the houses could easily be demolished by the council. Times have changed though. We never succeeded in getting working people much housing in Dockland. The developers moved in, and then the rich. The rich people have expansive river views. The council flats along the river had no views apart from the high dock walls.

I was gradually shifting my activities to Acton. I always believed in being in the AEU branch that covered where I was working. Acton was famous for giving jobs to militants, so its union branch was good. There was also a Party Branch at Acton Rails which had been organised during the war. It had a broad reach, particularly on the maintenance side. They were fine comrades: Denis Birdseye, Pat Warwick, Don Cook and Billy Taylor among them.

The branch sold about 50 copies of the *Morning Star* each day and printed its own leaflets as well as those of the national Party. We got together at Communist Party London Transport Advisories with branches at other works. One of our recruits who will agree he was trained by these comrades is Bob Crow. When he became famous as RMT General Secretary he still acknowledged his formative years.

CPGB West Middlesex District had well-organised factory branches generally. There was a branch at Chiswick Bus Depot to equal Acton. Chiswick was another major London Transport base that repaired the bus fleet and trained drivers on the grease pad. It was closed under privatisation. I remember a mass meeting of London transport members in opposition to the Chiswick closure. I proposed we get off our seats and do a mass walk to the London Transport HQ on 55 Broadway. This was opposed by the platform. It hadn't been agreed with the police. I stood up and said I was going in any case and I hoped the meeting would follow me.

Five of my comrades joined me there and then and we walked out. On the street I looked round. No-one else had followed. By the time we reached Victoria Street, though, we had grown into a trickle which gradually became a march. The police stopped us nevertheless. But when the bus drivers saw our posters they switched off their engines and refused to move. Most would have been trained at Chiswick. We received great publicity. A little initiative paid off but it was a gamble. A demonstration of just five people would have been dispiriting but giving a lead had proved worthwhile. When privatisation came the firms to whom the infrastructure was sold had hopes of the workforce being non-union, but TGWU worked hard and won a good percentage of the incoming staff to its membership.

The Acton branch met weekly to plan leaflets, education days and peace demos: we were always on peace demos. Jack Redding, the AEU convenor at Acton and a Communist, had been called up as a reservist during the Suez War, but he refused on the grounds of conscience. He was jailed.

The AEU shop stewards collected weekly so that his family never suffered. Such action is often unsung but it is definitive of the working class approach to peace.

I was also on the Supplementary Benefit Appeals Tribunal for the Department of Social Security. These bodies were politically neutral with employer and trade union representatives, and generally a lawyer or a long-serving tribunal member in the chair. The best tribunal I sat on during my Acton days was one where the employer's rep was a foreman from a London Underground depot and the chair was a bus employee. We were ruling on such things as cessation of benefits, rent grants or supplementary pensions. An officer from the DSS would present the case for the decision which was being appealed. Some officers could be quite helpful, making suggestions, when it was difficult to grant the benefit in question, as to how we could assist financially in other ways.

I would be inclined to agree with all the claimants, but I found it was necessary to discriminate. The Department could challenge our decisions citing precedents, and if the tribunal lost too many cases the Ministry would reconstitute the tribunal membership. You could only continue to do good work by deciding on the strongest cases. I learnt that ruling in favour of a pensioner, or a mother and her children, or a disabled person was doing more in terms of a long-standing effect than deciding for someone who was claiming a day's under-payment. You prepared the ground before the tribunal sat by walking in and greeting the Ministry officer with a 'Good morning, busy day. You've been a bit hard on Smith, etc', mainly indicating that you were going to battle for those cases. It was easy to think you were a superior being, deciding the course of someone's life from the dais.

In 1972 the Conservative government gave tenants the right to buy council housing. The Greater London Council had rebuilt Tower Hamlets while knocking down slums. Then, under Horace Cutler it welcomed the chance to start destroying the powerful Tenants Associations. Many tenants seized the moment to buy cheaply their council flat or house. I say buy, although the majority only exchanged paying rent for paying a mortgage. But for many ex-dockers with redundancy money it was seen as a great opportunity. This policy was never reversed by subsequent Labour governments, and it is to blame for the London housing scandal. It changed the East End.

The custom of marrying and having a family in the same area could no longer be followed. To be housed you had to move out. Now, with

Kevin at work at Acton Rails

the lack of council housing youngsters have to get a mortgage for expensive houses or rent privately. Many of the ex-council flats are now let by housing agents with rents so high that we have returned to the bad old days of multi-occupancy, with people living in a single room. What used to be bakers, greengrocers or hardware shops are now estate agents making a killing on what was once council property. The Communist Party is still fighting for council housing against housing associations.

One evening in 1972 Ron and Barbara Champion held a Branch social. There in the crowd, I saw a young lady. She was very thoughtful, but she looked great. I got chatting to her. Her name was Anita. I said I would like to marry her. She laughed. She seemed right. The booze was running out so I walked with her to where she lived nearby for some more vodka. The party went on. I saw her home afterwards. Again I thought she was just right. She said, 'Are you drunk, or mad? Come back later.' I did. Again we got on well. After a time I moved in with her. I proposed marriage again at the Euston Tavern. She walked along and said, 'On one condition; I would like a family.' I never had. I was always too busy. I thought about it and said, 'Agreed.'

I met her mum, Lillie, for lunch at an Italian restaurant near the Marlborough Gallery. Diners brought their own wine. We drank all we had and I walked out for another. To impress, I went up-market and bought a Barolo. It was a lovely lunch.

We went on later to meet her Dad, Hans Hess. He was then lecturing in Art History at Sussex University. I knew his history. He had written for James Klugmann on the artist and the artisan in *Marxism Today*. Before the war his family had made shoes in Germany. He was not the kind of person to easily impress, but at that time I was using a shoemaker; Trickers on Jermyn Street. Good shoes were required for all those hours I stood in the rain lobbying.

Hans and I had a long talk. He was not in the Party but he was political – very much so having lived in Germany until May 1933 when he fled. He startled me when I said I was going to marry Anita. He said he thought it might not be good for me. Anita had only been in the CPGB a short time, while I was a leading comrade and it might retard my progress. In contrast Anita had no form. We laugh when I remind her of this, now that she is so advanced in the Party and trade unions.

The Acton Rails Branch agreed that I should continue as the Parliamentary candidate in Tower Hamlets for the General Election in February 1974. I was the candidate for Stepney and Poplar. The Labour candidate was Peter Shore, not the worst Labour man, but the national Labour policy on former dockland, council housing, Europe, and Vietnam was enough to fight on.

We soon fell into the swing of things, driving round the constituency doing loudspeaker work with comrades meeting us on the way or following by car to give out leaflets and canvassing passers-by. This was how we worked all our electioneering, both Parliamentary and municipal; we always had a good few weeks on the stump.

In one election a comrade volunteered to drive me. He had a Daimler Sovereign, a rare breed of car, which he offered for service. He was a professional chauffeur who had, at one time, been Soviet diplomat Maxim Litvinov's driver. At first I objected to using it but I was assured that people would think their Communist Party candidate was successful as an East London car dealer or gangster or something, and was worth listening to.

We fitted the speaker gear to the roof. It was good to make an impression. We would drive up to our pitch with the Beatles playing full blast. *The Red Flag* went on for the drive away. I remember speaking at Watney Street when the market was still running.

During my address Peter Shore rattled up in a decaying Mini with a small loud-speaker tied to its roof by a piece of string. A thin warbling strain crackled out which scared off a curious sparrow that had flown down for a closer look. I refrained from blowing him away with some choice decibels but Peter could see it was a hopeless competition. I told him that when I left I would announce him: 'Now folks; next on the stump is a man you've probably never seen before – your Labour MP, Mr Peter Shore. Peter, it's over to you.' After that we started a bit earlier on Saturday mornings and quite often managed to get ahead of Peter at some of the best pitches.

We worked out our best tactics for large blocks of flats. We would set up in the courtyards whilst canvassers knocked at the doors with our policies. If the residents had any questions which couldn't be answered by the canvasser they could come down and meet the candidate; he was just below. This gave inexperienced canvassers confidence and I would recommend the method.

Many Bangladeshi people were living in the constituency. One of our comrades was Doctor Chakraborty. I got him to do loud-speaker work in Bengali but one day he took me aside and said it was no good, the people were wondering why a well-spoken educated man was speaking for Communists. Instead he translated leaflets and found that many Bangladeshis lived in communal flats with a Headman. We could ask the Headman to call a house meeting and speak to everyone there. Dr. Chakraborty was excellent at organising that.

A few of the docks and warehouses hadn't yet closed. The open-floor warehouses meant that we could move along the streets with the megaphone and the dock workers could listen to our case while getting paid. But it meant an early start. The dockers had an 8 o'clock call-on and often had a pint beforehand in one of the early houses.

In all I stood three times, twice in 1974 and then in May 1979 when Thatcher won and always had good support from the Acton Rails Branch, with Pat Warwick and Denis Birdseye leading the team, and Chiswick Bus also gave its strong backing. The Exchange Branch was drafted in in the October 1974 election. This was an industrial branch comprising comrades working in London telephone exchanges; John Haylett , later to become *Morning Star* editor, was the branch secretary.

In May 1979, the National Front stood in both Tower Hamlets constituencies. My strategy was to decry its fascism as an insult to Stepney since so much of its population had family members who had been slaughtered by fascists on the continent.

NF leader Martin Webster stood in Bethnal Green and Bow against Labour's Ian Mikardo and, the comrades agreed to send a team of our best canvassers to bolster Labour's campaign. Mikardo led a strong fight against a loud cabal of fascists who were making trouble in the constituency, Moseley's old stomping ground. I had been over the boundary to bolster the attack. In the end Mikardo won well, but the resolution at the next meeting of Labour's GMC to thank the CP for their help was ruled out of order by the chair.

My own campaign that year began somewhat inauspiciously. I was out doing loud-speaker work in Poplar. I'd only just started the Saturday morning round in Crisp Street market, denouncing the NF, when the old amplifier finally conked out to many taunts and howls from the crew of fascists. I was so incensed I packed up, pooled the cash Anita and I had to hand, and bought the best loudspeaker system I could find. It was guaranteed to blow the NF off the streets. It could address thousands with ease and it has now been well-used at rallies and during elections over many years.

We went to the 1979 count which was held at York Hall for both Stepney and Poplar and the neighbouring seat, Bethnal Green and Bow. The Party line was unequivocal; we would never share a platform with fascists. This stance contributed to the 'No Platforms' position which many progressive organisations now take.

By this time Anita was my agent and it was down to her to try and get agreement from the other eight agents at the count. Labour's agent was arrogant; he said it didn't really concern them as they would win in any case and would already have spoken by the time the NF came to the mike. To give them their due, I don't think that was Peter's or Ian's decision. Every other party except the Liberals agreed. The Tory candidate Robert ('Bob') Hughes was especially supportive and all his people at the count wore anti-fascist badges - a black clenched fist on a white background - in the middle of their blue rosettes. Once Labour had spoken, there was a disciplined walk out by well over 90%, including many council employees who had counted the vote. It was a very heartening moment. All our campaigns yielded some fresh recruits - one of whom went on to contest the June 1983 election - and a clutch of new *Morning Star* readers.

It was during the early 1970s that I made what I believe has been my biggest political error. With my branch I had gone to a great many anti-Vietnam War demonstrations at the US Embassy in Grosvenor Square. However I had come to the conclusion that the Vietnamese fight for freedom called for a different approach. I felt that the drugging of US soldiers and slaughter of civilians epitomised by My Lai was going to continue. Agent Orange would be sprayed indiscriminately to kill crops and the B52s would keep dropping millions of tons of bombs (not many were shot down but I remember buying a ring made from the metal remains of one plane sold by the great solidarity movement).

All this led me to speak of the war as being irretrievably lost. I argued that with its massive resources the US could retreat from Vietnam and destroy it from off-shore. I was hopelessly wrong. It is an important lesson hard learnt that you can have a war, win militarily, occupy the ground, and destroy the military machine: but then you have to fill the space. The Marxist tenet 'believe in the people' is correct.

In the USA body-bags were being counted. You can be in favour of a war and cheer your son going out to fight, but having him sent home as a dead hero is hard to take. I had to remember that the USA doesn't just consist of the impersonal frontages of New York and Chicago. There are many small towns. The soldier killed was a boy well known, who had played, courted and married in those same several acres. His death changed that town's collective opinion, from support for the fight to free a supposedly tyrannised people to disilluagsion in the face of an unwinnable battle. And so our brave comrades in Vietnam continued the war of attrition.

I was wrong in my estimation of the value of military might. I was glad when I saw the US scrambling for the last helicopters, but I had learnt a lesson worth remembering: people count. No-one ever commented on my lack of politics. There were other reasons to keep me off the CPGB Executive. Had my lack of judgement been quoted I wouldn't have stood. But living is about learning.

In October 1974 I stood once more as the parliamentary candidate for Stepney and Poplar. The selling of GLC housing was one of the key local issues we addressed, together with the question of who should benefit from the dock closures; the people who had lived there throughout the life of the docks, or rich people moving in from Surrey.

Again Peter Shore was my Labour opponent, and the fascist Martin Webster also stood again. Webster got some support from the bottom end of the working class. One square off Wapping High Street had been bombed in the war and people were still living like rubbish in prefabs. No Communist could canvass there, we were told. However I assembled a heavy team and we argued our case to the residents. No-go areas might be tough, but so were we.

The prefabs had been built in an emergency but by now they were dilapidated. I remember one from my Dagenham days. The family used it for holding stolen goods from the docks. In the middle of July temperatures inside the prefabs soared to punishing levels and in the winter they were permeated with frost and ice. One February the police found it full of Argentinean frozen beef. The man who lived there was caught. He became the laughing stock of Dagenham: worse than being jailed.

In Tower Hamlets the Party put up ten candidates for the local council elections. I had to ask Jack Dash to stand. He was very well known for leading many of the struggles in the docks. It earned him a soubriquet – 'the Red Rooster'. Unfortunately, there were many in the traditional industries who accepted redundancy. 'Take the cash and go' was the prevalent attitude.

Of course I knew the temptation of a four-figure offer after years of so little. But I was shaped by Ford where we opposed seasonal work and went down to three days to keep the jobs. This was hard to hold, but the position was clear. The job wasn't yours to sell: what of the youngsters behind you? Accepting redundancy and watching the job disappear accounted for the appearance of many social problems. The young people couldn't follow their parents who had known where they were going as they grew up.

At Acton I was now the AEU steward on the negotiating committee. Jim Mortimer had become the new Industrial Relations Manager for London Transport. Jim was ex-DATA (the Draughtsmans' union), and a progressive. At this time Labour was in a progressive mood, having taken over aircraft manufacture and British Leyland. Jim devised a nine point plan for the improvement of working terms and conditions at London Transport. The plan's main points were an improved pension scheme, higher apprentice wages, and a shorter working week. It also stipulated that clean overalls were to be issued at work. This meant that they no longer had to be taken home to be washed by the good woman, stopping the transmission of asbestos.

One of the notable features of this period was the passing of the 1974 Health and Safety Act. This transformed working lives. Dangerous working practices were widespread. Often peoples' lives were routinely at risk. A typical example of the situation in the docks was the running maintenance given to the cranes. If the top wheel pin needed replacing, safety dictated that you had to lower the crane by letting the lulling gear down. The operation took two hours. But the ships had to be unloaded, so someone would climb 90 feet, haul up the new six-inch diameter pin, and drive it in. I always insisted the crane driver slewed over the dock so I could land in the water, but there was so much driftwood about you were still likely to bang your head. Before the Act employers, cushioned by insurance policies, were quite happy to accept claims from mangled employees: now they had to provide safe working conditions or put up with the penalties.

However there were still not enough factory inspectors, so trade union reps had to fill in. I was appointed Acton Rail's Health and Safety Representative. Some of the depot's working processes were obviously out of date, having been formed when the works was built in 1929. Not only management, but some of the workers were resistant to change. It was hard work ensuring people knelt on cushions, or wore a hard hat while standing underneath a train.

Even the wearing of eye protection while chipping or turning was a difficult habit to instil. Eye injuries were a curse. The medical surgery at Acton, though excellent, sent people with steel shavings in their eye straight to Moorfields Eye Hospital. There the patient was met by a formidable Irish casualty sister. She would always start by asking the injured man if he had been wearing goggles. Even if he said yes she didn't pull any punches. He was accused of lying and sent to the back of the queue. When his turn came she made sure his head suffered as she administered the treatment. After boxing ears for a time she sent for both me and the manager and asked why we were allowing these idiots to work. We couldn't answer. Not wearing goggles became a certain disciplinary offence.

The other safety concern at Acton was asbestos. It still is today. At a union branch meeting as late as February 2008 members were alleging that MetroNet was ignoring their worries about asbestos. East London Cemetery holds many late employees and the wives who washed their overalls. Asbestosis was not then certified so people died of a 'bad chest'. Cape Asbestos always defended asbestos claims.

I remember in ship repair when asbestos had to be removed from steam valves. It was indiscriminately knocked off with a hammer and the people doing it were laughed at as 'snowmen'. At London Underground, as well as the brakes, wheel axles used to be wrapped with asbestos to reduce noise. An asbestos sheet was used also under the floorboards of the carriages. After a time it was reduced to powder by constant use.

Just after the Health and Safety Act became law we had a train of 1962 stock in Heavy Repair and when we opened the floor and found powdered asbestos I had the men out of the shop. I went next door where the same models were being worked on. Asbestos was all over the floor and being blown into the air by the wind of the air drills. I stopped the job. The steward protested it would cut their bonus and he had also negotiated an early shut for working on it. The shop manager was furious at my decision. He argued it wasn't blue asbestos. There were varying degrees: blue was the worst, then white, then pink. He argued as this stuff was only pink it wasn't bad. I asked if he used pink asbestos to make blancmange for his kids.

In the end London Underground was forced to strip down trains in an exclusive part of the works, with the workers wearing protective suits. Members gradually saw the end of negotiated danger money, but they lived longer. I always opposed working in dangerous conditions being compensated by a few extra bob. A company prepared to pay danger money was a grim admission of disdain for a person's well-being.

In 1975 I was again nominated for the National Executive Committee of the CPGB, but there were other engineers in the frame and I had had another set to. The Party executive had seen the successes of the LCDTU, and they wanted to co-opt it for other issues. They saw a big organisation with a mass following as a ready-made structure to ground campaigns against, for example, nuclear weapons, rent rises, and apartheid South Africa. LCDTU's opposition to this, no matter how worthy the cause, was one of long struggle with executive members. We resisted on the principle, established on the advice of Julie Jacobs during LCDTU's formation, that we were a single-issue organisation: this was our strength. Sharp debates followed but we remained firm, even though the Committee's leadership comprised many Communists. It must be clear that sticking to this founding tenet was correct. Insisting that LCDTU's resources be concentrated on the defence of trade union activity didn't make me popular with King Street, and again I was runner-up on the EC ballot.

While waiting for our wedding day Anita and I had a great difference. Anita had a non-malignant growth on her face which needed to be removed by a very delicate operation. It could leave her face badly scarred if unsuccessful. If that happened, she said, she wouldn't inflict herself on me. What rows we had: that I loved her as a person regardless, that if I had a disabling accident at work she would marry me. But she was stubborn and it was a hard time waiting for her admittance to surgery which fortuitously fell between the end of the February 1974 General Election and the start of electioneering for the May local council elections. The operation took about nine hours, involving the painstaking untangling of nerves and negotiation of muscles. It was successful. The wedding was on.

I invited everyone at the Acton Rails Branch to the wedding, held on the Friday of the summer holiday shutdown. Everyone would take the day off. However, there was an issue. We were selling about 50 *Morning Star*s each morning outside the gate. Who was going to sell if we were all at the wedding? Most of my comrades couldn't because their wives were not in the Party and wouldn't understand: they wanted to be taken to the ceremony. There was only one person left. 'Anita won't object,' I was assured. I was deputed to come into work before going to the Hampstead registry office. I went in and sold the papers. I gave a chit to the foreman saying I was leaving at 10 o'clock. 'No problem,' he said, and took it off to the office. He came back shortly: 'You can't put 'getting married' as a reason for knocking off. They'll think I've gone mad.' I told him it was a fact. I had to be in Hampstead at 11 o'clock. He shook his head then told me I should have let the shop know so they could have had a collection.

At 10 o'clock I left the factory and hurried up the road to Acton Town station to catch the North London Line, then (as now) a notoriously fragile service. The train had been cancelled. The Richmond train arrived on the opposite platform. I hailed the driver and told him to be sure he came back; I needed to get to my wedding. He did come back, pulling in with his horn blaring. I had arrived just on the right side of late and rushed in to the clerk's office to pay for the licence when the situation again became troublesome. In my exertions I had managed to lose my wallet. Anita's dad offered the cash but I couldn't take it. I wasn't being bribed to marry Anita. I went outside and asked the assembled crowd. Could somebody lend me a score? Derek Wedgwood shouted, 'Blimey, he's taking a collection at his own wedding!' but Denis Birdseye took pity and gave me £20. I was married. What an investment by the Party.

Being married to me has sometimes held Anita back. She has my greatest respect as a comrade. When I stood for parliament in Tower Hamlets Anita advised me to wear a suit and tie. It was a good idea, although I avoided the East End tradition of two new tailored suits a year. Hans and Lillie came to a rally at Limehouse Town Hall. They talked with Bert Ramleson, and drank beer with us. Afterwards her mother joined the Party and Hans sent a poem. The last time I saw Hans was the evening before he died. He was critical of the Party's anti-EEC propaganda. He had particular insight in this area having worked for a company that advertised some of the biggest products in Paris and New York. He died that night. How proud of Anita he would now have been.

The caretaker
in the Limehouse Library
impartially, as a public servant should act
places a jug of water and glasses
on the table of the speakers
at a Communist election meeting.
Blue rexine chairs
municipal in price and style
in straight rows
would seat one-hundred-and-eighty inhabitants
if one-hundred-and-eighty inhabitants
had had the urge to attend.
Actually thirty odd did so
and the other one-hundred-and-fifty
are unaccounted for.
How can a man know
that there is a seat for him
if he does not go and look for it?
We live in an age of empty chairs
it is not the only
emptiness in our lives.
But it is the one which matters.
Not before the chairs are full
at a Communist meeting
will our lives be full.
Do not stay away for too long
or you may not find the way.
*Hans Hess, 26/2/74*

# 12 High days at Acton Rails

Acton Rails was a good place. The management were pure railwaymen with great experience. You could have sharp negotiations but there was respect on each side and if anyone argued from a lack of knowledge they were given short shrift.

It was an industry with a long-term future. The progressive Labour government of 1974-79 had appointed Tony Benn as Secretary of State for Industry, and he in turn had appointed Jim Mortimer as Industrial Relations Manager at London Transport.

However, I blamed Jim for the fact that London Underground had twice blacklisted me when I applied for a job at Lifts and Escalators, and our relationship was strained. So much so that when, years later, we were on an anti-apartheid march, walking together behind the TASS banner, we entered into a discussion in which I accused him of espousing progressive policies but being, like all personnel management, an anti-militant. We were raving at each other. Jim took his coat off and told me to leave the march and have it out with him. Comrades intervened which was just as well as we were outside Buckingham Palace, opposite the Bag O' Nails. After that, for many years we met only formally. However, I'm glad to say we made up many years later.

After 18 months at Acton I became Heavy Repair steward. The first time I stood I lost as a result of a right-wing campaign from surrounding union members ('He will always have you on strike, the red bastard.'). I gained a seat on the AEU negotiating committee and was given the brief of dealing with the apprentice engineers.

Acton was a strong centre for apprentices as both management and workers saw the need for specialised skills. The skills we taught were not used exclusively in the rail industry; apprentices could go on to work on cars, ships, machinery, and cranes. The London Transport Board had built a marvellous modern training school with instructors who were devoted shop floor workers. The LTB school was a classic example of the trade union movement's traditional stress on the importance of apprentices. The mechanical fitters for instance would work in all the sections: heavy repair, lifts and escalators, and signals. It was a very varied experience which addressed both theory and practical learning. The intake each year was 12 engineers, 12 electricians, a couple of bodymakers and one sheet metal worker. The apprenticeship lasted four years. Only a very few gave it up.

Applicants for the apprenticeship were interviewed jointly by a union rep and a training officer. There were always more applications than places; even more as firms employing apprentices closed down or didn't want the expense, preferring to hire craftsmen trained by other firms. It was very difficult to select just twelve engineers and reject the rest. Generally agreement on who to apprentice was reached without much difficulty.

Only one time did we really fall out over a decision. A young West Indian woman called Anita had applied. Of course she hadn't been taught metalwork at school so she couldn't produce specimens of her work, but she answered the questions impressively. During the interview the training officer, a white, Anglo-Saxon Protestant, had asked her whether she knew that the work was heavy and not suited to women. Anita replied that she was an amateur weight-lifter with medals and trophies and if he stood up she would lift him over her head – which she did.

When we were reviewing the candidates the training officer casually rejected her, saying airily when we came to her name, 'We'll pass on.' He smiled when I said he had two choices, the Commission for Racial Equality or the Equal Rights Commission. 'We will pass on,' he said. 'In that case, I'll appeal the Equalities Tribunal first.' When he could see I wasn't joking, he blanched and Anita was apprenticed.

She was a great education for me. After two and a half years of her apprenticeship the same training officer called me in and said, 'Anita's got herself pregnant.' I asked if she got pregnant by herself but he insisted on her dismissal. Being on the CPGB's Women's Committee I knew exactly where to turn and I was given step by step advice by Tess Gill and other comrades. It was hard work negotiating with people saturated in the prejudice of the default male position. Eventually Anita was given leave of absence for 12 months. It was trade union women who would later ensure maternity leave by statutory right. Anita went on to work in the heavy repair depot, becoming an AUEW steward, and a good one.

Though I defended many I only had one apprentice dismissed in my time. Throwing-stars were all the rage among gangs and one apprentice was found to be making them. They were forged in half an inch of steel, weighed half a pound and were lethal. Thrown well they could stick in a wall, never mind a human body. The apprentice was suspended for three days and when he did the same again I persuaded him to leave to avoid a bad reference.

As the apprentices rotated round the factory some of the jobs were a bit tedious and repetitive. My shop was most intensive. Most of the foremen didn't bother but Peter Cudmore in Heavy Repair and Development used to call in the apprentices at the end of each week, and ask to see their log and question what they had done. Some used to complain to me but I took the attitude that they were there to learn and thought that Peter was a good foreman. Together Peter and I used to skim off the best apprentices and earmark them as future heavy repair fitters. A peculiar feature was that the best apprentices were also the brightest politically. So I finished up with a shop that would stock the demos and picket lines: years after I still meet some of them at events, and they haven't changed.

The only failure we had was with one who was made Apprentice of the Year, an award that made him smug and superior. He worked with me on a big job, making towing couplers for the imported Plasser locos. I started telling him how to mark out the inch-thick plates and check them, but he told me he knew what he was doing and to leave it to him. I decided to follow his instructions. After all, you can make a mistake marking out, but the plates are not lost until they are cut by the burner. He went on to say that the plates didn't need checking and sent them straight to the burner. The finished articles were well out and the foreman had to be told. The smug expression disappeared for a long while. Peter and I agreed it was worth it to take him down a peg.

Acton Rails in the 1970s was a regular job without boom and slump, but it was badly paid. There was a pension scheme that returned a pittance, but if you were fit and capable you could work until you were 75. Then, to make room for younger people, the company reduced the retirement age to 70, then 65. This caused protests.

While earlier retirement gave some relief to the unskilled and semi-skilled who did the most lifting and humping, the skilled bench-worker did not have the same concern. The best way of dealing with this was to improve the pension.

Jim Mortimer could be counted as a progressive, but he had to sell any scheme to the directors. He was on a hard rock to stony ground position. A joint pension was ground out. The worker paid £1 and the company £10 a week. The board was half company and half employees, unlike other schemes where the board was entirely comprised of the directors who started and stopped schemes on their own whim, and gave themselves pension holidays whenever they felt like a break. Joining the Acton scheme was an agreed condition of employment. There were some who objected to paying, but I am sure they were delighted they had when they retired.

When our negotiations opened I found I had an advantage. I had been part of the team that negotiated the Ford pension scheme, and Ford was a lot harder to deal with than London Transport. The Ford pension was based on service and you benefited if you had worked at Briggs before the buy-out. When I retired I applied for my Ford pension for 13 years service, to be told they had no record of me working at the company. I said that if they consulted their minutes they would see I was a founder of the pension scheme. They replied that because I had been dismissed I was not entitled and a government Court of Inquiry asserted the same.

London Underground pensions were always negotiated annually. When asked why I put pensions in negotiation submissions each year I would say because pensions were deferred wages. I always won the vote although some younger members couldn't see that far ahead.

Thatcher depleted many work pension schemes by giving people the right to opt out at a portion of their fund's value. This led to an influx of insurance carpet-baggers offering cash to join a private policy. What people didn't see was that these schemes had no employer contributions and many were carried away with the thought of a new car or a holiday abroad. London Transport, with its 25,000 employees, was a prime target for insurance agents. Although there were advantages for the company in savings, the pension committee came to a unanimous decision to fight against withdrawals.

London Transport agreed to furnish the trade unions with the names of applicants to private schemes. These staff would be seen jointly by stewards and managers and the disadvantages of the schemes explained to them. Equally, we argued, if wages and pensions were jointly negotiated, by turning their back on one how could they register an opinion on the other? Moreover, they weren't going to be able to negotiate anything under a private policy. This approach was successful and I believe fewer than 100 rail and bus workers left the company scheme. I appreciate the pension now. It's not large but reasonable compared to the state pension. It's better than a gold watch, at any rate.

The wages at Acton were slow to increase. When they were at least £10 a week less than dock pay some skilled workers such as body makers used to rotate jobs. There were several car body firms in the area that paid better than Acton Rails, including Rolls Royce at Neasden and Park Royal Bus Builders. Members would apply there in a jobs boom then move back to Acton when the wind changed. It was usual practice in a casual industry. However with a decent pension scheme at London Transport this job migration slowed.

Acton works also had a bonus scheme. It was paid shop by shop, it was long and costly in its operation, and it created massive divisions. Additionally, it wasn't much. You might expect to be given £30, at a time when dockworkers were earning £40-£50 per week.

Jim Mortimer's nine-point plan brought in a flat bonus rate alongside a higher rate based on the top bonus earnings, making all the shops equal. There was a bit of a protest from the shops that had been pulling in the higher bonuses, but as everyone was getting a rise it was accepted. It saved a lot of arguments. The single bonus rate was welcomed by Communists as it gave a better basis for unity, although the settlement did give differentials.

The Toolroom, which traditionally took the highest bonuses, drew 15% of the works' earnings. Heavy Repair was only on the works flat rate when I took over as steward. I unearthed a claim for 3% of earnings and pursued it. The shop banned overtime (quite a feat), and work being sent outside the shop until 18 months had passed. The tunnel cleaning train on which I had worked from the first girders was under threat of being sent to a contractor, so the project was held up. No one else could work on it because it was 'black', i.e. not recognised as a dispute. After a long fight we won the 3% and the cleaning train rolled.

The union members were solid at Acton. When major negotiations took place, union officials had to be involved. Often during adjournments the officials would say to the management, without the least scruple: 'That's a good deal. We'll accept.' The stewards would then have to step in and make it clear that the officials were only negotiating on behalf of the members – the stewards would declare whether or not the deal was acceptable. To decide this we would call a members meeting of all the shops.

It wasn't easy organising this around the various shifts but we insisted there be democracy. Some of the members would grumble: 'We don't need a meeting; we trust you.' We replied that we could be talked into a bad deal, and then what? Overall the democracy was appreciated. Not only were wages and conditions dealt with like this, but also all major solidarity issues.

Later, when I became chair of the all London Underground negotiating committee, I solved the problem of adequately reporting back by insisting on mass meetings day and night in paid working time. Before there was always the problem of jealousy arising between sections with suspicion that the other shops were getting a better deal. Holding mass meetings during negotiations killed that distrust.

But it wasn't only the big issues that were given support. Individual member's cases were prone to be dismissed by the stewards committees or put on the back-burner but we stopped that tendency. After all, if a bloke wants a set of overalls or boots that is the main thing on his mind. The member who gets his boots remembers it and is more likely to offer his support on other issues.

Individual cases were sometimes unbelievable. A person who has worked in rail for a bit becomes absorbed by the culture and begins to feel affinity with railways all over the world.

One long-serving member approached the management with his dearly-held ambition to travel across Canada by train, from Montreal to Vancouver. Acton Works wrote to Canadian Pacific Railway, which was pleased to issue him with a complementary off-peak return ticket. There was a delay in Vancouver for the return leg so CPR agreed to fly him back to Montreal to enable him to catch his scheduled flight to England. In a sudden expression of gratitude he touted his train ticket. As it was marked for CPR employees only, the purchaser was challenged attempting to board the train, and the fraud unmasked. CPR raised hell with Acton management, who on the basis of their recommendation were now being accused of a serious breach of faith.

The management decided to dismiss the miscreant instantly. He was not an honourable person and had put the company into disrepute. I was inclined to agree with them, but negotiated a reprimand, conditional on him paying back all his costs to CPR. The Canadians had initially wanted him extradited and charged in Canada, but the repayment of costs, with an apology, satisfied them. We even managed to find him time to pay.

I told this story to an NUR member who worked the main line to the north and he said he could beat it. The St Pancras Station Hotel on Euston Road had stood abandoned since the end of the war. One railwayman decided he would like the enormous clock that was still in the hotel's tower. Each night, on his own initiative, he removed the clock's innards bit by bit to his house in Essex; a long and arduous job. That done the enterprising railwayman turned his attention to the clock-face and began with the massive minute hand. The next morning the whole world noticed it was missing. British Rail was concerned. Had the hand fallen and damaged anything, or killed someone? On investigation they found the clock's workings had been filleted and began to suspect a conspiracy. A secret watch was placed and the culprit was caught as he came back for the hour hand. Dismissal appeared to be inevitable, until NUR intervened and it was agreed that the clock be brought back from the railwayman's house and reassembled in his own time. Now the same clock is working again on the revitalised multi-million pound hotel at the Eurostar station. If you go past, remember its journey to and from Essex.

Other negotiations come to mind. I remember that the four weeks paid holiday allowed each year led to problems. Holidays could only be taken two weeks at a time so as not to upset production. A large proportion of Acton's workforce originated from other countries and there was a demand for a four week holiday to allow them to visit their families. It was obvious that the cost and time involved made a month essential. After prolonged discussions the holiday ruling allowed a four week break during slack periods to allow such visits. This was welcomed by workers as a good show of solidarity.

Members then proposed one year's holiday allowance being saved until the next year to give eight weeks. This was more difficult because you accrued holiday week by week. You would be getting holiday pay without putting in the credit. We negotiated that it had to be taken after six months in the second year. There were great celebrations. I did very well in West Indian rum, and also once in beer in a pub in Ealing. It was full with Sikhs who lived thereabouts. I was told my pint had been paid for and I wondered what was going on until along the bar I heard a shout of 'Cheers Halpin!' Three lads from Acton were in.

Wider issues were also discussed. The Peace Camp at Greenham Common had been established and we endorsed its appeal for funds. The AUEW shop stewards committee had always supported CND and took its banner on all marches. However we had difficulty securing support of the EEPTU Committee. Its hierarchy was right-wing and welcomed any action against socialist countries, including beating them over the head with the threat of dropping a nuclear bomb on their people. The NUR could be won, though, and the Sheet Metal Workers and NUVB.

We sent supporting delegates to the Women's Peace Camp at Greenham Common, but it was clear that the women didn't need cheering on. We could give them a bit of cash, but we decided we could also help out with the supply of food. Around the North Circular there were big factories such as Heinz and McVities. Many of our AEU members had worked at these and through their contacts we were able to buy products at cost price. We ran a food convoy up to Greenham once a week. This came out of shop stewards' funds, but shop collections were also agreed and members contributed. The women were delighted, though I doubt whether any of them ever willingly opened a tin of Heinz soup or baked beans after leaving the camp.

We also had very good contacts with the Guinness brewery at Park Royal, but despite repeated offers dry stout didn't seem to be high on the list of priorities at Greenham Common. We also supported the Trico Windscreen Wipers strike. My team from Heavy Repair leading the way, we all turned up at the factory on Friday at 5pm to put pressure on the scabs when they were paid. Pay-day picketing led to a worthwhile night out. It was a bit heavy in the West London bars, before the West Ealing Trade Union Club was set up.

A memorable picket was one held at Canterbury prison, where Malcom Pitt, the Kent miners' leader, was imprisoned for breaking a court order banning him from approaching a local power station. He had been arrested for passing by in a car. That morning I had received a bonus cheque from London Undergound for suggesting how to make the hydraulic jacks used to hold up trains stronger and safer, and I thought it would be a good idea to subsidise the trip. Outside the prison I addressed the picket from a wall. It was fortunate I climbed up before and not after our refreshments, or I may have fallen off before elucidating my main points.

Malcom Pitt was a good comrade. He always supported class and international positions. He had a jail education. In class terms the Kent mines were similar to, or better than, Acton, which is high praise. The secretary was the ever-solid Jack Dunn. The four Kent pits were relatively new and the men had been recruited from mining communities across Britain. They settled in a country scene with squire traditions and proletarianised the area. The Kent coalfields helped in the ousting of the right-wing who had been long entrenched in the NUM. Soon after losing his position as NUM General Secretary, Joe Gormley was seen in a morning suit and top hat at Ascot racecourse.

# 13 CPGB leadership and Euro attacks

In 1977, after 27 years of Communist work, industrially and electorally, I was voted on to the National Executive Committee of the CPGB. I was elected with nine other new members, of whom three were good mates: Sammy Barr, an LCDTU member from Upper Clyde; Ron Halverson, a leading engineer; and Mick Costello, who had been industrial correspondent for the *Morning Star*.

It was the first time I had been on the list of nominees recommended by the outgoing EC. I owed my nomination to Bert Ramelson, and to Jack Askins, a TGWU comrade from the Party's North West District. Bert and I had worked together on many issues. We had also fought together over many issues, but his class instincts were finely tuned. We may have disagreed on tactics but never on the aims.

I had met Jack at Hastings during one of the Schools. He was then fit and playing volleyball. Now he was wheelchair bound. They both had to battle hard for my nomination and I go on the record with my thanks. They argued at Congress and on the EC that it was enough my being chair of LCDTU and for securing the pan-industry agreement for a complete stoppage after the arrests of the Pentonville Five, resulting in the TUC General Council's call for a General Strike. But in addition I was chair of the powerful West Middlesex District. With 1,100 members it wasn't the biggest about but many of our number were in the big industries. Also West Middlesex included a powerful branch at Heathrow Airport led by Freddy Gore, an EEPTU militant debarred from office by the right-wing leadership of the Les Cannon/Frank Chapple type.

Anita put my election down a little to politics but mainly to my newfound respectability in marrying her. For a few years I had drifted around. The British Communist Party had certain attitudes arising, I think, from Scottish religious traditions.

The first EC meeting I attended went through the election of committees. I had always been on the National Metal Committee, the advisory body for engineering comrades. The National Metal was very strong during the Second World War. It had many stewards, and district and regional organisation, as well as providing three CPGB comrades who were elected AEU National Industrial Organiser: George Crane, a rough diamond but a great agitator; Wal Hannington, once a blacklisted worker who helped found the 30s National Unemployed Workers' Movement; and John Foster, a great comrade and intellectual. John always brought his young son, also called John, aged five or six to the National Metal meetings. He was a lovely kid; we used to give him pencil and paper to draw and amuse himself.

After school young John worked as a typographer and was active in union politics. He was never a CPGB member but because of his father he never forgot his class. He became a good friend of Anita at the NUJ, first when he was an organiser and then as General Secretary. We still have one of his exquisite line drawings on our wall.

The Political Committee made recommendation on committee membership, among these Tess Gill for the Women's Advisory Committee and me for the Economics Committee. Tess complained that this was stereotyping both of us, so we agreed to swop. The reaction was uproarious; some were doubled up with laughter. I was seen as a typical craft-union comrade far removed from the nature of women's politics in the 1970s. Of course my education by the women workers at Briggs wasn't widely known.

That said, this committee was the hardest body I ever sat on. I sometimes faced considerable hostility. I was sitting with the Woman's Organiser Jean Styles, along with Jean French, Maggie Bowden and Tess Gill. These comrades held good class opinions compared to the rest of the Committee members, who generally argued from the radical end of feminist politics, seeing men as the enemy, not capitalism.

The two Jeans, Maggie, Tess and I continually argued that exploitation of women was primarily a class position. This was rejected by our opponents. They were allies of the Eurocommunists who were just then breaking away from class positions and accusing members of 'economism'.

Debates would frequently become highly-charged, and there were occasions when members would weep in frustration. Sometimes I thought the tears were working against me, as if to condemn me for attacking them even though I was scrupulous in keeping to criticisms of their politics. I would attend the Committee socials. I kept my hands under close scrutiny, somewhat nervous of allegations questioning where they had been. The radical feminism in the Party seems to have given way in its opposition to straight class politics, and the legacy of the Jeans, Tess and Maggie is evident. Many advances won by trade union women were influenced by leading women comrades.

The Party Congress in 1977, chaired by Mick McGahey, was memorable. Grunwick was in full swing and the floor passed an emergency motion urging the TUC to cut off gas, electricity and water. This could have won the dispute but the TUC didn't act on it.

The same Congress supported devolution in Wales and Scotland to allow those countries to control their own economies. This was moved by Arthur True, a councillor from Wales. While the Congress was in session the firefighters' national strike was on. Merlyn Rees, the Labour Home Secretary, attacked the strikers in a right-wing speech he gave in Parliament.

The same year LCDTU took Friends House for a conference opposing public spending cuts and unemployment. This was attended by upwards of 1,200 delegates. The West of Scotland Secretary, Josh Shaw, commissioned a sleeper train from Glasgow. It was an excellent Conference. At this time my good comrade Jim Hiles was the Committee's National Secretary and he did a fine job. One of the major speakers was Ben Rubner, General Secretary of the Furniture Makers Union.

As the working class was organising, preparations for the Silver Jubilee were afoot. Anita and I were living in the East End. Anita was chair of the local Tenants and Residents Association, and a governor at the primary school at the bottom of the road.

Ideas were floated for a street party, proposed by Iris, Secretary of the TRA, and born and bred on the street. The police agreed to close our road to traffic. The Unicorn, my local, was trapped in the middle. What do Communists do at times like this? Boycott the party and suffer isolation? We took part, not in support of Queen Elizabeth, but in support of the community.

It was a typical East End bash: booze, food, bunting, a stage, a piano, the lot. It was a good night. I even sang a few songs. A television film crew turned up during my second encore. I was wearing my best yellow silk-knit shirt which made me look, on the television, like an oversized canary. The remarks next day at Acton were predictable, especially those from the Irish republicans. I had to hold my hands up. Perhaps I am preserved in the archives somewhere, chirping at the Jubilee in my finest plumage.

But 1977 was also the year that Eurocommunists, clustering around Martin Jacques, first made themselves felt in the CPGB. The

Eurocommunist movement was led by the Spanish, Italian and French CPs who had massive Parties with strong industrial roots. They exhorted us all to get together as European Communists, in which state we would be stronger. This was part of a general strategy to diminish the role of class and class struggle.

The notion that class wasn't important ushered a gradual decline in the Italian and French Communist Parties. To say there was hostility from some sections of the CPGB executive committee to my election would be putting it mildly. I think the Eurocommunists hated the working class more than the employers did. If you moved 'open the window' they would oppose.

The dilution of class politics also had a detrimental effect on Party membership in Britain. After reaching a peak of 56,000 in 1942, by 1946 membership had fallen back to 42,000, and when I joined in 1950 the Party had around 35,000 members.

After Hungary and the resignations following the controversy over Inner Party Democracy in 1957 this fell to 28,000; and a similar drop occurred between July 1977 and March 1979, the inaugural period of the denigration of class politics, during which membership declined from 25,295 to 17,756. London suffered the biggest loss, falling from 4,124 to 3,125. The YCL had the greatest percentage loss, 1,663 to 699 members. Only a few Young Communists were now going on to join the CPGB.

The death of James Klugmann, the editor of *Marxism Today*, can now been seen as a watershed. James was the leading Marxist theoretician of the post-war period. His history stretched back to Cambridge in the 1930s where he joined the Party (with Donald Maclean, his schoolfriend). During the war James joined the Special Operations Executive as an intelligence officer and worked in Yugoslavia assisting the recognition of Tito's Partisans and the isolation of the Royalists. Among his publications are the first two volumes of a history of the Communist Party of Great Britain.

After James's death Martin Jacques was elected as editor of *Marxism Today* and he used the journal as a tactical vehicle for Eurocommunism. It was outwith democratic centralism and IPD to hold meetings opposed to Congress policy except during the period of pre-Congress discussion. The reason was that only Congress decisions should be carried out between congresses to forestall the Party pulling in different directions, and prevent the consequent problems in our approach and public work. It was also argued that those with the equipment and finance to organise would have the advantage over working class comrades without these facilities or cash. But in seeming contradiction of this tenet, the EC agreed to set up *Marxism Today* Discussion Groups which were free to have theoretical discussion on the journal's contents. Apparently innocuous, in effect these became legitimised factions as the EC had also made *Marxism Today* an independent commercial entity and the editorial board ceased to be an elected sub-committee of the EC.

Shortly after the appointment of Jacques, *Marxism Today* published an essay by Eric Hobsbawm. It argued that the forward march of labour predicted by Marx had come to an end 25 to 30 years ago, and claimed that the working class were in crisis with sectarianism and 'economism'. This was 1978, and there were verging on 12.5 million people in the TUC. Arguably the working class was at its height.

Hobsbawm's attack on class politics led to a lengthy debate in the pages of *Marxism Today*. Many opposed his views (including Jack Jones and Tony Benn) and I aligned myself with the critique of his argument. Ken Gill argued that the growing wages fight within organised labour was leading to political solutions, a consequence made evident by the anti-union laws imposed by the ruling class.

My criticism centred on whether a Marxist can accept the concept of a halted movement. Class movement can be forward or backward, but a halt isn't possible in Marxist theory. Hobsbawn's article came after the successful injection of public funds into a declining capitalist manufacturing sector. Of course, we criticised the unchanged management structures, but in contrast with later Labour governments it was a big advance. Nevertheless the Hobsbawmites had a marked effect on our trade union followers and allies.

The Euros continued with criticism of our Party's support for socialist countries. Since then I have been criticised by both Eurocommunists and Trotskyists about the defence of socialist countries in the face of their collapse.

My reply has been that those countries were good for all the people, not just the local intelligentsia. I use the word intelligentsia in Leninist terms: people trained in a certain discipline, rather than thinkers about society overall, who he termed intellectuals. I have no doubt that the intelligentsia's ascendancy accounts for the massive numbers of billionaires in the former Soviet Union: none but the trained could have had the knowledge to gain control of state enterprises (a good subject for some research).

That socialist economies were struggling by the late 1970s was inevitable given the great anti-Soviet campaign designed to convince western populations of the overwhelming need to defend their countries from the spectre of Communist aggression. This forced the Socialist Republics to match the West's massive spending on weapons; the difference being that western arms expenditure was funded by colonial sources, the US exploiting the whole of South America, for instance, and Britain doing the same in its former colonies. By contrast socialist governments were forced to limit the resources of their own people. Ending support for the socialist countries was aiding imperialism and attacking our class.

The 1977 Congress saw the clearest indication of the Euro attack on the Party. Ominously, at the start of proceedings it was known that the charismatic Clydesider Jimmy Reid, who had left the Party in 1975, had finally been accepted into the Labour Party. He had done a good job at the Upper Clyde work-in, and one forgets that Jimmy had been a full-time worker for the YCL and for the Scottish Committee. When he wanted to return to industry his CV hardly recommended him to employers but our comrades in Clyde shipbuilding fought to get a job for him. Jimmy was a good comrade spoilt by Communist adulation. He was put up as the parliamentary candidate for Clydebank in 1974. He was widely tipped to win and his defeat disillusioned him.

The grave ideological differences which were to beset the Party became most apparent during the Congress debate on *The British Road to Socialism*. The executive committee's recommendation to change direction to a 'Broad Democratic Alliance' was seen as removing the Party from its proletarian foundation. This 'Alliance' hinged on representing all who worked for a living. A position which would necessarily include judges ruling on anti-union laws and police attacking pickets was too broad and diminished the class imperative.

The 'Alliance' was opposed by Rowan Roenig from Leicester with support from John Foster from Govan and Mary Davis from Tottenham, who moved to substitute it with an 'anti-monopoly alliance'; which was in turn opposed by the executive committee's speaker Jack Woddis, Sue Slipman from London Students, Tom Bell from Greenwich and (young) Pat Devine from Salford University. In the end the EC won with 69 votes cast for the 'Broad Democratic Alliance'. This was a significant warning as to how non-class our Party was going. Against this background I suppose it was a surprise to find myself elected, or even recommended, to the EC.

After this victory the Euros were stronger in their dissent from established rules. The preparations for the 1979 Party Congress at the meeting of the National Executive in November 1978 included the job of electing members to Congress committees. I was nominated for the Inner Party Democracy Commission by the Political Committee. On being questioned where I stood on the constitution in view of my 1957 stand in favour of semi-federalism, I stated that I didn't think that was an issue, because again there was a serious attack coming on the principles of Democratic Centralism. I was elected along with Dave Priscott from Yorkshire.

At the 1979 National Congress the Euros decided to attack the method of election to the Party's Executive Committee. The National Executive Committee was elected at each congress. Outgoing EC members studied the list of names nominated for the next years' Committee and decided on a balance of industrials, women, regionals, intellectuals, *Morning Star* staff, etc.

This 'recommended' list then went to an Election Preparations Committee comprising of two people from the EC (not mandated but with the duty to put EC recommendations) and delegates nominated from every Regional and District Committees. After this the list was put to delegates at the start of the Congress. Before this process was established it was the view that in the absence of any wider recommendations an EC would be elected of comrades who had gained publicity through the *Morning Star* and Party publications, but which didn't reflect the membership or trade unions.

The lesson was learnt and subsequently it was ensured that the recommended list contained comrades with a range of experience broad enough to make policies that were capable of winning support. The Euros argued for this procedure to be replaced by open lists without recommendations from the outgoing EC. I was one of two members on the EC to defend the status quo publicly at the Congress.

The opposition to EC recommendations was led by Dave Cook, National Organiser, behind whom was a whole list of Euros; but it was not enough. The Congress rejected the proposal for open lists by 212 to 71, showing that the Party had not gone over to the Eurocommunists quite yet.

The 1979 Congress also adopted the recommendation made in a report by the Election Preparations Committee that, after a vote, EC members should cement support for its decisions while reporting to the rank and file. I decided to use the Inner Party Democracy report to record instead my opposition to EC policy, the section moved by my good Acton comrade Pat Warwick. At line 524 there is the following: 'EC must report all votes taken and individuals shall have the right to have their dissent recorded and the reasons thereof'. I would record my vote, go back to my West Middlesex District bearing the majority decision, and dutifully ask for support. I would give the results of the votes and state the recorded opposition by name. Asked why I had voted against I could give my reasons. My District comrades would then give me unqualified support in opposition.

There was consternation on the executive when it received the minutes, but I quoted the rule under which I acted. West Middlesex's rejection of the Euro direction of the Party was ensured. National officials were sent to check my meetings but there was nothing the Euros could do. I was in the clear and this was the routine for my reports back. This went on to 1985. The problem the executive faced with me was that while I opposed its every motion I retained my credibility through my position on the LCDTU; although in the end it was prepared to defeat any opposition by disciplinary action.

On Boxing Day 1981 I read the obituary of Betty Sinclair, the fine Irish Communist. Her funeral was to be held on 30 December. I got hold of Gordon McLennan, then General Secretary, and suggested to him that the CPGB should be represented. Gordon agreed but said it was impossible for him to go, and he didn't think that any members of the Political Committee would make themselves available. I believed it was important someone should be there. It would be a significant political gesture that would remind people that the Irish Communists had not been left isolated.

At the height of the violence I don't believe Communists were touched. Comrades like MSF officials Joe Bowers were famous for their trade union stand for members at Shorts Bombardier, the aircraft manufacturer. Betty Sinclair was secretary of the Belfast Trades Council, one of the few organisations in which both sides of the sectarian divide were united on policies to strengthen Belfast's economy and social provision. It had the status of the old London Trades Council. I volunteered to attend the funeral, saying it would be an honour to represent the CPGB.

I landed in Belfast. I had to meet a minder. I had walked two yards out of the airport when I realised I had passed through the wrong door. I turned to go back. As I did so there was a shout from an armed policeman who was sitting on his own by the side of the road under a small canopy. 'Go in and come out the other way!' 'Sure; I only walked two steps past you.' 'Just do as you're told,' the policeman said. I realised I was in a different place. 'Hello, Kevin,' said my minder, 'don't roam off and make my job hard.' We had a couple of hours to spare so we met up with comrades in a pub.

It was a massive funeral. The coffin arrived covered with the Red Flag. A good choice: funerals of political figures in Ireland typically showed either the Union Jack or the Irish Tricolour. The orations included one by Michael O'Riordan, chair of the Communist Party of Ireland. It must have been a job getting the balance of mourners correct.

My minder gave me a run-down. Not, 'That's an uncle, and she's a sister' but, 'Him and his group are leading Provos. See that lot? Top ranks of the loyalist hard-men.' Others were more amenable but overall it resembled to me a stand-off at the OK Corral.

At the wake I was introduced to a medley of people: civil dignitaries, trade union leaders, businessmen, and so forth. Among them, to my surprise, was the chair of the All Ireland Licensed Victuallers. He told me he was there like I was to pay his respects. He added that not to attend would reflect badly on his organisation.

The price of drinks must have been a united decision. A pint was £1 or 1 Irish punt. I can't remember the price of the Jameson's, but the principle was no different. I left Belfast thinking I had done a job, and Gordon McLennan thanked me at the January EC.

I knew Gordon McLennan quite well. He had a good Scottish pedigree, and led a successful strike of apprentice engineers. When the Pentonville Five were inside he addressed comrades at an emergency meeting to back the call for an all-out strike. It was a very good speech with about 150 present. People have been critical of Gordon's role during the miner's strike: correctly so. But he fitted with my appreciation of the role of the individual in history. There have been many who had a turn of politics which didn't diminish their stand at the Historical Moment.

As a delegate from the CPGB EC I also went to the Hungarian Socialist Workers Party Congress. Jenny Williams was with me as a fellow delegate. On the opening morning the Congress platform was empty. Someone came to the rostrum and proposed a comrade for the chair. The proposal was put to the vote and the chair endorsed. Once the chair was occupied he thanked his comrades and the Congress opened.

The business proceeded placidly. A Programme for A Better Life was debated. I stumbled over the language. It's strange that the Magyar language didn't spread more widely given than Hungary was part of a large empire in the 19th century. It's the nearest language to Finnish.

I was pressed by our hosts to agree to a joint Parties conference. I couldn't give an answer. The CPGB EC was suspicious of socialist countries. Jenny and I had discussions in the swimming pool in the manner of James Bond. There wasn't a chance of interception there. We decided to contact London discreetly.

During the afternoon session I sneaked out of the back entrance and found a public telephone. Don't agree to anything, I was told by the EC, and bring the proposed agenda back. I attempted to smuggle myself back into the hall. The receptionist at the front desk saw me. She was surprised I had gone out of the Congress. I wasn't allowed back in. I supposed she would get in a row for not keeping an eye on me.

We met Charlie Coutts, the *Morning Star* reporter. He had been living in Hungary for a couple of years before 1956. Coutts' eyewitness reports in the *Daily Worker* replaced those of Peter Fryer who had been sent to Hungary at the time of the counter-revolution and had sympathised with it. Charlie was good company. Together we went to the Matyas Pince restaurant, reputedly the best in Hungary.

The Congress reception was held at a former Cavalry Club. I could easily imagine what the Club was like in Empire days. The wide staircase was lined with a Romani orchestra. This was a tribute to the Party's recognition and support of the Romani people after their persecution at the hands of Hungarian imperialists and German fascists. I doubt very much whether there would be such a tribute these days. Of course, everyone political is aware of the persecution of Romani by the Nazis. Communist governments in Eastern Europe addressed that history by giving them space, and land to move to if they wanted, not enforced settlement.

One of the evils of the return to capitalism is a revived intolerance of travellers. Romani people are now scapegoated and an oppressed minority in many former Communist countries.

This is not peculiar to Eastern Europe, as I have found. One of the most difficult things of British politics is the hidden attitude to 'gypsies' or, as McColl wrote in his song, the travelling people.

When I was growing up in Preston the families who worked the fairground would to try to educate their children. At the local schools there was opposition to them joining the classes; the children were accused of being dirty, of being ignorant, of being criminals. I was once invited inside a caravan: it was beautiful, clean, and shining. The

Kevin next to Jenny Williams arriving in Hungary for the HSWP congress

father couldn't read, but he could count the number of people on a big ride and instantly add up the fares he had received.

Todkills would paint the fairground rides when they were laid up in winter. I used to block in the signwriter's colours and so I got to know the fair people and I was given the job of mending the roundabouts and carousels. On rough Saturday nights the wooden horses would sometimes have a leg broken, or an ear knocked off, or their tail pulled out. The fair was forbidden to open on Sundays and I would take my tools and make running repairs. This carried with it the privilege of free turns on the big rides. In fact, you only had to mention Todkills to a fair worker and you were on quite a good perk all round.

Many years later my scooter broke down one evening near a north London encampment. Out of courtesy I knocked at a caravan door and told them that I was leaving a scooter and would return tomorrow to pick it up. Back in the East End I was informed that it would be nicked or stripped. I was surprised at the attitude of people who were considered progressives. I argued against them but they were unshakeable. I would see them proved right all too soon. I went back the next day and found my scooter not only intact but protected from the rain by a tarpaulin. As I repaired the engine I was brought cups of tea and some sandwiches. When I showed my crowd the scooter I was told they couldn't have been real gypsies.

I remembered this when I was a convenor at Acton Rails. I had called for a lunchtime meeting of AEU members. It was an issue over which we had differences with the management so I suggested we met outside on an open space not far from the factory. As we gathered I recalled reading in the *Acton Gazette* about a local campaign to get rid of some travelling people who had pitched on this forsaken spot. I foresaw complications. I could understand their worry at a crowd of 450 people suddenly massing in their space. I decided to walk over and explain why we were meeting there.

I could sense the travellers' suspicion and several came out to stand prominently on the caravan steps. There was an expectation of hostility. I explained what we were up to, addressing them all, hoping that our right to meet was compatible with their right to camp. We would just be half an hour and then we would be off.

We finished our meeting and afterwards as a few of us were packing up, three or four of the travellers came over. They thanked us for giving them notice and asked who we were. We said we were trade unionists. I wouldn't say they joined up but I hope they had a better opinion of unions at least.

Whilst in Hungary I saw the original Rubik Cube. It had not yet been launched in the West. If I had got a concession I could have made millions for the Party. Instead Jenny and I came back with a dozen and half bottles of wine and spirits, including some marvellous top grade Bulls Blood wine, vintage brandy, and liquors.

I declared mine as we came through customs at Heathrow. The customs officer didn't know what the bottles were. I said I had met a bloke who gave them to me: they were probably foreign rubbish. 'Give me five pound,' the officer said. I paid and he turned away. Jenny was behind me: 'What about mine?' she asked. 'Keep walking,' I said, 'it's been settled.'

Officially though, the booze didn't belong to me; it was the Party's. I reported it to the Centre but I was told that if I left it there anyone would drink it. I got onto Denis Elwand, the treasurer, and said I would like to do something; Anita and I would keep it and give a donation to the value. We did and enjoyed the drink with a clear conscience

I took Anita and our son Boris, aged five back to Lake Balaton for a holiday the next year. We didn't want the Party hospitality at its large place on the shores of the lake. Instead we stayed as paying guests at the Volan holiday resort. Volan was Hungary's long-distance truck driver group. The holidaying truck drivers and their families were a good crowd although it took them a while to get used to foreign Communists who spurned the Party place to be with their own people.

While we were there a CPGB school was being hosted across the lake. A few days into our stay I was approached by a Hungarian comrade. The English were getting drunk and causing hostility. They were embarrassed to have to complain, and didn't want to offend, but was there anything I could do? I called a meeting of the English contingent and told them that if there was any more of a problem I had, on behalf of the executive committee, instructed the Hungarians to ship those responsible back on the next Malev flight. Happily the school was soberer after that.

We visited the vineyards at Eger. We were shown around by a man in overalls. I thought he was a peasant. Somewhat hesitantly, I asked him if the vines had suffered from phylloxera. Later he appeared in a suit and I learnt he was head of wine. He had studied for three years in Bordeaux, and for two in California. We were given an excellent meal, but I had too much wine and nearly had to be poured out of the car when we arrived back.

The CPGB executive committee continued to move to the right. In 1981, the book *The Forward March of Labour Halted?* was published, which reprinted Hobsbawn's divisive article and the responses to it, along with some new contributions from among others Bob Wright and Jack Jones.

This was followed in the September 1982 issue of *Marxism Today* by an article written by Tony Lane that amounted to a savage attack on rank and file organisation and its shop stewards, who he accused of 'collaborational corruption'. I objected to the article's unrelenting denigration of the working class and warned of the dire consequences this would have for industrial work and the Party as a whole.

At the next Political Committee meeting Mick Costello, myself and a few other comrades discussed and criticised Lane's article. Tony Chater commissioned a reply for the *Morning Star,* written by Mick Costello. This provoked uproar, orchestrated by a Euro clique which shouted 'Factionalism!' while it had a permanent faction acting as the *Marxism Today* editorial board.

Gordon McLennan attacked Mick Costello at the Political Committee, and rounded on Tony Chater for printing such an attack on *Marxism Today,* claiming that the journal had a duty to print Lane's piece. Tony Chater defended the response on the grounds that the *Morning Star* had agreed an editorial policy consistent with *The British Road to Socialism*. By now there were sharp divisions on the EC over the Party's relationship to the *British Road*.

Needless to say the majority supported Jacques, even Mick McGahey. I can't understand why to this day. By 1982 Eurocommunists made up the majority of executive committee members. Tony Chater remained at the *Morning Star* but the Euros soon had another scalp. In February 1983 Mick Costello was forced to resign as Industrial Organiser. I applied for the open post. My opponent was Peter Carter, a Birmingham builder. The prospective candidates were debated.

One of the strangest comments came from Mick McGahey: 'Kevin couldn't talk to trade union leaders.' I don't know why he said this. It's possible he was parroting the line from Scotland: the Scottish Secretary had been converted from class to Euro politics. In any case Peter Carter was given the role. (Some problems arose. He found it difficult gaining admittance to large hotels to lobby officials in meetings as he was always dressed for a building job. I advised him to get a suit.)

This was the start of the break-up of the CPGB. Large sections of the Party's rank and file supported Chater and rebuked the EC. The EC attacked these sections using disciplinary measures: suspensions and the cancelling of District Committees. It went on to press for the resignation of Tony Chater.

The editor of the *Morning Star* is chosen by the People's Printing Press Society's elected Management Committee, and only it has the right to remove an appointment. The PPPS Management Committee resisted calls that Tony and his deputy David Whitfield be ejected and replaced with Chris Myant and Frank Chalmers, that Ken Gill be dismissed as chair of the PPPS Management Committee, and that the CPGB executive committee nominate five comrades to sit on it. This last was carried by the EC with five against. I had my name recorded as one of the five and reported back to branch and district.

In 1984 I went again to the GDR. It was the 35th anniversary of the socialist state and I attended the celebrations as a representative of the Political Committee of the CPGB. I went with Frank Chalmers, the Euro-communists' man for the Morning Star; and one of the anti-Marxists on the EC who hated socialist countries. He wasn't keen on the British working-class either.

We stayed at the Hotel Palast in Berlin. The hotel had two sides: one for people like us and the other for Western business and all that goes with it. My co-delegate's liking for the business bar was not looked upon with favour. Our rooms had a fridge filled with wine, beer, vodka and brandy.

Kevin being welcomed in the GDR, Frank Chalmers directly behind him

As leader of the delegation I had a small conference room attached. Frank complained about this and moaned that my fridge was bigger than his. 'Look here, comrade,' I said, 'you would have to drink 24 hours a day to empty your fridge and be lagging drunk the whole time. But when you have drunk yours, you can start on mine.'

Some customs always seem strange. Walking around the city we passed a busy bar and went in for a drink. Our minder said we couldn't drink without a table. I couldn't get over it.

There was a large dinner for the anniversary. Afterwards there were speeches. I was not called on to speak. The main speech of the evening was given by Soviet foreign minister Andrei Gromyko. He spoke on peace and praised the growing peace movement in the West. He classified it as part of anti-imperialist forces.

I took exception to this. The peace movement would not see themselves as an anti-imperialist force. It was sectarian to refer to them as such and was doing western comrades a disservice. I told Chalmers what I proposed we do. I had expected agreement given his criticism of the Soviet Union but he raised concerns: we didn't know what would happen, and anyway we weren't authorised by the EC. I replied that Gromyko was like him and I, a Communist, and we should try to stop him repeating the mistake.

With Frank in tow I explained my concerns to the minder who organised a meeting with the GDR Theoretical Representatives at 8 o'clock the next morning. We had a big debate over whether peace was in essence anti-imperialist. My position was that it could be so strategically but that the peace movement and the British Party saw it primarily as a movement of people who simply didn't want to be killed or kill others in useless wars. I didn't convince them but they agreed to put my objections to Gromyko. They must have done so. After the anniversary military parade we were on the rostrum when Gromyko walked past. He looked over and spoke to our interpreter before moving on. He asked if I was the person who had raised the objection to his speech. My co-delegate was very worried.

Frank Chalmers was a funny comrade. He kidnapped his own judgement with his anti-line. After all the hospitality we had been shown he pronounced that, after all, the show was put on by the Government. There was an audible sucking of breath from our GDR friends. They told him that the event had been funded on the back of a Party Congress decision that every member should donate 1% of their salary over the previous five years to host the celebrations and invite guests like him. Collapse of stout party.

I had the good fortune (maybe it was Gordon trying to win me over) to be given the honour of chairing the last session of the CPGB executive held at 16 King Street. Comrades were a bit put out at leaving the historic site. I made a short speech: 'The Communist Party can be proud of its actions in this building, but the Party doesn't exist in buildings but in Marxist ideas.' It was well received, even by the opposition.

The *Morning Star* called its 1984 London section AGM at the Wembley Conference Centre. There was so much controversy, it was obvious that the usual venue would be no way near big enough.

I spoke in favour of Tony, Ken and the *Morning Star* Management Committee. Gordon McLennan made a great plea for the paper to return to the Communist Party; misguidedly, as the paper was always owned by PPPS members. He got carried away as he spoke, running from the platform down the aisle shouting, 'Vote now against the editor!' His exertions were in vain: the PPPS and Tony Chater won the vote of confidence.

There was a celebration afterwards at the Hackney Empire. Anita and I went. During the whole of this period I had the support of my District and Branch, but just as importantly Anita's backing.

When the LCDTU was at its most active the miners were a strong support, and their 1972-74 strikes for better wages were a noticeable success in a burgeoning union movement. However, in 1978 the NUM executive, ignoring a ballot vote but in support of TUC Conference policy, chose to restrict its members' wage claims to 10% and embrace instead a productivity rise.

The 1978 LCDTU Conference condemned the restriction of wage rises to 10% at a time when profits throughout the industry had risen by 28%. The government's position was even meaner than the NUM's: Jim Callaghan was talking of wage rises for miners capped at 5%, while Merlyn Rees, the Home Secretary, advocated 4%, and suggested all public workers be restricted to this. The LCDTU policy was to raise purchasing power; a policy won at TUC: but TUC leaders appeased the Labour government.

The 1978 LCDTU Conference declared a commitment to put pressure on the TUC to state boldly and clearly that there would be no tolerance of government interference in free collective bargaining; no norms or ceiling guidelines which would restrict trade unions in winning back and advancing their living standards.

The 556 delegates endorsed this with a long list of speakers: Ann Field from Print, Bernard Dix from NUPC, Ken Gill from TASS; Bill Mulholland from Dunlop, John Nulckel from the Times, Frank Smyth from Corby Steel; Scots miner Tony Steel, Mike Perkins from the civil service, Sid Harraway from Ford, and George Samson from Dundee. Among the speakers were two black workers: Eric Lynch from Liverpool and Mr Mahoub from the 13-month long Garners strike. George Guy from Sheet Metal was the opening speaker. The collection was organised by Betty Crawford (Manchester took a big collection). Jim Hiles as secretary gave an organisation report. I closed, moving 'Declaration carried unanimously'.

The miners' gains in the early 1970s stored up the enmity of the Tories, and the party's return to government under Thatcher saw a deep-seated hatred manifest itself. The NUM executive's policy of wage restraint led only to the programme of enforced pit closures.

The NUM leadership was attacked by the Eurocommunists, who took the capitalist line that the miners must have a national ballot. Pete Carter wrote a Party pamphlet which wouldn't have looked out of place in the *Daily Mail.* He concluded that mass picketing rather than balloting was a grave mistake. Previously Mick McGahey had sharply rebuffed this call: 'NUM members don't need a ballot. They have had a show of hands for a stoppage and are voting with their feet to come out and man picket lines.' But now he said never a word.

The call for a ballot was influenced by the claim that workers didn't strike freely but were coerced by left-wing leaders. That was the basis of the bedevilment of Arthur Scargill and his so-called cash from Libya. Undoubtedly miners needed solidarity funds because their own had been sequestered.

The Liaison Committee ran appeals for cash amongst all its affiliates in print, rail, transport and white collar members with great success. At Acton we put into action our food organisation, buying it at cost through our well-placed stewards as we had done for the women at Greenham Common.

It was at one of the food collections that I came into a jar of caviar. At first I thought it was blackberry jam, but Vince, an AEU friend, put me right. He had worked for Wilkinsons Sword in the Soviet Union, replacing dilapidated razor blade factories, and had returned with a case of caviar. I took my jar home with me that evening.

The strike went on and after a local support social I put two miners up for the night. When we got back it was late and we had little to eat in the house. The only food I could find was a sliced loaf and the caviar. It got a mixed reception from the miners and I'm sure that in Yorkshire there was talk of rich fitters in London living on caviar; what, no champagne?

LCDTU backed a solidarity march to Trafalgar Square. I was a lonely figure at the microphone on the platform waiting to greet the marchers as they came in. From there I heard the battle in Whitehall where the police and army in police uniforms had attacked the march. A leading MP urged me to send the families already waiting in Trafalgar Square down to Whitehall. He asked for the microphone. I refused. We had called the families out and the street fighting could cause injuries to their children. I felt responsible for their safety.

Maybe I was wrong; maybe the ensuing injuries would have led to the public sweeping away the Tories in anger. It was the biggest personal decision I ever made, and I have thought about it over and over again, regretting that there was no collective to take responsibility. I think the decision I made was the right one, but you as a reader will consider it.

The preparation for the watershed special CPGB Congress in 1985 included the appeals against a number of expulsions for organising opposition to Eurocommunism including EC members, 22 members of the London District committee, comrades from the North West District Committee and *Morning Star* PPPS Secretary, Mary Rosser.

North West and London District Committees had been taken over by Eurocommunist appointments made directly by the EC; and in the 1984-5 card exchange whole branches were dissolved and many comrades were not re-issued with their cards, among them Anita Halpin. The 1985 Congress was clearly meant to be an administrative victory for Eurocommunism. Except for the steadfastnesses of the comrades in the West Middlesex District I felt isolated and beleaguered.

Before the EC meeting which handed down the expulsions I was called in by Gordon McLennan. He told me he was preparing his list of EC recommendations for the Congress Election Preparations Committee. He was prepared to put my name forward if I changed my views. I told him that I had respected him when he led the Glasgow apprentice strike but now I thought he was not the same man. What had changed him? He replied that he owed the Euros. A young close relative had been won back from Trotskyist organisations. I said he would do better to give up his relative than the Communist Party, as he was on the brink of doing. At that we parted. My name did not appear on the list.

The Congress was held in Hammersmith in the town hall where I had held rail craft union member reports. There was a loud demonstration of opposition to executive decisions. It was the last time any effort was made to turn the Party from the Euro machine.

I lobbied with the protestors outside, not speaking on the microphone as I was a delegate to the Congress and could have been excluded for public dissent.

Inside I sat quietly through the business until the item of appeal against the expulsions. Gordon McLennan spoke to recommend the punishment: among other accusations was that they had falsified membership records so that their branches showed more members and could therefore send more delegates to the Congress. That this was in fact the Euros' tactic was never in doubt.

None of those expelled were allowed to hear McLennan's condemnations. On arrival at the Congress they had been escorted to separate rooms under the guard of stewards, even being 'escorted' to the toilet. No contact was allowed between them. After McLennan had finished speaking they were led in one by one to the platform, given three minutes to make their defence, and then escorted out. Among those accused were Maggie Bowden, Margaret Witham, Mike Hicks and Tommy Durkin — all great members of the LCDTU and who all played a leading role in working class politics: it was a disgraceful scene. I stood up and spoke for them, exposing the false records for what they really were. I cited branches where I went as a parliamentary candidate to organise canvassers not only did I not find any willing comrades, but the buildings had ceased to exist years before. I went into the Euros' need to win. The microphone was switched off in an attempt to move me. I carried on speaking. I could be heard without it. I finished my speech. There were howls.

The Congress vote backed all the expulsions and other measures to silence opposition. It was a victory for the Eurocommunists; a definitive step to turn Communist parties across Europe away from factory-based politics and into non-representative lackeys. Yes, Marxism had a set-back, but the working class in Europe has paid the price for this betrayal, and we are still fighting back.

The 1985 Congress and its aftermath saw the creation of the Communist Campaign Group. Its base was the *Morning Star* and all those who were expelled or disenfranchised. Although I had retained my Party card I began to work with the CCG. West Middlesex District continued to oppose the Euros. Its members were not going to be expelled: they had their own premises.

However, life doesn't stand still while the CPGB argues: as the debate over 1956 and Inner Party Democracy occurred when my base in the motor industry was under attack after Suez, so now began moves to change the employment structure at Acton Rails. The idea was to send the overhauling of trains outside the Works and for the heavy repair shop to concentrate on component repair. It meant the loss of 400 jobs and the implementation of 'double-skilling' — training electricians to do mechanical work and vice versa. (Although training was restricted to the bare specifics required for the job; management didn't teach the workforce enough to make them full craftsmen with skills applicable outside the rail industry: you weren't shown how to wire a house.) My heavy repair shop fitters had to learn to do pipe-work, hot riveting and welding.

Of course the main opposition was to the loss of jobs by redundancy. There were handsome pay-outs. The trade unions were then to be reorganised with a Joint Shop Stewards Committee rather than the five separate negotiating units.

The management approached me personally. No, I didn't want redundancy. They pressed me on the Joint Shop Stewards Committee. They said I knew it would work; I had operated it successfully at Ford. It was difficult to argue. Of course many members, as usually happens, volunteered to go and take the redundancy cash. The aftermath was horrible. Many leaders at Acton took the redundancy. I went to the first Joint Stewards meeting with standing orders mapped out and was given the chair.

It was a downhearted workforce. My shop had a dispute and went on strike. The standing orders (decided by the previous works committee — a right-wing lot) stated that after 24 hours there had to be a mass meeting to confirm support; failing that a return to work. The vote was lost as it was felt that the strike's aim would only benefit the shop. I learnt the lesson: standing orders were made for action, not to prevent it. Not long after we were able to try the durability of the vote order. The compressor fitters wanted a higher pay differential. I negotiated but there was a failure to agree.

I called in union officials who pressed the claim but agreement still could not be found. The lads stopped work. They were quite a powerful group. The compressors on trains frequently needed replacing and without a compressor there was no train. The right wing stewards pressed for the stipulated mass meeting to be held to approve the action, but this was resisted.

I believed we could win this dispute and turn things around. The compressor lads weren't calling for a factory stoppage. The stewards were persuaded back to their shops to collect £1 a head to help keep them out. The management called the Stewards Committee over and asked us to carry out our standing orders. I told them the standing orders were our business. They ran the factory and we ran the trade unions. The levy was a success and the compressors had a wage every week. Our doctrinaires said that the strikers shouldn't enjoy themselves, but should sit in the canteen for eight hours a day. I said they could play golf for all I cared as long as they kept out.

The compressor fitters won their claim in full. I called a meeting to move a return to work the next day. This created a small row; they wanted to stay out for the rest of the week. I said I had played the game with them, now they must do the same or I would be under attack for paying them for a holiday. They accepted. The resolution of this strike led to a change in the atmosphere at the works. It broke the despondency that had set in after the redundancies and put us back on a keel.

I was a member of the Joint Crafts negotiating body which met regularly at 55 Broadway. Because meeting times were of undetermined length, and members had to put on decent clothes (this was in the days before lockers), it was accepted that attendance precluded a return to work. However, after one meeting I returned first to Acton to see a member who was not at work with a problem before going home as usual in the afternoon.

The following day I was called in to an inquiry. The secretary of the Joint Stewards Committee, Bert Salisbury, told me management was gunning for me and I had better call a mass meeting. Bert was known as a right winger so his sources were reliable. He had also learnt the Steward Committee's tactic of calling an interesting mass meeting to address extraordinary issues, and he recommended we use it to put the matter of myself on the agenda.

The stewards called a meeting on the pretext of an overtime issue and over 1000 members attended. The quickest move from the floor came from Derek Wedgwood: 'Whatever happens to Brother Halpin, we support him by action equal. If sacked, we all go out of the gate; if suspended, we all stop for the length of suspension.' Further speeches from the floor carried this unanimously. I attended the disciplinary and was given three days suspension with a warning that my next offense would meet with dismissal. 'Thank you very much,' I said, and reported back to members that I was on an appeal procedure.

This was delayed and I then had the most peculiar experience in my chequered career. Members began to ask when they were having 'Halpin's Three Days'. The West Indian contingent pressed to have it when the Test was on at the Oval. The Irish wanted it during the big meet at Cheltenham. In fact, could we switch it to a two-week shut down? It was no good telling them that I could win the appeal. The appeal went to the top level and the disciplinary was dismissed with no stain on my record. It would have been a cause to celebrate in most trade unions, but not at Acton Rails that year.

There was great concern at the loss of Halpin's Three Days. Sometimes working people are hard to weigh up. After all, they knew that they would lose three days' pay if they followed me out. But it was a lesson to management.

People were suspicious of Bert Salisbury's right-wing background and I was accused of not defeating him. But like many in trade unions, although he might not like a decision taken, if it was made by members then Bert gave his support. The Shop Stewards Committee was asked to give its assistance to the lobby of South Africa House. Bert insisted that we present a letter to the Embassy. It would have to be a collar and tie job.

As we walked past the lobby outside some of the demonstrators shouted out, 'Where do you think you're going, Halpin?' Inside we asked for the International Secretary and were shown to his office. We gave him the stewards' headed letter expressing the members' concern at Mandela's internment. The Secretary asked if we would convey to our members his Government's reasons for its action, which he then expressed. Afterwards we were shown out. It had been a very interesting afternoon.

The canteen at Acton had a piano. It was only really played by Percy on Christmas Eve. Taking advantage of some idle time one day the supervisor called in a van and it was taken away. This was at the time of reorganisation and redundancies so shop steward meetings were busy; even so, the Committee wanted me to put the lost piano on the agenda. I wouldn't take the motion.

There was a challenge to the chair's ruling. The item was moved again and carried. At the next meeting with management we came to the end of the agenda: 'A piano, Mr Halpin? You're not serious?' I replied that it was a sincere concern, and cited several witnesses who had seen the instrument being purloined. The manager shook his head, dumbstruck for a moment: 'Well, if you can prove the piano is the property of Acton I will act to get it back; but I need proof.' I think he thought that would be it.

Three days later a dusty Bert Salisbury came up to me. He had an old minute book in his hands. The rail industry probably keeps more records than any other. Having to record when trains leave and when trains arrive, how many passengers each carried, how many tons of coal, and so forth, instils the habit of meticulous note-keeping. The evidence lay in Acton Works' Minutes: March 1940.

The BBC was broadcasting *Music While You Work*, a radio programme to increase morale and boost wartime production. Acton Works was asked if it would allow a broadcast from its canteen. The Stewards Committee agreed and after a successful show it was given a piano to keep. Later in the war another broadcast saw the Works awarded another piano, which was given to HMP Wormwood Scrubs. It was lucky we gave it, or I could have been instructed to retrieve it; the Committee would probably have insisted I nick it back.

At the next meeting the manager asked if any evidence of the ownership of the piano had come to light. I handed him the minute book. He nearly collapsed, but the piano was returned. I came into the canteen to great applause. You would have thought Mafeking had been relieved.

The working class are funny people and it's quite wrong to put labels on them. I believe I was right about Bert Salisbury.

# 14 Founding the CPB, Last Days at Acton

The terrible defeat of the second miners strike was followed by Wapping. I remember that in the 1970s the new Dockland Committee badly needed firms to move to the desolate wastes, and there was the prospect of a cheap offer of a built site for the *Morning Star*. I made the proposal to the paper's Management Committee but it was rejected for being too far from the major titles on Fleet Street and from mainline railways. Ten years later Murdoch's rags moved into their well-fortressed site at Wapping. The time to take action was before Fleet Street closed.

The print-workers knew what was coming and could have shut down the papers until there was a trade union agreement in place for the new works. But unfortunately the print unions were over-confident. The assurance that no one could publish and print without them was ill-founded. Five hundred print workers were sacked and replaced with trained EEPTU workers.

Murdoch, benefiting from Eddie Shah's Messenger Group's defeat of the unions at Warrington, used Thatcher's anti-union laws, and police willingness to commit illegal action, to hold up and turn round pickets arriving in coaches. Three other factors undermined the strength of the strike at Wapping: scabs, the new electronic processes, and journalists working off site.

Massive picketing took place every Saturday. The police cavalry would clear the streets and the locality was locked up. Eventually peaceful demonstration turned to battles, but the papers still came out. In retrospect it might have been better tactics to picket local distributors.

I was on the picket line most Saturday nights. I turned out with my neighbours. Twelve of the houses in our street were involved in picketing; they were either printers, or Communists and supporters. One evening we all came back to the local pub. A big bunch of police walked in just before closing time, whereupon the doors were shut and there was a lock-in. We didn't mingle though.

The LCDTU held a special conference on the strike issues and the use of anti-union laws. There was also condemnation of Ken Jackson's EEPTU, and calls for its expulsion from the TUC. This was taken up by the TUC executive, and the union was only readmitted after merging with the AUEW and apologising and promising never again.

Some journalists to their credit turned down handsome offers and made up a group that didn't go in to the new offices. They became known as refuseniks. They numbered such leading NUJ members and distinguished journalists as Barry Clement, Paul Routledge, Pat Healey, Don McIntyre and David Felton. Several militant trade unionists condemned journalists, but some at least should be remembered for their stand.

Scabs came from afar, organised from EEPTU's Southampton office. They were given high wages and bribes by Murdoch. After the dispute Murdoch's thanks was to reduce their perks and wages. They protested but to no avail: neither Murdoch nor the unions wanted to know.

The house in Cable Street was used for banner-making as those coming and going from the demonstrations with placards and signs were being stopped by the police. I spoke at several mass meetings. The best one was New Year's Eve 1986 when I had a glass of Scotch in my hand during the speech to give a toast to the crowd at midnight. Some comrades thought it inappropriate, but the atmosphere called for it.

The suppression of those who dissented from the CPGB's embrace of Eurocommunism resulted in the formation of the Communist Campaign Group (CCG). I was supportive of the CCG while remaining chair of West Middlesex District and a member of the Party's Political Committee.

In 1987, by arrangement with the Soviet Communist Party, I made a trip to Moscow to discuss the official division and re-establishment of the British Communist Party. At Moscow airport I was met by a welcoming committee which took me and my Scotch straight through customs and into a waiting ZIM which drove to the hotel. Anita and Boris followed behind in a smaller car.

I met the Soviet Party functionaries and explained the situation: the British Party was abandoning class politics and excluding opposition. There was a ten to one debate. We should fight to win back the Party, the functionaries said. How could we if members were being excluded? Communists don't divide their Party was the line firmly held by the ten mouths. I tolerated this for over an hour then went on the attack. If there was an inviolable policy not to divide, how did

Kevin speaking at a West Middlesex CPGB meeting during the inner-party battles of the 80s, also on the plaftrom (left to right), Dave Green and Ian McKay and Bob Newlands

Lenin set up the Bolsheviks against the Mensheviks in the Russian Social Democratic Labour Party? This was met with hand throwing. These were not comparable historical circumstances. I remained firm. We were not committed to division but if the next Congress decided to continue its support of exclusions there was no alternative but to re-establish the Communist Party.

Afterwards Anita, Boris and I had a holiday in Yalta. We stayed in a sanatorium. Yalta was beautiful but, following a bizarre edict from Gorbachev, dry. It felt like a misjudged attempt to discourage the population's fondness for heavy drinking.

Nobody was ever consulted in the matter; he just laid it down. He might better have begun by banning bars having half-litre bottles of vodka on the boards. I had my illegal whisky which was surreptitiously poured into bottles of coke. The childrens' bottle was opened; the adults' stoppered.

A car was provided for trips out of the sanatorium complex. One afternoon I gave it the slip and walked down the road looking for a bar. I came across one with the ubiquitous zinc counter and no seats selling kvass, a distillation of stale bread with about 1% alcohol. I noticed a group of people heading into the forest behind the bar and went for a look. I found them sitting together on some logs. I explained that I was a British Communist and like them wanted a drink. They gave me a glass of their homemade vodka. I returned the following day with a lemonade-bottle of whisky and was made very welcome.

Over the next year the Communist Campaign Group prepared to re-establish a party based on the ideas and class politics of *The British Road to Socialism.* When the Communist Party of Britain was re-established in 1988 it was decided it would be based on the historic experience of the CPGB. I never resigned or was expelled from the CPGB: I just didn't consider myself a member any more.

For industrial comrades there was a better atmosphere in the CPB. Mike Hicks, the printworkers' leader, was elected General Secretary. Mike had recently been arrested and charged with assaulting a policeman by sticking a loud-hailer in his face. He did a few months in Parkhurst, during which time he learnt that some prison officers were sympatico.

Derek Robinson was made chair because of his experience at British Leyland. I had known Derek for years, but I couldn't agree with him dropping out of engineering. He took a job as the *Morning Star* Midlands Organiser and we weren't such mates after that. He eventually left the scene altogether. The death of his first wife, an ex-sewing room steward and leading comrade at Austin (British Leyland as it became) had some effect; maybe also the fact that he remarried after a time. I was asked to be Industrial Organiser with the job of returning the Party to our industrial base. Alongside were Mary Davis, John Foster, Joan Bellamy and Ron Bellamy.

After debate at the Re-establishment Congress it was decided to drop the 'Great' from Britain in the party name as a left-over from the old Empire days. The party emblem also aroused discussion. There was large support for the hammer and sickle. Those opposing argued that it was a symbol of Russia and, in terms of the sickle, Britain had no peasantry as such; but it was countered that farm workers were exploited as much as their industrial counterparts and the sickle could just as well stand for them as for a mass peasantry. Eventually the Committee settled for a hammer and a dove of peace; a good decision, I think. It was agreed that the structure, rules and historical stance of the CPGB should be adopted, and this was settled at the inaugural Congress in 1988.

The CPB tried hard to overcome the set-back to industrial work caused by Eurocommunism. As Industrial Organiser my strategy was that comrades from trade unions should meet and agree policy. We would set this meeting for the CPB EC following the TUC Congress, so that we could develop policies after examining the frailties of the TUC's positions.

One of the TUC's biggest weaknesses was its great belief in Brussels and the EEC. This was so enthusiastic that when Jacques Delors spoke at the TUC in 1988 he was given rousing, prolonged applause. We had to expose Brussels, Public Private Partnerships, Public Finance Initiatives and anti-union legislation, the gender wage-gap, arms production and imperialist wars, to name but a few.

In addition we examined TUC structures, particularly the equalities conferences. These were good, but there was no room at the TUC Conference for motions from these satellite conferences. Anita was the great battler for the women's, gay and lesbian, disability and black workers conferences, and also for young workers and the trades councils to have their motions put further up the TUC's agenda.

The CPB had some good industrial advisories, or occupational advisories, and tried to use these more effectively, giving greater attention to policy before deciding who would be the best candidate to enact it in office. I decided the best way to make contact with union leaders was to sell the *Morning Star* outside conferences. This meant I would meet people I had known from LCDTU: Derek Fullick from Waterloo, now general secretary of ASLEF and TGWU general secretary Ron Todd, who I had first met in my Ford days when he had represented a small factory in Walthamstow.

We put out Needs of the Hour — key strategic model motions which were agreed by the September EC. Often as a result there was a big debate in the TUC Congress. Even our opponents had to admit it made for a lively discussion. We tried for a return of workplace branches but the run-down of industry made it hard.

After Gorbachev took the leadership of the CPSU, the *Morning Star*'s troubles had increased. The Soviet Union did not directly subsidise the paper but it had bought 14,000 copies daily to distribute to its schools and colleges for their English language classes. (I believe many of today's 'oligarchs' must have learned their English with our paper). This massive loss of revenue created grave problems. Several years earlier, Tony Chater decided to cut costs and opened discussions with the political committee of the CPGB. The PC elected a sub-committee on which I sat. It comprised management committee comrades, editorial staff, and printers. It also met with SOGAT officials.

It was known that on the traditional rotary press the papers could be printed in half an hour, with another half-hour for plate-making. The paper was put to bed by 7.30pm when the working day ended. This meant the printers could go casual after that and see if there was any work at SOGAT or call on at its Britannia Street office. This was before supplementary sections were printed in advance.

After considerable debate it was decided to run-on the *Sporting Life* after the *Morning Star* had printed, re-plating the press and printing for about another hour. Privately I was dubious and thought it would be hard to get printers to give up long-established practices brought in to achieve the best deal from newspaper proprietors when Fleet Street unions were king. I couldn't say this publicly for fear it would look like sabotage.

It turned out my prejudices had some substance. The press was at 75 Farringdon Road, near to Marx House where we held many industrial meetings. Ted Crook and I used to go to a pub nearby. One evening, after the *Sporting Life* deal had been agreed in principle, we sat there quietly and listened to a group of *Morning Star* printers. They were having a laugh about the new agreement. At that time presses contracted printers by applying to SOGAT which allocated the next on the list; a good practice to stop newspapers black-listing, but not good for ensuring that a paper could pick politically reliable people. Ted and I overheard that the printers' tactic was to accept the contract for *Sporting Life,* then when it came to print demand a separate agreement by arguing that as it was a separate title they should be paid at the full rather than the run-on rate. This would not be any saving and the proposal, though pushed by the union, was shelved. The *Morning Star* was saved by increasing the fighting fund and by the political loyalty of its staff, who would accept delayed wages.

Once, the paper didn't appear for two days and I turned up at Farringdon Road to find out what the problem was. The press motor had burnt out. It wasn't easily replaceable. It had been built as a prototype in the GDR and ran on 393 volts, at odds with the English standard of 220 or 440 volts.

I decided to try my luck in Acton. It had the best rewind shop in the country. I wondered if, as an AUEW convenor, I could get away with negotiating a rewind without compromising myself. I went to see the manager. I asked whether he could fix the press as a commercial job. His first reaction was not enthusiastic. 'Why should we? Your crowd is always stirring it up.' I could only reply that we never reneged on agreements, and besides, if he helped us out here he would have a good name and other opportunities might come his way. He said he would have a think and told me to go away. After a short while he called me in. I was a cheeky bastard but he would do it.

I went back to Farringdon Road with Percy, the winding foreman. Without going down the two floors to the press Percy said, 'Bad news, Kevin. The armatures have gone. Burnt out field coils would have been easier.' He could tell this by sniffing the air. The motor would have to go back to Acton to be stripped and rewound. It was at least three days work with overtime. I had a pint with Percy and found out that he was a sympathiser. He used to be in the winders' exclusive branch of ETU and knew a lot of our comrades of old.

It was Friday so to have the motor running again by early the next week the weekend would have to be worked. The problem was I had been responsible for banning overtime by persuading management to hire extra workers instead. If a meeting of members clamoured for overtime I would call a mass meeting under the slogan: 'I am the overtime you didn't work last week.' It became easier as time went on and people remembered being hired on the slogan. The EEPTU right-wing convenor laughed at my predicament. Eventually I managed to argue that we could legitimately call the job plant work and plant workers had overtime; and it wouldn't affect the train schedules in any case. The motor rewind crew worked all weekend and delivered the overhauled motor on Monday afternoon. The *Morning Star* was back on the streets the next morning.

When the paper eventually received the bill the charge was far less than the standard rate. In the end I think it might actually have been waived. Acton Rails got a terrific name and deserved it. It became known as a Friend Special of the paper. The supervisor never asked me for any favours in return either.

When I came out of Ship Repair and found work at London Transport I left behind my good mate Ted Crook, who remained at one of the last Harland and Wolff shops in St Katherine's Dock – now the city's great expensive yacht area.

When he was made redundant from there we had to find him a job. I was friendly with John Davis, the leading steward in the Lifts and Escalator shop. He pushed and Ted was interviewed and immediately taken on. He got on with the job in his usual exact manner, studying the work closely. 'How do lifts stop falling if the cables part?' he once asked me. I didn't know. 'Well, the claws on the lift bite into the wood uprights....' Ted by then had married Jean French (I don't think they merged their TU branches).

That year Anita and I went to the Boxing Day meet at Kempton Park with the Crooks. In one race Anita bet on a horse at 33-1. I had a big bet on the evens favourite. The first time around the track we could see two of the jockeys having a chat. By the second circuit they had decided to race and I was shouting for my horse. Anita said I must be mad; I would only win £20. Now if hers came in it would pay for us all to have a night out. Hers came in. It was a good day.

When Jean died Ted asked me to make the oration. I was uneasy about it, but I couldn't refuse. In the end it went well. I spoke for the class politics Jean so firmly advocated. Everyone felt it was what she would have wanted.

A few years later Ted fell ill. John Davis and Iwould visit him in south London and push him in his wheelchair to his local, where he would drink out of his own pint pot. Then one day I had a call from John. Ted was dead.

He had no known relatives so John and I had to make the funeral arrangements. We called in a solicitor to look at his will, of which John and I were co-executors. The will asked if I would speak at his funeral, and instructed every worker in Lifts and Escalators to go back to the pub round the corner from the crematorium where the executors would buy the beer. I did the usual 'cash behind bar – shout when more needed'. Working people can be hard to fathom. After a couple of pints they insisted on paying.

Suddenly Ted had relatives. They seemed to own farms, and were certainly not poor, but they wanted to know what they had been left. They told me it was usual to read the will at the funeral. John and I demurred and said the first thing stated in the will was that there should be a good send-off. The relatives became a bit aggressive and we had to tell them to contact the solicitor. They weren't a happy crowd.

Ted's will was clear. After the house was sold and the insurance paid out, the cash from himself and Jean was to go to the Party. A few bits and pieces of furniture were left to some named relatives. The solicitor sent letters to the beneficiaries. A reply came back asking for the goods to be packed and sent around the country to their various addresses. By now I was a bit fed up and wrote them back saying Ted's pieces were at his house and if they wanted to collect them would they let us know.

John Davis was not in the Party but he was nonetheless honest. He didn't believe Ted did the best thing leaving everything to the CPB but he would see it through. All told there was a sum of £150,000. This led to a fight on the EC of CPB. It was moved that the cash be given to the *Morning Star*. Some EC members working for the paper said that as it was the Party's money they could do what they wanted with it. I refused. The majority of the EC and several quoted rules were against me, but I was clear: Ted had left his money to the CPB. As executor I would challenge them in court if need be. Scottish CPB leader John Foster backed me. There was a good deal of disgruntlement but I shrugged it off. In the end an amicable solution was found. The CPB had no premises but the *Morning Star,* after a dubious sale of 75 Farringdon Road, was having new offices built at Ardleigh Road. It agreed to the CPB's tenancy of the ground floor, and Ted's money would be saved for the Party. Thanks, Ted – it was a rough ride being your executor but together with John I think we carried out your wishes.

Acton Works was changing. London Underground Limited was being privatised. The business was taken out of the hands of railwaymen and put into the hands of accountants. Every square metre of space was valued. We had a store of extruded aluminium pillars which were used for the trains. We always bought extra in case of damage. These were laid on top of the toilet block. They couldn't be used for anything else. 'Sell for scrap' was the instruction. I pointed out that the cost of setting up the extrusion die for a few replacement pillars was enormous. Management agreed but the instruction had to be followed and the scrappage invoice entered in the books.

Due to the implementation of double-skilling, at the age of 63 I had to take on heavy riveting. The shop manager came to see me and laughed. He forgot the rivet gun was heavy. I finished what I was doing and threw the gun down. Luckily for him he jumped out of the way or his foot would have hurt.

I transferred to the new works built for my shop opposite Acton Town Station, designed for the engineering component work that was now our task. Heavy repair was split between contractors and depots. But of course the train lines still ran into the old shop, and plant work for other depots continued to arrive there. Management proposed that Heavy Repair and Plant have a dual role. This was rejected by the members. It was not in the Acton Works agreement, and it could have excused a further cut in the labour force.

Management brought in two officials – from the AUEW and EEPTU. They presented themselves at a meeting of members. Without consulting any stewards they had discussed the issue with management and had come to an agreement. They were now insisting on addressing members and submitting the agreement to the meeting; their meeting, as they put it. It was an unheard of situation. The members decided they hadn't asked for the officials. They didn't want them at the meeting and voted not to agree to their attendance. The officials began to rave. The members shouted. I closed the meeting, noting in the minutes that there was still a 'failure to agree'.

I was then away for a couple of days and when I returned I found Heavy Repair on strike. After the fitters had been told to do some unscheduled pipe-clipping the shop had formed a resolution: 'No work outside the flexibility agreement.' The management said, 'Do it, or else.' The shop decided that 'or else' meant not work. As there hadn't been a ballot management had got on to the union's head office, invoking anti-union laws and threatening sequestration.

My EC member at that time was Roger Butler, a good left-winger and ex-LCDTU member. He advised me to convene a meeting to propose a return to work on the basis of holding a ballot the next day, a Friday. If I could take the completed ballot forms to Roger over the weekend a vote for action would have EC approval by Monday. The members agreed, they returned to work and a ballot was held the next morning. It was unanimous in favour of a strike.

The result went to the AUEW EC who notified Acton management that there would be an official dispute which could affect other members if they were instructed to do similar work. Management thought about it, then negotiated a settlement.

The shop manager seemed to be bearing a grudge. I was still chair of the joint LUL Craft Committee. One day I was in the union office with the permission of the foreman. The manager came in and over-ruled the foreman, ordering, 'You get back to your job'. After some argument I decided to return to my shop. The new process was only to work to written instructions and these hadn't been given. The manager didn't know this. He followed me into the shop, told me I wasn't working as instructed, and said I was on a disciplinary.

As he was at once accuser and witness the case had to go higher up. I was given notice to appear at a chief engineers' disciplinary hearing. By this time technicians who I had known as apprentices had stated that instructions were not available. So did the foreman. The manager couldn't squeeze a better statement from them. Allowed an official to represent me I took Billy Taylor, a very reliable member. The manager read the evidence, then turned to us. 'Mr Halpin, I don't know why you're here.' 'Pardon me,' I replied, 'but I don't go around disciplining myself.' My manager was not called. The case was dismissed with the statement, 'I don't know why you're wasting my time, Head Manager.'

People say we mellow with age. I refused redundancy at 62, took on rough work at 63, and defeated a disciplinary at 64.

I also managed to secure myself a summons to Bow Magistrates Court. I had joined the mass non-payment of the Poll Tax and was one of over a hundred people notified to appear. To save the magistrate's time we were to be dealt with collectively. Instead we insisted on our right to trial as individuals. Sheer numbers made this impossible and the cases were never brought to hearing. Apart from doubling and trebling the rates bill, the poll tax weakened the long term health of democracy in this country. As it was based on the electoral register millions didn't add their names. As a result turn-outs at elections declined significantly and haven't recovered.

I was still the chair of the Works Committee. During one meeting the Committee Manager said to his secretary, 'Make the tea, Joyce.' I thought this was uncalled for. 'But she isn't employed to make the tea,' I said. 'Well who is going to make it?' 'I am this time, and it's your turn at the next meeting.' I made a friend of Joyce. She would always type me a report of the meeting that I could photocopy and have on the union notice boards the following morning.

After a time the Manager formed an idea of what was happening. Could I not have my notices read like the firm's? I made them a different style by leaving in a few literals. Incidentally, my editor owes this secretary a lot. Joyce couldn't read my scrawls and showed me the benefits of unconnected letters.

At 64 I was coming up to retirement. Bert Salisbury told me I should be given notice of my allotted retirement date 12 weeks ahead of the day. If not I would receive the pay in lieu. I made a note of this. That October at the Committee the disgruntled manager said, 'I'll be fucking rid of you soon, Halpin.' I pulled him up for his language. If he didn't apologise I would take him to the industrial relations department. He apologised with a red face.

At the November meeting he asked when I was retiring. I go, I replied, when I'm old enough. At the end of the December meeting I said I was going soon. In fact I wouldn't be coming back on 4 January. 'By the way,' I said to the Manager, 'you're giving me 12 weeks pay to take away.' 'Rubbish, we knew when you were going.' I told him to ask the Industrial Department. He called me in later and, gritting his teeth, informed me that he had no choice but he had to pay me 12 weeks. Boy, was he sorry. I made him announce it at the next Committee meeting and insisted it be minuted. Everyone in the Works was jubilant:

'Halpin even beat them on retirement!' My mates had all known, of course, but no one had let the cat out of the bag.

I decided to hire the Railwayman's Club at Marylebone and throw a party. Eve Bland – Claire's daughter, for whom the East End seamstresses had stitched the dress – put on her band. She had gone to acting college and specialised in cockney songs and these were loudly appreciated. I laid on food and drink and enjoyed it all. I took the thank you speech to a big crew, including those of LCDTU now up for General Secretaryships. I also invited Jim Mortimer. A retiring Acton manager had told me that Jim had urged management to give me a start if I passed the interview. 'Put him on a job and check him,' he had said. So I gave an apology to Jim. He and Pat have been great friends and left comrades ever since.

The Acton Shop Stewards Committee presented me with an electric jig-saw, obviously knowing I was going to work in my retirement. It was of the finest quality, lasting years. ASLEF, one of the key LCDTU support organisations, gave me the great award of a brass engraving of Salisbury, a Southern Region 'West Country class' steam locomotive. I was touched as these plaques are given only to ASLEF's most respected members.

Then I was made an even rarer presentation. Very occasionally the *Morning Star* gives a replica of a front page that tells the life story of the recipient. It does not come from the editor or management, but from the journalists and production staff who make it for someone they believe has done outstanding work for the paper. I was in the company of JR Campbell, Allen Hutt and Barbara Champion. It was a most unexpected present and the best thanks I ever had. Bylined by P. Reston, it hangs on my wall to this day.

# 15 Retirement work

Upon retirement I had more time to give as the CPB's Industrial Organiser. I had already set the seal on our work: the Needs of the Hour which established strategic aims. These tried to avoid smaller issues, although that could be a difficult task. After EC approval I would take the Needs on the road.

The work-place advisories which I convened to consult on union policies were very interesting. What members wanted to advance through their unions was constant: no cuts to public services, more social housing, and job security. The Needs were never under CPB-headed paper. It was too easy to go back to the Cold War period. The defeat by the right wing was not possible through debate, but by attacking the origins of the motion.

As industrial organiser I was able to attend many trade union conferences as an observer. While there I could keep up with selling the *Morning Star*. The Party's profile was maintained by *Unity*, which dealt with trade union politics in general, and particular issues relevant to specific unions. I stood outside the conferences and saw the different cultures. If delegates were late at the NUR conference they had to publicly apologise to the chair and pay a fine. Five minutes after it started I could give up selling. At others, such as UNISON, I could sell for half an hour after the start time and start to wrap up when another clutch of delegates would arrive. I enjoyed standing outside conferences. It was better than being inside.

One of the best experiences in my new role occurred at the General and Municipal Workers conference. Comrades had discouraged me from attending, saying its membership was intractable. A motion came from the North East Area: 'That this Union gives its full support to the *Morning Star*.' Roy Jones, the paper's industrial reporter, came out to let me know. I expressed misgivings. It was a right-wing union: suppose it was rejected? No question. It would be OK. The two women who got up to propose worked with Mary Turner, the GMB president, who had a good team of dinner ladies. They spoke well. Mary asked for a show of hands in support; 'And I don't want to see any hands up against.' The motion was carried unanimously. I invited the proposers to the stall and we broke open a bottle of champagne. There have been advances in the General Municipal Union, now the GMB. Paul Kenny became its General Secretary and recently it has courageously organised sex workers. Paul usually gave me a tenner when I sold the paper at the London Regional conference.

Making my way round the conferences could be hectic. Sometimes it meant leaving MSF in Llandudno on Friday to get to the Unison pre-meeting in Bournemouth on Saturday night. In Llandudno once, late in getting away, I dumped unsold papers on a shop. There was no time to count how many there were. The newsagent ran after me as I hurried down the road. He couldn't have counted them so quickly? No, he had dashed to give me a fiver in thanks for sales. No excuse; I had a drink on it.

So this was my career of choice and I spent 20 years in this way: talking to comrades, agreeing agendas, and defining Needs. Who we would support to be officers and national secretaries was not the foremost of the CPB's priorities. We were a party of politics, not individuals.

The AEU was taken over by EEPTU so that EEPTU could rejoin the TUC after it was expelled for its collaboration with Murdoch at Wapping. The AEU *Gazette* was assured that AEU rules were sacred by Jimmie Airlie and Roger Butler, who then left the field. The AEU became the AEEU. It was a disaster. At conferences officials sat at every delegate's table. The delegates were told that if they voted against EC recommendations they wouldn't be attending again. Each delegate had to vote using a numbered card. When the *Gazette* gave out leaflets the heavies would turn up and push and shove.

The AEEU conference in Jersey was notorious. Vertical banners advertising major firms hung from the hall roof. We were informed these companies sponsored the conference. On the last day trucks brought in skips of Guinness and lager with promotional bags to take away.

I mistakenly supported the setting up of the Electrical and Plumbing Industries Trade Union (EPIU) after the left walked out of the EEPTU following its expulsion from the TUC. Members wanted to be affiliated to a TUC union. But it was the merger of AEU and EEPTU that showed a weakness. The new rules gave parity to both sections so executive seats were balanced and each area had one candidate each from engineering and electrical. The AEU *Gazette* put up candidates but we had problems finding left electricians and this gave Ken Jackson a big lead.

Engineering held the presidency of the union; always a bigger job than the General Secretary's role. We elected Dave Hall only to be stunned by his resigning on being offered a job as Northern Organiser. By this time the AEEU was a right wing union with full-time workers running and controlling the branches.

Ken Jackson became AEEU General Secretary in 1995. The AEU's old left-wing continued to lobby and fight for policies agreed at *Gazette* meetings. To our disappointment one of our EC members was offered a Jackson job and left. Just before his 65th birthday Jackson was given EC approval to continue as secretary for another year without having to stand for re-election. Immune to the shock, the left soldiered on.

It was early in 2002. I had been to the RMT to have a chat about anti-union laws and Bob Crow's stand on them. Present was the union's QC, John Hendy. As chair of the LCDTU I counted John an indispensable advisor. He was one of the originals when I spoke against anti-union laws very early on. He would agree that the laws brought massive fees from the unions to the legal profession, but John was not impressed or corrupted. Hendy continually led campaigns for free trade unions and was prominent in the group of lawyers and trade unionists that founded the Institute for Employment Rights. The Institute has drafted opposition to the Tory repression and even got the Labour Party to agree to the removal of one part of its Election Manifesto that supported regressive legislation initiated under Thatcher, although Labour infamously reneged on the pledge under pressure from the CBI.

As we walked down Euston Road afterwards John asked why AEEU's left-wing wasn't challenging Jackson's extra year as Secretary. I said that the Conference had taken the decision and there was nothing we could do about it. He argued that employment laws stated national TU leaders had to stand for re-election after five years. I doubted that the engineering left would want to go to court over the matter. The law was prejudiced against them. We argued quite sharply. In the end I agreed to bring together a representative body from the *Gazette* to hear his opinion and decide.

About a dozen AEU stalwarts from across England, Wales and Scotland met one night at my house. The meeting agreed to give John a hearing, and he would then withdraw to let it come to a decision. John made clear that we would have to challenge first through a solicitor, but that if it came to court he would represent us. After a long debate it was decided to challenge Jackson. We went to an industrial court and it was ruled that a leadership ballot must be held.

Jackson backed down under legal pressure and angrily declared an election. We then had to decide which candidate stood the best chance of defeating him. Our usual position would be to choose a well known national official but the Jackson machine had either bought off the obvious candidates or they were retired. The only possibility was Derek Simpson, once a leader in our Sheffield heartlands, although since transferred to a right-wing area in Derby where his influence was less.

We ran a massive *Gazette* campaign in support of Derek. Jackson mobilised all officials to visit AEEU branches. The South East regional officer pledged that in the London area Simpson would not get a branch nomination. I thought my West London branch at least was secure, but on arriving at Hoop Lane Working Men's Club for the nomination meeting Bill Taylor met me and said we would lose. He had looked at the number of union cars in the car park, all belonging to officials and their office staff.

A right-winger had taken the Chair and the branch secretary, Kevin Gallagher, was a full-time appointee of head office. Nominations were called for and Derek Simpson and Ken Jackson were put forward. Then the members challenged the presence of the officials: they were acting as though they were members but they had never before been seen at the branch. Gallagher produced a computer print-out which was said to prove that all present were Branch members. The nomination was a tied ballot. The Chair gave Jackson the casting vote.

Afterwards we enquired about the previous night's meeting at the Ford branch. The same officials had attended and nominated Jackson. The same had happened at the South London branch. We made a challenge, known as the 'Greysuits Challenge', but nothing was done. However progressive industrial correspondents put out the story.

The national count took place at the Electoral Reform Society. The result was called in the evening. Jackson had won narrowly. I wrote a piece for the *Morning Star.* Yes, we had lost, but we put up a good fight and only lost by a few votes.

I was lucky. The paper had gone to bed so I was too late to file for the next morning's edition. Kevin Maguire had written the same story and it ran in *The Guardian*. The following day as the count was being cross-checked by the tellers a bundle of votes was discovered on the Jackson pile that had been cast for Derek Simpson; enough to give him victory. At that year's TUC Kevin Maguire was awarded Golden Bollock of the Year. I told Kevin (now associate editor of the *Mirror*) how a matter of minutes had kept me from sharing the award with him.

Kevin speaking in Glasgow on *Britain's Road to Socialism*

The result was a great boost for the trade union movement. John Hendy was delighted. It was rich revenge for his father, one of the Communist leaders who were expelled by Jackson and his cohorts in the ETU after a vicious press campaign. The industrial correspondents who exposed Jackson's fiddle at the local branches deserved our thanks – running the story undoubtedly influenced the final vote.

In the late 1990s, I was on the Political Committee of the CPB when Tony Chater retired as editor of the *Morning Star*. Arguments followed over his replacement. The *Morning Star* is autonomous but without comrades buying, selling and financing, there would be no paper, and the Party has the right to call a meeting of Management Committee members who were also in the Party to discuss editorial policy. The paper's support of *The British Road to Socialism* is endorsed at each AGM (open to all shareholders). The Party hoped to see John Haylett be made the new editor, but while it could have an opinion it couldn't make the decision: that was up to the People's Printing Press Society. Despite this Tony Chater led the camp of those who argued that the CPB had no authority to even nominate an editor. A vote for discussion of the editorship was carried 15-13, with many of the 13 walking out of the meeting.

After the AGM of the PPPS John Haylett was appointed. The opposing candidate favoured by Mike Hicks and Mary Rosser was their son-in law, Paul Corry. The matter came to a head. I had been a friend of Mike and Mary for many years, I had even made and iced their wedding cake, but I couldn't agree with this dynastic approach. John Haylett's tenure was short. Mary Rosser brought disciplinary proceedings against him and he was dismissed by a committee of three: only one of the three was on the PPPS Management Committee. The NUJ staff backed John, and Amanda Kendall, the mother of the NUJ Chapel, called a meeting which agreed that if there was no reinstatement they would take strike action.

As the CPB Industrial Organiser I backed the strike. The NUJ executive made it official, paying hardship pay from day one. John Haylett had a good case for victimisation. The strike committee was using the Party offices on the ground floor of the *Morning Star* building. I met them to oppose this. I reasoned that, in order to strangle the claim made by Mary Rosser's supporters that the issue wasn't an industrial struggle but an internal Communist Party argument, the strikers needed to physically distance themselves. My argument was accepted and the committee applied to the NUJ for premises. It then produced the *Workers' Morning Star.*

Amanda Kendall did a good job. She had to counter the argument that the strike could finish the paper, and she did this effectively by firmly stating that a paper that opposes victimisation and victimises its editor can have no credibility. The Management Committee met on Saturdays and the CPB backed protests in support of the strikers. I supplied my loudspeaker gear. We could drown out the Committee. It supported Secretary Mary Rosser but eventually had to agree to arbitration. The panel decided John Haylett had been wrongfully dismissed and handed down the verdict that John be reinstated.

The sacking of John occurred after the CPB Executive had elected Rob Griffiths as General Secretary in January 1998. Mary's action appeared to be revenge. During the dispute the Party sent letters to every CPB member explaining their executive's support of John Haylett.

I believe John was the only editor to have the conviction to sell his product. When John said he would be at my stall outside union conferences at 8.30am you could bet your house on seeing him at 8.20am. The most pressing seller I had with me was Mary Davis. She wouldn't just stand there but accost the delegates: 'Have you had your paper today? Why not?'

When Anita Halpin became a member of the TUC General Council she was the first Communist to take the *Morning Star* to the Council each morning during Congress and sell. I had always sold to members as they arrived at the entrance but they began to refuse me: 'I can't buy off you, Kevin. What would Anita say?' Of course the *Morning Star* has made big advances, and at some of the most progressive union conferences the executive buy in bulk and distribute it free to each delegate. At most trade union conferences you will see many of our CP strategic motions on the agenda.

In 2006, I travelled around China with a CPB delegation. It was a rich experience. We visited a colossal car factory. It was organised as we had been at Ford. The shop elected a steward answerable to a shop meeting. The shop stewards then elected a works committee with a chair and secretary who could be voted out at any time. In this factory stewards had reps at the management committee. There was a national wage rate. If a factory was successful more workers were taken on; often brothers and sisters from poor, rural areas.

I asked the convenor what happened if there was an issue requiring strike action. He said his members could decide to work with less effort – a 'go slow'. Overtime was limited to eight hours a week and was voluntary. The convenor told me that during festivals management gave workers a gift. I thought it would be a bunch of flowers or a turkey, but it turned out to be a cash bonus of up to one month's pay. The amount was decided on the basis of the factory's prosperity: negotiated, in other words.

We went to Xinjiang, a Muslim region. In the West we are often told that the Chinese language is imposed everywhere and no religious freedom is allowed, but here the shop notices were not in Chinese, but the local Uygur language, and we were shown round a huge mosque by the daughter of the imam.

We drove through hundreds of miles of desert filled with wind farms. In the distance were ice-capped mountains. I asked why water was not piped from the mountains to irrigate the desert. My hosts gave me polite but funny looks. We pulled up at a desert town famous for grapes and raisins and wine. The water for the vines came from an underground stream that had been reached by carving through the rock, with wells sunk every 5km for raising silt by donkey wheel. It was the work of an emperor well-educated in many subjects (Chinese emperors did not descend through the eldest son: the father selected the most proficient and learned). The local council owned the water. A man with a vineyard opened his sluice gate and recorded the hours for payment. It had run like that for 3000 years.

I asked a shifty East-Ender question: 'What prevents a farmer using the sluice for nine hours and only recording four?' It provoked bemusement: 'Why would he do that?' I was trying to explain how capitalism works to a field-worker in China. 'To make more money,' I said. It was like speaking to a blank wall. If you fiddled the books the town would ostracise you, they replied. You couldn't live with the contempt. You would have to move on.

I tried to buy silk on the Silk Road. There was none at all, not even in Beijing. It was explained to me that silk is supplied exclusively to manufacturers. It's more profitable that way.

# Postscript

I have written about what happened in politics and on the shopfloor. It isn't a history of events, but written in order to give some details to explain how many people got a better life – not given them, but which they struggled for.

I was, of course, in the middle of this. Middle – not meaning on one side, but leading and welcoming the change. Many on the shopfloor said they could and would write a book about it, but left it too late.

Maybe I was lucky being in the right places at the right time. I owe a lot to Communists such as James Klugmann who educated me and ones I had rows with.

To mention names of people would be dull. That is what I hoped to avoid – boring you. To quote lessons would be presumptuous. The only lesson I learned – to trust working people and I was not let down. There were setbacks yes, but they were overcome through class solidarity.

I hope to have left a better life for my son Boris and his wife Jerusa and my grandchildren Sophia and Hans Kevin. I never set out for a family, but Anita made the change and made it worthwhile.

# Index